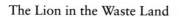
The Lion in the Waste Land

The Lion in the Waste Land

*Fearsome Redemption in the Work
of C. S. Lewis, Dorothy L. Sayers,
and T. S. Eliot*

✠ ✠ ✠ ✠ ✠

Janice Brown

The Kent State University Press ⬚ Kent, Ohio

© 2018 by The Kent State University Press, Kent, Ohio 44242
All rights reserved
ISBN 978-1-60635-338-7
Manufactured in the United States of America

Cataloging information for this title is available at the Library of Congress.

22 21 20 19 18   5 4 3 2 1

To Phyllis, my mother,

who taught me to love books,

excellence, and God

Contents

✠ ✠ ✠

Preface

✠ ✠ ✠

T. S. Eliot believed that no poet or artist "has his complete meaning alone" and that in order to truly appreciate a writer, we must set him among other writers "for contrast and comparison" ("Tradition and the Individual Talent" 15). This book places side by side the central ideas of three writers: C. S. Lewis, Dorothy L. Sayers, and T. S. Eliot. I hope to reinforce the impact Lewis has had, and draw attention to the strong Christian witness in the work of Sayers and Eliot. The significance of Dorothy L. Sayers has been largely overlooked in recent decades, while T. S. Eliot is regarded by many as an esoteric poet who has little relevance to Christian thought. I hope this book will help correct the tendency to undervalue Sayers and misconstrue Eliot's central concerns.

The Christian message is a message of redemption that offers hope in every age and in every culture. The bleakness and spiritual destitution of modern culture is depicted in T. S. Eliot's *Waste Land*. This poem, published in 1922, was hailed as an expression of the disillusionment of the era. It continued to be regarded by many as a work that accurately depicted a world devoid of all that was wholesome and life-giving, a world without the hope of redemption. The ensuing decades, the middle decades of the twentieth century, were dark with the memories of World War I, the new horrors of World War II, and the bitter residue of failed idealism. One of the apparent failures was the Christian Church, an institution that had provided stability and hope to earlier generations. Yet, surprisingly, during these same dark decades—the 1930s, 1940s, and 1950s—Christianity reemerged as a source of hope, partly because of C. S. Lewis, Dorothy L. Sayers, and T. S. Eliot.

The doctrine of redemption through Christ does not offer a cheap and easy solution to the complexity and anguish of life. The gospel, Dorothy L. Sayers declared, is "a thing of terror," and Christ, "the Lion of the Tribe of Judah," is aptly represented by the lion Aslan in C. S. Lewis's Narnia books as good, but not safe. The process of salvation is fraught with danger and pain, but the Christian message, illuminated through the work of C. S. Lewis, Dorothy L. Sayers, and T. S. Eliot, still offers hope to those wandering in the Waste Land. Although the offer of redemption is a fearsome thing, like the image of a lion, it is also glorious.

Acknowledgments

✠ ✠ ✠

In writing this book I am indebted to my Grove City College students, whose love of Lewis, Sayers, and Eliot inspired me to explore the works of these writers more deeply. I am particularly grateful to two former students, James Witmer and Emily Jefferis, whose appreciative and thoughtful responses to the original draft of my first chapters encouraged me to go on writing. Dr. Jerry Root (of Wheaton College) played a key role in determining my initial conception by suggesting that I use historian Adrian Hastings's linking of Lewis, Sayers, and Eliot as my starting point.

I received much support and scholarly help from friends, particularly the Right Reverend Donald Harvey (St. John's, Newfoundland), Dr. Michael Ward (Oxford, England), and Dr. James Dixon (Grove City, Pennsylvania).

My daughter, Stephanie Miller, and my brother, Dr. Carl Hudson, gave generously of their time to proofread much of the manuscript, and made insightful suggestions. Above all, I am immensely grateful for the patient and tireless assistance of my husband, Cliff, who supported and advised me at every stage, reading and rereading, questioning and affirming. The book could not have been written without him.

Author's Note

✠ ✠ ✠

Unless otherwise indicated, the quotations from the Bible are from the King James Version—the version commonly used by Lewis, Sayers, and Eliot. For Lewis's poetry, I have consulted two different collections: *Poems: C. S. Lewis,* edited by Walter Hooper and first published in 1964 (New York: HarperCollins, 1994), and *The Collected Poems of C. S. Lewis: A Critical Edition,* edited by Don W. King (Kent, Ohio: Kent State University Press, 2015). In quoting Lewis's poetry, however, I have used the versions given in the former work, because the collection edited by Hooper includes the previously published versions of Lewis's verse, while that edited by King reproduces, in some instances, earlier, unpublished versions less familiar to readers. In referencing certain of Sayers's plays—*The Zeal of Thy House, The Devil to Pay, He That Should Come,* and *The Just Vengeance*—I have cited the collection in which they occur, *Four Sacred Plays.* Quotations from Eliot's journalism come from variously named phases of the critical journal he edited: *The Criterion: A Quarterly Review* (1922–25 and 1928–39); *The New Criterion: A Quarterly Review* (1926–27); and *The Monthly Criterion: A Literary Review* (1927–28). For most of the quotations from Eliot's poems and plays, I have used *The Complete Poems and Plays, 1909–1950* (New York: Harcourt Brace and World, 1971). For several poems and one play (*The Confidential Clerk*) that were published later than 1950, I have used other sources. Because none of these Eliot sources give line numbers for the poems and plays, I have indicated the location of quoted passages by giving page numbers.

I

A Meeting of Minds

✠ ✠ ✠

The image of traversing a Waste Land[1]—a sterile, death-ridden landscape—appears most notably in Sir Thomas Malory's *Morte d'Arthur,* a composite work written in the late 1400s. Malory recounts the myths of King Arthur and the knights of the Round Table who, in their quest to find the Holy Grail, journey through a region blighted by "pestilence" in which all vegetation is "withered and [will] not grow again" and all water has become "empty of fish"—a region called "the Waste Lands" (Malory 410). The Waste Land image reappeared in T. S. Eliot's iconic poem of 1922, in which the landscape is littered with "stony rubbish," "broken images," "withered stumps of time," "bones" of the dead, "exhausted wells," "tumbled graves," and "falling towers." The scene is peopled by haunting figures: shadows "striding behind you," a "hanged man," abused and demeaned women, a drowned sailor, and a mysterious "gliding . . . , hooded" figure (*The Waste Land* 37–55). *The Waste Land* depicts a world that is falling apart and lives that are blighted. Blending a variety of poetic forms, the poem is a collage of bits and pieces: scraps of conversation, fragments of scenes, and disparate images. Startling and contrasting impressions bombard the reader. The poem appeals to the senses and emotions, requiring the reader to respond to constantly shifting scenes and a bewildering array of vague characters that crowd in and then drop away again. The diverging and converging fragments that make up *The Waste Land* spoke for a whole culture in crisis in the early

1920s, and the poem was viewed both as an eloquent expression of the dismay that underlay modern consciousness and as the ultimate example of a modernist poem. Although written almost a century ago in a time of great anxiety, *The Waste Land* continues to speak powerfully to later generations. Writing of *The Waste Land* in 1994, Jewell Spears Brooker remarked that the crisis it addressed was an ongoing one (233). "We still," Brooker observes, "live with the possibility that contemporary people will . . . literally annihilate themselves and their civilization" (233–34). The bleakness and uncertainty of the 1920s, and of the ensuing decades of the mid-twentieth century,[2] are paralleled by the bleakness and uncertainty of our own age.

From the late nineteenth century, the visibility and influence of the Church had declined steadily, yet during World War II there was an unexpected "re-appropriation of Christian faith as 'the key to the meaning of life'"—a reappropriation that British historian Adrian Hastings attributes to the "Anglican lay literary and theological writers C. S. Lewis, T. S. Eliot, [and] Dorothy L. Sayers" (388). Hastings connects this revival of Christian faith with the harsh realities of World War II, which prompted much "moral fumbling" but also "simple, almost crusade-like heroism" and a widespread return to rudimentary values. The work of Lewis, Eliot, and Sayers was, Hastings observes, surprisingly "of the same sort." Through the literary output of these three writers during the 1940s, he argues, the "popular religious apologetic of modern Britain was . . . being composed almost at a stroke!" (389). Though they occupied very different niches, all three writers were well-known public figures by the early 1940s. Eliot, luminous among the cultural elite, had by 1925 become widely recognized as a leading poet and critic and was regarded as the quintessential representative of modernism. Sayers, more closely connected with popular culture, began writing detective fiction early in the twenties—that golden age of the whodunit—and within a few years had become one of the best-selling writers of the genre. Lewis, well respected as an eloquent Oxford academic, did not become widely known outside Oxford until the early 1940s, when his popular radio talks inspired renewed respect for Christian teaching.

The Christian message that Lewis, Sayers, and Eliot delivered was not, however, easy to embrace. The challenges it presented were enormous: the call to submit to the lordship of Christ, the invitation to forsake all and become a disciple, the disruption of ordinary life by the interference of the unexpected, the opportunity to endure great suffering with hope and peace, the prospect of arduous pilgrimage, the disquietude of finding oneself a stranger in a hostile age. In chapters 3 through 8, I will examine these six frightening but redemptive extremities as they are illuminated in the work of Lewis, Sayers, and Eliot. The overarching image in all six is that of Christ himself: the Lion[3] in the Waste Land.

Three Voices, One Message

My focus in this book is not on what these three writers had in common as individuals, and my purpose is not to prove that the similarities among them were greater than the differences; the three were strikingly different in their natures and their literary output. Instead, my purpose is to explore the complementary nature of what Lewis, Sayers, and Eliot had to say on a number of important subjects—subjects connected with the central Christian doctrine of redemption through Christ. Although the universal Church includes much diversity, there is agreement on core issues. As St. Paul wrote, there is "one Lord, one faith, one baptism" (Eph. 4.5). It is not surprising, therefore, that there is harmony in the view of these three writers on such subjects as the nature of Christ, the experience of conversion, the reality of angels, enduring suffering, struggling with time, and the failures of modernity. By the very nature of their differing backgrounds and perspectives, they bring to these subjects insight and clarity that, when viewed collectively, enhance one another. Eliot said that no writer "has his complete meaning alone," because his significance lies in his relation to others. To fully value individual writers, he explains, we must set them, "for contrast and comparison," among others ("Tradition and the Individual Talent" 15). This book will place three writers side by side: first by showing the ways in which their lives connected (ch. 1); next by showing the struggle that each experienced with the calling of poet-prophet (ch. 2): and then by examining their complementary convictions under six different headings (chs. 3 through 8).

Common Ground

Three things that Lewis, Eliot, and Sayers had in common were Christian faith rooted in conservative Anglicanism, higher education in the humanities, and searing power with words. While many writers exhibit these characteristics, they are particularly important to the work of Lewis, Sayers, and Eliot.

All three writers were members of the Church of England, but the flavor of their affinity to it differed, partly because of differences in their early religious experiences. Though Lewis's parents faithfully attended the Church of Ireland[4] and though he was regularly taken to church and taught to say his prayers, Lewis recalled taking no interest in religion in his early life, and regarded his childhood as devoid of significant "religious experiences" (*Surprised by Joy* 4). The insipidity of his early religious experiences bred no lasting animosity, however: it was the established Church and its traditions that he espoused when he became a Christian in 1931. Lewis particularly loved *The Book of Common Prayer*. Praising its sobriety, artistry, and strength, he described it as shining "with a white light hardly surpassed outside the pages of the New Testament itself" (*English Literature in the Sixteenth Century* 221). Lewis was not comfortable with the extremities of the Church of England: he was equally uneasy with extremes of High Church ritual and Low Church casualness. Even in the Anglican mainstream of his local parish church he felt somewhat detached from the paraphernalia of corporate worship. Nonetheless, he believed in the necessity of church attendance, observing that "the Church is not a human society of people united by their natural affinities but the Body of

Christ in which all members, however different . . . must share the common life, complementing and helping one another precisely by their differences" (*Collected Letters of CSL* 3: 224).

T. S. Eliot was born and raised in St. Louis, Missouri, in a Unitarian family. Though Eliot remained devoted to his parents and siblings, by the time of his public confession of faith at the age of thirty-nine,[5] he had moved a long way from the religious position of his family. As Eliot knew it in his early life, Unitarianism had strong liberal and rationalist leanings and placed so little emphasis on the core doctrines of Christianity that he described himself as being brought up "outside the Christian fold" (letter to Bertrand Russell, qtd. in Gordon, *Imperfect Life* 19). The blandness and coldness of Unitarianism offered nothing that Eliot wanted or respected. In a 1934 lecture, he spoke with disapproval of the liberalism in the American Episcopal Church reflected in the Church's wish to have "Unitarian infidels recognized as fellow-believers" (*After Strange Gods* 22). He saw orthodox Anglican doctrine as the essence of Christianity and was instinctively drawn to the living tradition of the Church of England that had begun in Canterbury in AD 597. This tradition was, as Russell Kirk points out, especially appealing for being "interwoven with the great body of literature [Eliot] knew so well" (120). Kirk observes that "the preachers and scholars of the Church of England, from the reign of Elizabeth onward, had filled [Eliot's] mind" for many years before he was baptized into the Church (120). From the time of his first confession in March 1928, Eliot practiced Anglicanism devoutly, meeting regularly with his spiritual director and receiving Holy Communion at least three times a week (Gordon, *Imperfect Life* 224).

Dorothy L. Sayers was also a regular communicant, but unlike Eliot she was a "cradle Anglican." The daughter of a Church of England clergyman and an only child, she continued in the faith of her parents and remained closely associated with Anglicanism throughout her life.[6] In her later years, she was actively involved in parish life in central London, serving for a time as church warden of St. Anne's Church in Soho. Like Lewis and Eliot, Sayers found in

The Book of Common Prayer the structure that defined her faith. Indeed, she spoke and wrote much on the *BCP*, recognizing it as the bedrock of Christian orthodoxy and particularly emphasizing the importance of the creeds.[7]

Lewis, Eliot, and Sayers had similar educational backgrounds and academic interests. All three were scholars. Lewis's achievement as an undergraduate at University College, Oxford, led to his being made a fellow (i.e., a faculty member) at Magdalen College, Oxford, in 1925. He continued to hold this post as a tutor and lecturer in English literature for the next twenty-nine years, until his Cambridge University appointment in 1954. Eliot's initial academic focus was philosophy, which he studied at Harvard University, in Boston, between 1906 and 1914, as both an undergraduate and a graduate student. He also studied at the Sorbonne in Paris, and at Merton College, Oxford. Superbly trained as an academic, Eliot did not take up an academic profession, but distinguished himself as one of the most scholarly and widely read men of his generation. Dorothy L. Sayers was also a scholar. She studied medieval French Literature at Somerville, Oxford, between 1913 and 1915, and throughout her life she was a voracious reader in a wide range of subjects. Her scholarly gifts were most fully exercised in the last decade of her life when she immersed herself in Dante, producing a new English translation of *The Divine Comedy* and lecturing extensively on it.

In addition to their commonly held faith and devotion to scholarship, the three were all highly gifted writers, sharing a talent that was, to use a phrase from Lewis's description of Mercury in his poem "The Planets," "the spark of speech from spirit's tinder" (*Poems* 12). Eliot's power with words—the "tinder" that sparked some of the greatest poetry of the twentieth century—was first apparent in 1915 with the publication of the poem "The Love Song of J. Alfred Prufrock," and then in 1917 with the volume of poetry *Prufrock and Other Observations*. Five years later, *The Waste Land* became the "poem that fired the imagination of the 'lost' generation" (Gordon, *Imperfect Life* 146). The first readers of Eliot's early poetry, Kathleen Raine records, found that it, "more than the work of any other poet," enabled them to "know [their] world imaginatively" (78). Other high points in Eliot's career as a writer were *Murder in the Cathedral* (1935), perhaps the greatest of Christian plays, and *Four Quartets* (1944), regarded by many as "the greatest twentieth-century achievement in the poetry of philosophy and religion" (Kirk 240).

Lewis's power with words is as indisputable as Eliot's. His works of Christian fiction and apologetics had unprecedented appeal, and his prowess as a speaker was widely recognized. Harry Blamires, an Oxford student in the late 1930s, reported that he was the most popular lecturer in the English faculty: "He could fill the largest lecture rooms . . . his lectures were meaty . . . arguments beautifully articulated; illustrations richly chosen" (qtd. in W. Lewis 38).[8] Outside the formal lecture room, his fame as a rhetorician was equally great. "When I was a student at Oxford between 1942 and 45," one student recalls, "Lewis was the uncrowned king, not only of the English faculty, but of the whole university. . . . We made our way through the blackout to hear this extraordinary man . . . in his element, the apologist, and popularizer, 'the true wayfaring Christian' in Milton's phrase" (Trickett 61–62).[9]

Lewis's radio broadcasts in the early 1940s drew enormous listening audiences. His "Broadcast Talks" were published first as several separate groups of essays and later as *Mere Christianity*. In October 1944, the *Times Literary Supplement* wrote of them, "Mr. Lewis has a quite unique power of making theology attractive, exciting and (one might almost say) uproariously funny" (Review of "Beyond Personality" 513). Another reviewer commented that because of "his clarity of thought and simplicity of expression [the talks had] a magic about them which makes plain the most abstruse problems of theological speculation" (Homes 12).[10]

Dorothy L. Sayers's skill as a wordsmith has been less well known than that of Lewis and Eliot, particularly in America. Yet in England in the 1940s and 1950s her name was a household word. In the tribute C. S. Lewis wrote for Sayers's memorial service,[11] he thanked "the Author who invented her" for the "delight and instruction" her work brought to so many and praised her enormous success as both "a popular entertainer and a conscientious craftsman" ("A Panegyric for Dorothy L. Sayers" 91–95). The Rev. James Welch, the BBC's director of religious broadcasting, acknowledged the success of her radio plays on the life of Christ, saying she "put the Christian Church in her debt by making Our Lord . . . 'really real' for so many" (16).[12] By 1940 Sayers's popularity as a speaker almost equaled her fame as a writer; she was flooded with demands to lecture on religious themes in person and on the radio. Her eloquence in this media pulpit was praised by a columnist in the BBC magazine the *Listener,* who said, "In the way of accomplished exposition I have seldom heard anything more admirable than Dorothy L. Sayers on the essentials of Christian belief. . . . In one of his moods of elephantine obstinacy Dr. [Samuel] Johnson ridiculed the notion of a woman in the pulpit. I'd back Dorothy Sayers to put the case for Christianity better than many of our wireless padres . . . I will gladly listen to her for a month of Sundays" (Williams 248).

Increased literacy in the first half of the twentieth century produced a much larger reading public, and the *spoken* word, via radio, was just coming into its own. From the 1920s through the 1950s the world was reeling in the aftermath of the Great War, suffering through the Great Depression, and enduring the horrors of yet another war. In this bleak Waste Land, Lewis, Sayers, and Eliot emerged as three eloquent communicators who offered hope. Their message was redemptive.

The Tension between Lewis and Eliot

Lewis and Eliot eventually came to hold each other in great esteem, but a distinctly negative feeling existed between them early in their careers. The negativity seems to have been largely on Lewis's side. During the 1920s and 1930s Lewis clearly expressed his intense dislike of Eliot's poetry, but the dislike—largely arising from differences in literary perspective and literary taste—does not seem to have lasted beyond that time period. Lewis was an Oxford academic of the old school and Eliot was part of a modernist avant-garde milieu. The initial difference in what each viewed as good poetry arose, for the most part, from the divide between the traditional and the modern in literature. As the years went on, however, the divide between their positions as literary figures greatly diminished. It became increasingly apparent that Eliot was not in the truest sense a modernist in his thinking, and that his claim to be a classicist (in the sense of being intrinsically respectful of and connected with the past) was reasonable and valid. With respect to literary style, the divide between the traditional and the modern was real, but while it eventually became clear that Eliot, in his worldview, was not on the modern side of that chasm, this was not apparent to Lewis (or to anyone else) in the 1920s and 1930s, and during these years Lewis frequently expressed dislike for Eliot.

C. S. Lewis's first reaction to Eliot's poetry was scorn. In a journal entry of June 1926, Lewis indicates that he has written a nonsensical parody of Eliot's verse, with the thought of sending it in to Eliot's journal, the *Criterion,* to see if he "might be . . . taken in" by it and publish it. "If he doesn't," Lewis writes, "I shall have proved that there is something more than I suspected in this kind of stuff" (*All My Road Before Me* 409–10). The writing of "Eliotic" poems (as he called them) and the idea of playing such a joke on the *Criterion* created a brief humorous diversion for his "anti-Eliot group" of friends (411, 413). However, Lewis's suggestion in the journal entry that he might be mistaken in his dislike of Eliot's sort of poetry—that there might be "something more" in it—is significant. It shows, even this early, a slight willingness on Lewis's part to reconsider his negative view of the new movement in poetry.

It is not surprising that Lewis's literary tastes and preferences made him unable to appreciate Eliot's drastically unconventional style. In his poem "A Confession" Lewis directly belittles Eliot's first significant poem "The Love Song of J. Alfred Prufrock" (first published in 1915), in which an evening sky is compared to "a patient etherized upon a table." That opening image of the poem is meaningless to

Lewis, and is, he ironically suggests in his poem, equally meaningless to most ordinary people—people who are "coarse" and unsophisticated like himself: "For twenty years I've stared my level best / To see if evening—any evening—would suggest /A patient etherized upon a table; / In vain. I simply wasn't able" (Lewis, *Poems* 1).[13]

Eliot's most famous poem, *The Waste Land,* was equally unpalatable to Lewis. In a letter written to Paul Elmer More in 1935, Lewis harshly expressed his view of it, observing that "no man is fortified against chaos by reading the *Waste Land,* but that most men are by it infected with chaos." He judged that people liked Eliot's poem because they confused poetry that depicted disintegration with "disintegrated poetry." He clearly viewed *The Waste Land* as the latter. He compared *The Inferno* with *The Waste Land,* observing that while Dante's work (though depicting hell) was not "infernal," Eliot's poem was. He evaluated Eliot's criticism with similar negativity, noting that, though Eliot called himself a classicist, "his sympathy with depraved poets (Marlow, Jonson, Webster) is apparent: [and] he shows no real love of any disciplined, and magnanimous writer save Dante." He categorized Eliot as "one of the enemy: and all the more dangerous because he is sometimes disguised as a friend." This intensity of dislike is modulated, but very slightly, by his concluding remark on the subject: "Of the man himself I know nothing and will do my best to believe any good that I may hear from you or other authorised sources" (*Collected Letters of CSL* 2: 163–64). These observations are particularly disturbing in that they come in response to a letter from More that had said, "Eliot is a dear friend . . . , and on the whole I do not like to see him placed among the enemies" (*Collected Letters of CSL* 2: 164).

Our uneasiness over Lewis's outspoken antagonism toward Eliot might be partially eased if we could assume that he thought of Eliot as an "enemy" only in a literary and cultural sense. However, in *The Pilgrim's Regress* (published in 1933) Lewis expressed an equally dim view of Eliot's religion through the character Neo-Angular. In a letter to his publisher he admitted that he was parodying Eliot (*Collected Letters of CSL* 2: 94), and in another context, he explained that what he was attacking through Mr. Neo-Angular was "a set of people who seem to me . . . to be trying to make of Christianity itself one more high-brow, Chelsea, bourgeois-baiting fad," and added, "T. S. Eliot is the single man who sums up the thing I am fighting against" (qtd. in Green and Hooper 130).

Mr. Neo-Angular of *The Pilgrim's Regress* represents Lewis's unease about Anglo-Catholicism in general and his disapproval of the religious stance of T. S. Eliot in particular. The key point is that Lewis suspected Eliot's religion of being just that—a *stance*. At this stage, just six years after Eliot's baptism and two years after he himself came to faith in Christ, Lewis was unconvinced of the genuineness of Eliot's faith. Lewis's skepticism toward Eliot's claim to be a Christian would dissipate completely over time, however, and the change would begin very soon. Surprisingly, in a letter written the very next year, in 1934, Lewis referred to Eliot as the leading spokesperson for the "side" of Christianity that he was part of—Anglicanism (*Collected Letters of CSL* 2: 134). By 1940 he had come to believe that Eliot's faith was genuine. In a letter of September 1940, Lewis responded to a correspondent who had complained of Eliot's "collapse into Anglo-Catholicism" instead of "newer and stranger things" by saying that he found such a critical view of Eliot "profoundly disquieting." He continues, "You don't seem to consider the hypothesis that he might have embraced this belief because he thought it was *true*—that he might be looking for the true, not the 'new and strange'" (*Collected Letters of CSL* 2: 443).

With respect to literary matters, the two most important contexts in which Lewis spoke against Eliot came in the late 1930s and early 1940s. These are *The Personal Heresy: A Controversy,* written jointly by the critic E. M. W. Tillyard and Lewis and published in 1939, and *A Preface to Paradise Lost,* published in 1942. The first is a short book made up of six essays (of alternating authorship) in which Tillyard and Lewis debate the nature of poetry: Lewis writes one essay expressing his position and then Tillyard writes the next, expressing an opposite position. One of Lewis's key contentions in the three essays he contributed to this collection is that much of modern criticism presupposes, illogically, that poetry has "su-perhuman" or transcendent characteristics, yet the critics do not themselves believe in any ultimate transcendent reality (Tillyard and Lewis 27). Since the larger issue of the debate is modernism in literature, one of the key exhibits for both sides of the debate is the poetry of Eliot. Tillyard quotes from Eliot's choruses to the religious pageant play *The Rock* to illustrate the freedom of scope of mod-ern verse and the "poetical personality that quickens our pulses" (36–37). Lewis's response denies the superiority of such verse. Til-lyard describes a passage from *The Rock* as having a rhythm that is "tense" and "subtle," and that "exploits to the utmost the startling mixture of biblical reference and golf balls" (36). Lewis responds to such approval of Eliot's style by disputing the "merits" that Til-lyard finds in the passage referred to, and by rejecting the idea that it is even "startling." He concedes that it may have a kind of power, but argues that it is not the right sort of power. "If I allow myself to attend to the kind of man thus speaking of the suburbs, then I find myself carried into realms of thought and feeling which are fatal to the reception of poetry." The kind of poetry Eliot wrote appeared to Lewis to be fatally imprisoned in the soul-destroying suburbs of modern London, and—with such horrific limitations—could not possibly offer passage to that grander, larger world to which poetry should, in Lewis's opinion, transport the reader (63–64).

As Lewis expresses his disapproval of modern poetry like El-iot's in these *Personal Heresy* essays, he connects modernism with unpleasantness and a complete absence of virtue. Responding to Tillyard's reference to Wordsworth's definition of a poet as "a man speaking to men" (Tillyard and Lewis 80),[14] Lewis questions the value of such a "Naturalistic" theory of poetry. He challenges Wordsworth's belief that a poet actually surpasses the average man in "'tenderness, enthusiasm', and 'knowledge of human nature,'" contending instead that "a poet . . . is sometimes . . . a man inferior to the majority" in those qualities, "—not to speak of information, common-sense, fortitude, and courtesy" (106). Lewis condemns the new poetry of the 1920s and 1930s as succeeding only in "commu-

nicating moods of boredom and nausea that have only an infini-
tesimal place in the life of a corrected and full-grown man." Rather
than a poet having superiority over the common man in his sensibilities, as Wordsworth suggested, Lewis considers modern poets to
be different from the masses "only by defect"—if at all (106). Passages like this, taken in isolation, sound like total rejection of Eliot
as a poet, perhaps even as a man.

We must not, however, take such accusatory passages in isolation: there is a bigger picture—a larger context—that must be considered. First, it is significant that the opening essay in *The Personal
Heresy* had been written by Lewis nine years earlier, in 1930. This
essay,[15] like the collection it later became part of, takes a very different approach to poetry from that of Eliot, but unlike the later
collection, it does not directly mention Eliot. Surprisingly, Lewis
had sent this essay (blatantly critical of Eliot's own poetry) to Eliot
in November 1930, asking him to consider publishing it in the *Criterion*. Although Eliot did not publish it, the letters on the publication issue that passed between him and Lewis in the spring of 1931
contain absolutely no hint of personal animosity. Eliot, typically
gentle and respectful to authors whose works he did not accept for
publication, was not affronted by Lewis's suggestion that he might
publish an essay that criticized the type of poetry he himself wrote,
and Lewis had probably assumed that he would not be.

The second important aspect of the larger context is the tone and
content of the preface to *The Personal Heresy: A Controversy*—
i.e., the six essays by Lewis and Tillyard as they were published in
1939. The preface, written jointly by the two authors, is striking for
its scholarly graciousness. Despite their disagreement, the two critics are extremely cordial in the preface, assuring readers that the
publication of the debate is a respectful joint effort. The "controversy" between them was conducted with decorum and fairness to
such an extent that Lewis and Tillyard were able to admit in their
preface, without loss of face, that both of them "have found now
and then that the alley they were exploring was blind and have had
to retrace their way, with apparent waste of time and effort" (v).

The civility and respect between Lewis and Tillyard represents, to a large extent, the feeling between Lewis and Eliot.[16] The preface by Lewis and Tillyard indicates that scholarly men learned much from such literary controversy—things like increased appreciation for the opposing "camp" in critical thought and increased awareness of the danger of critics disagreeing "without ever meeting face to face" (v–vi). From this point on, scholarly courtesy did, in fact, temper the edge of Lewis's dislike of Eliot. A face-to-face meeting was yet to come.

Another significant literary context in which Lewis spoke out against Eliot was his lecture series on Milton's *Paradise Lost,* published in 1942 as *A Preface to Paradise Lost.* In chapter 2, Lewis challenges the view of Milton that Eliot had expressed in his essay "A Note on the Verse of John Milton." Lewis objects to Eliot's suggestion that only poets can truly evaluate poetry. But, even as he proceeds to set up his own line of thought in contrast to Eliot's, Lewis is careful to make it clear that he has no desire to attack Eliot on a personal basis. "Why should I?" he asks; and goes on, "I agree with him about matters of such moment that all literary questions are, in comparison, trivial" (*Preface to Paradise Lost* 9).

Eliot wrote Lewis to tell him that he liked his book on Milton, and on February 23, 1943, Lewis wrote in response to Eliot's "kind letter" to him about *A Preface to Paradise Lost.* His tone and sentiments are cordial. He begins by saying "I do not think we were really at cross purposes. . . . Charles Williams is always promising (or threatening) to confront us with each other [to] hammer all these matters out." He then apologizes to Eliot for the fact that he so often contradicts him in print, and hopes that he does not take offence. He says that "it is a kind of tribute" to Eliot that whenever he (Lewis) comes across some literary view that he wishes to refute he finds that it is usually Eliot who expresses it most clearly. He concludes, "One aims at the officers first in meeting an attack! I'm so glad you agreed about Virgil" (*Collected Letters of CSL* 2: 556–57).

There was much on which these two men agreed: they highly valued many of the same things and the same people. Both held

Dante in the highest esteem and were greatly influenced by *The Divine Comedy.*[17] They also had several significant mutual friends. William Force Stead, whom Lewis counted as a close friend from the early 1920s onward, became Eliot's friend a few years later, and it was Stead who baptized Eliot into the Church of England on June 9, 1927. Most important among their mutual friends was Charles Williams, whom they both regarded with deep admiration and love. Lewis described Williams as "irresistible" (*Collected Letters of CSL* 2: 196), and Eliot said of Williams, "he was somehow protected from evil, and was himself a protection" (Introduction to *All Hallows Eve* xiii–xiv).

Charles Williams, in late 1944 or early 1945, made good his threat to arrange a meeting between Lewis and Eliot: he brought them together for tea at the Mitre, an Oxford hotel. Father Gervase Mathew, who was present at that meeting, interpreted the feeling between Lewis and Eliot to be less than cordial, reporting that he believed that Lewis was unamused, if not offended, by Eliot's opening remark: "Mr. Lewis you are a much *older* man than you appear in photographs" (Green and Hooper 223). It is possible, however, that Father Gervase misread Eliot's intention and Lewis's response. Eliot, who was typically polite and often formal to a fault, nonetheless enjoyed making witty jabs. He quite possibly intended the remark as a joke, and Lewis was humble enough about his personal appearance, and good-humored enough, to receive it as a joke, even if he did not find it funny enough to laugh at. I doubt if he was particularly offended.

Another presumed moment of offense at this meeting in the Mitre also requires some explanation. Some of those present knew that Lewis had criticized Eliot in his *Preface to Paradise Lost*. When Eliot said, "I must tell you, Mr. Lewis, that I consider your *Preface to Paradise Lost* your best book," it is understandable for them to think, as Father Gervase did, that Eliot was being intentionally sarcastic and trying to make Lewis uncomfortable. However, in view of the letters between Lewis and Eliot mentioned above, this is almost certainly a misreading of the conversation. Eliot's comment might seem sarcastic if one did not know that Eliot had already written Lewis an appreciative letter about that very book, and received a friendly response from Lewis (*Collected Letters of CSL* 2: 556). Eliot's compliment was genuine and sincere.

Nonetheless, this initial meeting of Lewis and Eliot does not seem to have been a particularly cheerful encounter, and this may have been in part because most of those present presupposed that the feeling between the two writers was more strained than it actually was. Father Gervase considered that "a bad time was had by all" except Charles Williams, who seemed to have "enjoyed himself hugely" (Green and Hooper 224). The meeting certainly did not constitute the beginning of friendship between Lewis and Eliot; that was not to come until about fourteen years later, in 1959.

It was the archbishop of Canterbury who provided Lewis and Eliot with an opportunity to become friends by asking both men to serve on a Church of England commission. This commission, formed to review the Psalms for a revised version of *The Book of Common Prayer,* frequently met in London over a number of years. Eliot and Lewis became warm friends almost immediately, and in his (now frequent) letters to Eliot, Lewis soon replaced the typically formal opening of "Dear Mr. Eliot" with the style of greeting he used for his close friends: "My dear Eliot."[18] The letters of Lewis to Eliot in this period are chatty and witty; they refer to committee matters, literary matters, and mutual acquaintances. "Lewis could easily have been speaking of Eliot and himself," Walter Hooper observes in his book *C. S. Lewis: A Companion and Guide,* "when he said in *The Four Loves* [Part IV]: 'Friendship arises out of mere companionship when two or more of the companions discover they have in common some insight or interest or even taste which the others do not share and which, till that moment, each believed to be his own unique treasure (or burden)'" (654). Indeed, Lewis said of Eliot that after getting to know him he "found it easy to 'love' him" (qtd. in Hooper 91).

It is much more difficult to examine the relationship between Lewis and Eliot from Eliot's side, because there is little information about Eliot's perception of Lewis throughout these years, when they occasionally crossed ways, both figuratively and literally. The volumes of Eliot's letters that have been published contain no significant correspondence with Lewis, and Eliot's published works do not directly mention Lewis. Nonetheless, it is fair to assume that Eliot would not take Lewis's criticism of his poetry as a personal affront. In his preface to *After Strange Gods* (a lecture series) Eliot remarked that the extent to which he himself criticized authors was "some measure of [his] respect for them" (12). Other than in book reviews, Eliot typically avoided making comments, whether literary or personal, on contemporary writers. He admitted that many people are curious to know what any writer thinks of his peers, but he regarded such curiosity as having "less to do with literary criticism than with literary gossip" and felt uncertain of his own ability to criticize his contemporaries as artists (12).

In later life, Eliot came to admire Lewis as an artist. Most of the letters to Eliot in Lewis's published correspondence of the late 1950s and early 1960s are responses to letters Eliot had written to him—letters that had apparently been warm and appreciative. On June 29, 1959, Lewis responded enthusiastically to Eliot's invitation to Lewis and his wife Joy to dine with Eliot and his wife Valerie.[19] The letter of invitation reached Lewis while he was on holiday in Donegal, and he said that the letter had followed him "to the world's end—or to one of its ends" (*Collected Letters of CSL* 3: 1063), alluding to a passage in Eliot's magnum opus, "Little Gidding,"[20] and showing his appreciative familiarity with it. As the two men continued to meet frequently, their friendship solidified. Lewis's letters to Eliot of 1961 and 1962 indicate the camaraderie they felt: they acknowledge further dinner invitations, mention a desire to talk with Eliot about the complexities of the concept of punishment, thank Eliot for his expressions of sympathy regarding physical ailments, and thank Eliot for "all the kind things" he had said in a previous letter (*Collected Letters of CSL* 3: 1346).

Eliot probably never felt the degree of animosity toward Lewis that Lewis had initially felt toward him. He had less reason than

Lewis to feel his position challenged, and by temperament he would be more inclined to suppress negative emotions arising from intellectual controversy than to express them openly. Lewis's outspoken expression of his early negative feeling toward Eliot seems to have done little harm, and may even have been the catharsis leading to the firm friendship of later years.

The friendship and appreciation that Eliot felt for Lewis is well summed up by the part he played in the publication of Lewis's *A Grief Observed*. After Lewis's wife died of cancer in July 1960, Lewis recorded his grief and despair in the form of a journal. This poignant diary of pain is probably the most intimately personal of all Lewis's work, and the most ridden with spiritual desolation. Though encouraged to publish it, Lewis hesitated; he felt that if it did appear in print it would be advisable to use a pseudonym. Eventually, with Lewis's consent, it was offered to a publisher by Lewis's literary agent. The publisher was Faber and Faber, and it was Eliot, a director at that publishing house, who received the anonymous manuscript, with a suggested pseudonym attached. In response, Eliot wrote to the literary agent, Spencer Curtis Brown:

> I and two other directors have read *A Grief Observed*. My wife has read it also and we have all been deeply moved by it. We do in fact want to publish it. . . . We are of the opinion that we have guessed the name of the author. If, as you intimate and as I should expect from the man I think it is, he does sincerely want anonymity, we agree that a plausible English pseudonym would hold off enquirers better than Dimidius [the pen name that Lewis had proposed, meaning "halved" or "divided in two"]. The latter is sure to arouse curiosity and there must be plenty of people amongst those who know him, and perhaps even among the readers of his work who do not know him, who may be able to penetrate the disguise once they set their minds to working.[21]

These are the words and thoughts of a wise and caring friend—a friend with intimate knowledge of Lewis and a sincere desire to honor his wishes for privacy at this very vulnerable time.

In the final analysis, Lewis and Eliot stand side by side as friends. In the third movement of "Little Gidding," Eliot speaks of inspired people of the past who are "touched by a common genius" and who yet find themselves on opposing sides of a conflict.[22] Eliot depicts, in this passage, the strife that separates such men as ultimately insubstantial—almost translucent. The men are described as finally "united in the strife which divided them" (*Four Quartets* 143). This paradox may be applied to the strife that divided Eliot and Lewis. The marked difference in literary perspective that was particularly intense in early life was, ultimately, of little consequence. Another kind of striving was to unite them. They found themselves on the same side in the spiritual warfare required of those who proclaimed fearsome redemption. That was the strife that brought them together.

Sayers's Acquaintance with Lewis and Eliot

In the passage just mentioned, from the third movement of Eliot's "Little Gidding," the individuals who find themselves initially on opposing sides are miraculously "folded in a single party" (*Four Quartets* 143). It is something of a miracle that Dorothy L. Sayers should be considered of "a single party" with Lewis and Eliot, in any respect. For one thing, the academic world of C. S. Lewis was unapologetically a man's world, and so was the urbane world of T. S. Eliot. A female scholar of that time could never have a significant voice among the dons of an Oxford college or in the loud beef-beer-and-the-Church debates of the Inklings. Nor could a woman writer—unless she happened to be Virginia Woolf—be considered an equal among the contributors to the *Criterion* or the directors of Faber and Faber. Dorothy L. Sayers was, nonetheless, a significant presence in the broader literary milieu of Lewis and Eliot.

Another thing that would tend to exclude Sayers from the immediate company of such men as Lewis and Eliot was her personality. She lacked the subtlety and restraint necessary to win acceptability in academic and upper-class society. Sayers was frank and energetic, and never shrank from confrontation. Such traits served her well as a writer, but would make her an unnerving presence in many gatherings in which the presence of Lewis or Eliot would be congenial. But, figuratively speaking, Sayers stands side by side with them. It could be argued that she usurps a place next to them through sheer audacity. It is not, however, audacity in isolation from other strengths; it is an audacity supported by intelligence and literary genius. Set next to Eliot and Lewis, Dorothy L. Sayers the mystery writer may appear lowbrow and populist. Yet she was a brilliant and scholarly Christian spokesperson, and her impact as a writer was—like theirs—that of a prophet, a proclaimer of spiritual truth.

Adrian Hastings, in recounting the history of the Church of England in the twentieth century, observes that between 1945 and 1960, the field of religious literature was bright because "C. S. Lewis, T. S. Eliot, and Dorothy L. Sayers . . . produced a continued glow of literary distinction around the Church of England" (446). To some observers, however, what Sayers shared with Lewis and Eliot was not so much a glow of distinction as a cloud of notoriety. In 1953, Sayers was depicted as being cut of the same disreputable cloth as Lewis and Eliot when all three were among the writers targeted in Kathleen Nott's *The Emperor's Clothes,* a book described on the jacket as an "attack on the dogmatic theology of T. S. Eliot, Graham Greene, C. S. Lewis, and others." Sayers was among the "others." Lewis jokingly referred to himself as being pilloried by Nott "along with some of [his] betters" (*Collected Letters of CSL* 3: 428).

Charles Moorman, during his research for his book *The Precincts of Felicity: The Augustinian City of the Oxford Christians,* wrote to Lewis asking him to comment on how the Christian writers in his circle of acquaintances influenced one another. Lewis was dismissive of the idea of mutual influence and told Moorman that in trying to show common influences between himself, J. R. R. Tolkien, Charles Williams,[23] and Sayers, he (Moorman) might be "chasing after a fox that isn't there." Although he agreed that Williams had influenced him and he may have influenced Williams, he maintained that no one could ever influence Tolkien. He observed, "You might as well try to influence a bandersnatch."[24] Lewis told Moorman that though Sayers knew Williams well, she had no contact with Tolkien and minimal contact with the others that Moorman had designated as "Oxford Christians," since she was not living in Oxford when they were. He mentioned that Sayers was well established as an author before Lewis himself became known, and though he admitted that he and Sayers had a "common point of view," he said it had existed before they met, and that it was "the cause rather than the result of [their] friendship" (*Collected Letters of CSL* 3: 1049).

The friendship between Sayers and Lewis that had developed by the mid-1940s was maintained primarily through letters. Lewis corresponded regularly with an enormous number of people, including many distinguished writers, yet he placed Sayers above them all as a master of letter writing. He told her in a letter of December 1945 that she would someday be recognized as "one of the great English letter writers" (*Collected Letters of CSL* 2: 682). Their mutuality of thought is evident in their frequent references to one another in their correspondence with others. Sayers frequently recommended a work by Lewis as further clarification or support of her own position on a Christian doctrine. In *Miracles,* Lewis recommends Sayers's book-length essay on creativity, saying, "How a miracle can be no inconsistency, but the highest consistency, will be clear to those who have read Miss Dorothy Sayers' indispensable book, *The Mind of the Maker*" (*Miracles* 155–56). Lewis also recommended Sayers's translations of Dante (*Collected Letters of CSL* 3: 625). After reading her *Inferno* translation, he was eagerly anticipating the release of her edition of the *Purgatorio,* and his response to it was exuberant. He praises it as even better than her translation of the *Inferno,* observing that she had magnificently made the shift from the rugged style of *Inferno,* introducing "new modulations." He gives her the highest of praise when he tells her that after a short period of reading he had stopped thinking of evaluating her style of translation and was thinking "only of Dante" and then a bit later was thinking only of Purgatory itself (*Collected Letters of CSL* 3: 634).

Sayers's scholarship was nowhere more evident than in her Dante work, and for Lewis scholarly excellence was next to godliness itself.

Lewis was especially able to appreciate the magnitude and energy of Sayers's literary genius. He praised her creative accomplishments, small and large, saying "You are always producing noble and joyous things" (*Collected Letters of CSL* 3: 593). The small accomplishments were sometimes unusual Christmas cards she sent her friends, designed by herself and professionally printed. The 1953 Christmas card from Sayers, called "The Days of Christ's Coming," had little doors to be opened on different days, resembling those of an advent calendar. Lewis commented on the difficulty he had opening them, joking that the inaccessibility easily admitted "an allegorical interpretation" (*Collected Letters of CSL* 3: 387).

The letters between Sayers and Lewis show that, besides admiring and deploring the same things, they shared a delight in witty banter. In December 1954, Sayers acknowledged Lewis's recent appointment and inaugural lecture at Cambridge by sending him a card with an allegorical drawing. In response, Lewis sent her a humorous poem querying the meaning of the drawing and asking whether he should interpret it personally:

> Dear Dorothy, I'm puzzling hard
> What underlies your cryptic card.
> Are you the angel? and am I
> The figure pointed at? Oh fie!
> . . . .
> No matter, for I'm certain still
> It comes to me with your good will;
> Which, with my prayer, I send you back —
> Madam, your humble servant, Jack. (*Collected Letters of CSL* 3: 548)

Sayers responded in kind with her own poem (more than twice the length of Jack's), revealing that her allegorical drawing represented the conflicting good spirit (Genius) and bad spirit (Siren) of Academe that shed influence over both Oxford and Cambridge, and identified Lewis as St. Jack being led by the hand of the good spirit.

The poem concludes by encouraging Lewis to trust in the best traditions of the life of learning (*Letters of DLS* 4: 197–98).

Both their light-hearted communication and their serious interaction show the mutuality of thought between Sayers and Lewis. Sayers's newspaper review of Lewis's autobiographical *Surprised by Joy* insightfully points out the main stages in Lewis's journey to faith, and identifies the major thread of the narrative: "From the beginning to the end of the journey the pilgrim had known the fleeting visitations of 'joy'. . . . Those intimations of possible beatitude" which are the desire for that real Other, "apart from whom, as Augustine said, the soul can find no rest." The review praises Lewis's "humorous candour . . . and skill in translating complex abstractions into vivid concrete imagery."[25]

Sayers's view of Lewis was admiring without being deferential; she regarded him as a peer, almost as a colleague. Their affinity was, however, a concurrence of minds rather than a concurrence of temperaments. One instance of personality contrast appears in letters they exchanged about the drawings included in Lewis's Narnia books. Sayers asked Lewis why he had allowed such poor illustrations to be used—artwork that was, in her opinion, "boneless and shallow" and almost "blasphemous" (*Letters of DLS* 4: 253). In response Lewis admitted that he always had harbored serious reservations about the illustrator, Pauline Baynes, but that he put up with her poor art because she was a timid creature who badly needed the work, and who could be crushed by criticism or correction (*Collected Letters of CSL* 3: 638–39). Although Sayers must have respected Lewis's compassionate nature, it is doubtful if she would have been willing to sacrifice the quality of illustrations in any work of hers to avoid hurting the feelings of an insecure young woman.

It was this no-nonsense, demanding quality of Sayers that people sometimes found off-putting. Lewis's most telling comment on the intensity of her personality was that he liked her "for the extraordinary edge and zest of her conversation as [he] liked a high wind."[26] A high wind is the kind of thing one enjoys occasionally, in small doses. That is the effect Sayers's personality had on Lewis, and probably on most men of that era and vintage, who were not very comfortable in the presence of an assertive female. Perhaps they could have benefited from closer association with a woman like Dorothy L. Sayers, had the times been different.

Nonetheless, Lewis's esteem for Dorothy L. Sayers as a powerful personality and as an inspired writer was expressed conclusively in his "Panegyric for Dorothy L. Sayers," the tribute he wrote to be read at her funeral in December 1957:

> She is first and foremost the craftsman, the professional. . . . She aspired to be, and was, at once a popular entertainer and a conscientious craftsman. . . . She never sank the artist and entertainer in the evangelist. . . . While art and evangelism were distinct, they turned out to demand one another. . . . The architectonic qualities of [her] dramatic sequence [*The Man Born to Be King*] will hardly be questioned. I have re-read it in every Holy Week since it first appeared, and never re-read it without being deeply moved. . . . For all she did and was, for delight and instruction, for her militant loyalty as a friend, for courage and honesty, for the richly feminine qualities which showed through a port and manner superficially masculine and gleefully ogreish—let us thank the Author who invented her.
> (91–95)

Lewis recognized that Sayers, in assisting in the Church's ministry of evangelism, remained true to her art, and to her calling as a writer and as a prophet-poet.[27] What Lewis admired in Sayers was the same sort of integrity she admired in him—integrity that was simultaneously creative, scholarly, and Christian.

Although Sayers's connection with Eliot was much less intimate than her connection with Lewis, she was a great admirer of Eliot's work, particularly his drama, alluding to it frequently in her essays and letters. Drama was, in fact, the most significant common ground for Sayers and Eliot. Both played key roles in the revival of liturgical drama in the 1930s—a revival in which the dramas written for the Canterbury Festival had of great prominence. Eliot's *Murder in the Cathedral,* written for the 1935 Canterbury Festival and performed in London and in America numerous times in the ensuing years, resonated deeply with Sayers. It embodied spiritual themes and dramatic techniques that were part of her own vision. Her deep connection to the text of Eliot's play is apparent in the fact that she quoted the phrase "To do the right deed for the wrong reason," from act 1 of that play, several times in her letters (*Letters of DLS* 3: 253; 4: 145). The rich poetry of *Murder in the Cathedral* and Eliot's skillful revival of the ancient theatrical device of the Chorus influenced Sayers's developing skills as a dramatist, as seen in her own plays written for the Canterbury Festival: *The Zeal of Thy House* (1937) and *The Devil to Pay* (1939).

Sayers was equally responsive to the new direction in Eliot's drama in his later plays. Following the enormous success of *Murder in the Cathedral,* based heavily on the tradition and structure of the Christian religion, Eliot began to write plays for more modern tastes. These plays were not overtly religious, but they attempted, as David Jones observes, to demonstrate "the relevance of religion to all spheres of human activity" (214). The first of these were *The Family Reunion* and *The Cocktail Party.* Sayers was alert to the spiritual themes underlying the apparently secular subjects of these plays, and commented extensively on the themes of *The Family Reunion* in her 1939 article "The Food of the Full-Grown."[28] She points out that Eliot's play shows the uselessness of trying to escape from the past and depicts the play's hero as finally realizing that the "hounds of heaven" that pursue him are ultimately redemptive, concluding that he is being released, "not from, but into, reality" (21).

Sayers's spiritual connectedness to Eliot's unusual and disconcerting plays continued; in November 1953 she anticipated seeing Eliot's fourth play, *The Confidential Clerk*—and especially looked forward to the challenge of interpreting it. She told her friend Norah Lambourne that her interest had been piqued by the conflicting comments on it she had heard from some who had already seen it. She was not surprised that her friends' reactions to *The*

Confidential Clerk expressed conflicting extremes: "best . . . worst
. . . amusing, but no 'religious' message . . . [many] religious over-
tones" (*Letters of DLS* 4: 108). Sayers knew that such a range of responses was inevitable because she was well aware of the difficulty,
the complexity, and the necessity of what Eliot was trying to do.

Sayers's belief that drama could and should be a major venue for
proclaiming the message of redemption was one of her most important convictions, and one of immense lasting value. It is the conviction that places her side by side with T. S. Eliot. Writing about
Christian drama in 1952, she rejoices in the triumphant recovery
of drama by the Church, and makes remarkable observations, not
only about religious drama, but about the precarious and important role of Christian writers generally. She comments astutely on
how Eliot, Lewis, and she herself are viewed:

> When I was young, the common (and I fear usually justified) criti-
> cism of a Christian work of art was that it tended to be undogmatic,
> sentimental, cosily optimistic and intellectually contemptible. Today,
> the most common criticism of the work of such writers as, say, T. S.
> Eliot, Charles Williams, Ronald Duncan—and even of C. S. Lewis
> and myself—is that it is rigidly dogmatic, harsh, disquieting, and
> aridly intellectual to the point of obscurity. Christianity, once de-
> spised as soothing syrup for low-brows, seems to be in danger of be-
> ing feared and hated as a superior vintage for highbrows. Of course,
> whether the Son of Man comes fasting, or eating, or drinking there is
> always a rude word to throw at Him. ("Sacred Plays" 1: 22)

A key point here is her recognition that the message Eliot, Lewis,
and she herself proclaimed would be seen by many as "harsh" and
"disquieting." Sayers did not believe that the intellectual quality of
their Christian writing made it "a superior vintage for highbrows,"
but she was proud to be part of a proclamation of the gospel that
was anything but "cosily optimistic." She knew that the disturbing,
and sometimes frightening, plays of T. S. Eliot conveyed the terror
that is integral to redemption.

The perilous journey of redemption had been graphically delineated six centuries earlier in Dante's *Divine Comedy,* a work that was dear to the hearts of all three writers. As we have seen, letters between Sayers and Lewis had often spoken of Dante, and particularly of Sayers's translation work. Their extensive knowledge of Dante and their fondness for Charles Williams—who was a kind of priestly mediator for Dante devotees—are other areas in which Sayers and Eliot stand side by side. In a letter written on May 9, 1945, Sayers reported to Charles Williams that, before commissioning her to translate *The Divine Comedy,* the Penguin publishers had considered asking Eliot to do it (*Letters of DLS* 3: 141). Sayers was delighted to take on the assignment, but she told Williams she had some misgivings. Having accosted the Penguin editor and convinced him of her competence to do the job, she was left with the "solemn thought that . . . all [she had] done for poor dear Dante [was] to deprive him of the services of a better poet than [herself]"; but she comforted herself with the thought that "Eliot might have refused" (*Letters of DLS* 3: 141).

Six days after Sayers wrote that letter to him, Williams died suddenly, following surgery. It was a completely unforeseen and devastating loss to all who knew him. To Eliot, he seemed "to approximate . . . more nearly than any man [he] had ever known . . . to the saint" (Introduction to *All Hallows' Eve*). Sayers spoke of being so "proud of his friendship," and owing so much to "his encouragement and inspiration" that she now felt that "the whole direction of [her Dante work] had been cut off" (*Letters of DLS* 3: 146). Within a week of Williams's death, an obituary to him written by T. S. Eliot appeared in *The Times*—an obituary that Sayers believed to be the result, at least in part, of her "instrumentality." Immediately on hearing the news of Williams's death, she had rung her agent, concerned about finding someone to write an appropriate obituary. Sayers's agent then rang Eliot (seemingly on Sayers's behalf) and "suggested, or persuaded, or encouraged him to do it" (*Letters of DLS* 3: 147). Though Sayers hoped to involve Eliot, she seems to have felt uneasy about approaching him directly, even on a matter that would have been very close to his own heart. Such was the combination of esteem and awe that she felt for T. S. Eliot.

As a Christian writer committed to Anglican tradition and scholarly integrity, Sayers knew she was part of something much larger than herself, something immensely important. She also sensed that Eliot was a leader—perhaps *the* leader—of it. One of the two published letters she wrote to Eliot was written on January 8, 1948, to congratulate him on his being awarded the Order of Merit by the king. She discreetly but pointedly included herself as one of Eliot's "company" when she said, "Everybody who knows you and your work and is, however modestly, of the company of the 'Makers' [i.e., creative writers], has good cause to rejoice" (*Letters of DLS* 3: 348). In the same letter, she drew comparisons between her own first experience of reading Dante and Eliot's first experience of Dante, and told him that Lewis had challenged her statement that Dante was a "lucid" writer, but she was glad to see that, in his 1929 essay on Dante, Eliot agreed with her on this point.[29] Though Sayers had by this time become well known herself as a Dante scholar, she continued to defer to Eliot as a leading expert on *The Divine Comedy*, who understood the universal relevance of Dante's thought. She especially concurred with Eliot's assertion (in one of his Dante essays) that many modern people cannot grasp religious ideas simply because they have received no religious instruction (*Letters of DLS* 3: 430).

Eliot was an intensely private person, and although Sayers did not know him as a friend (as she did Lewis), she was able to discern the nature of the soul behind the public persona. She showed her sympathetic awareness of Eliot's personal struggles when she observed, in a letter written in 1954, that he was unfairly accused of having withdrawn into a "smug Anglican complacency." She believed that his spiritual journey had been arduous but triumphant, and defended him eloquently: "I think he has gone through the Waste Land and come out on the other side, and *that* [his critics] cannot forgive him. All his poetry has the mark of wounds on it— none the less because it is elaborately and beautifully made" (*Letters of DLS* 4: 142). Writing to Penguin editor E. V. Rieu in January

1957, she commented approvingly and insightfully on Eliot's second marriage at the age of sixty-eight to a young woman half his age: "I see, by the way, that Eliot has got married; if the young woman succeeds in delivering him from the wheel of self-reproach over that first wife of his, she will have done a Good Thing" (*Letters of DLS* 4: 363). Most of Eliot's close friends reacted with dismay to the unexpected and unusual marriage, but Sayers's optimism was entirely justified: Eliot's second marriage was indeed—despite the initially stunned response of his friends—a supremely "Good Thing."[30]

Divine Compulsion

Relationships are never static. The negative relationship between Lewis and Eliot changed over time to a warm friendship, and even the more continuous positive feeling between Sayers and Lewis and between Sayers and Eliot had a kind of shifting quality. The spirituality of all three writers necessarily developed and matured over time, and so did the dynamic among them.

Their spirituality included their understanding of the sacraments at the center of Christian worship, particularly the sacrament of Holy Communion. Adrian Hastings suggests that the starting point for Lewis was "a rather fundamentalist orthodoxy [characterized by] an almost instinctive shying away from the sacraments," but that his creative genius "flowered out of a predominantly catholic literary tradition and within a circle of Catholic friends (Roman and Anglican)" (494). In the phrase "shying away from" Hastings may be understating Lewis's commitment to the sacramental aspects of Anglican worship—a commitment that was firm from the time he became a Christian. Nonetheless, there is much evidence to support Hastings's observation that over the years Lewis was "quietly moving" toward a deeper appreciation of "the sacraments and mystical life" (494). Hastings recognizes that "a chief characteristic of the Christian revival of the mid-century" was a renewed emphasis on the liturgical and sacramental elements of the Christian faith (494).

This renewed emphasis amounted to a "movement" or a "revival" in which, he asserts, Lewis was "the most powerful single voice" (494). Surprisingly, in his apologetic works on Christianity, Lewis said little about its mystical aspects—particularly the sacraments. In the Narnia books, however, and in *Till We Have Faces* (the last of his works of fiction, and the novel that Hastings calls "almost mystical"), Lewis depicts Christian truths in a more visionary and sacramental mode. It is in this latter, more mystical, focus that Lewis comes closer to Sayers's emphasis on the importance of ritual,[31] and to Eliot's sacramental imagery.

As we think of C. S. Lewis, Dorothy L. Sayers, and T. S. Eliot, somehow standing together, we need to be aware that their fame came from literary output in dissimilar mediums and for quite dissimilar audiences. Sayers's lasting popularity on both sides of the Atlantic derived primarily from her detective fiction, which has remained in print for more than eighty years,[32] while in England for several decades her name was associated with the Christian drama, particularly *The Man Born to Be King* (initially a series of radio plays, but later used as a religious studies text in schools). Eliot's luminosity initially arose from the acclaim his early poetry received from the educated classes; later, his lectures drew large audiences on university campuses, where he was viewed as both the leading critic of the day and a cultural icon.[33] Lewis initially won prestige by his brilliance as an Oxford tutor and lecturer, but eventually his widest appeal was to a more specifically Christian group through his apologetic essays and imaginative fiction.[34]

Although the genres of literature in which their fame was rooted were quite different, Sayers, Eliot, and Lewis functioned similarly as prophets to their own generation. A young American studying at Oxford in the early 1950s tells of the Christian influences on him and his wife during their journey to faith:

> C. S. Lewis['s] science-fiction trilogy . . . showed me that the Christian God might, after all, be quite big enough for the whole galaxy. . . . Apart from Lewis, we read G. K. Chesterton. . . . And Charles

Williams, theologian and novelist, who opened up realms of the spirit we didn't know existed, was tremendously important to us both. . . . Dorothy Sayers made Christianity dramatic and exciting. . . . We had read T. S. Eliot for years, but now we began to see what he was really saying in *Ash Wednesday* and the *Four Quartets*—and it scared us, rather. . . . But there is no doubt that C. S. Lewis was . . . the most important reading for us. (Vanauken 84)

In the third movement of "Little Gidding," Eliot observes that an individual's intense focus in a particular area begins as something peculiarly personal and specialized, "an attachment to our own field of action" (*Four Quartets* 142). All three writers began with strong attachments to a particular vocation—Eliot to poetry and literary criticism, Lewis to scholarship, and Sayers to the writing of crime fiction—but, as Eliot's poem goes on to observe, a person eventually "comes to find that action [or sphere of work] of little importance / Though never indifferent" (*Four Quartets* 142). So it was with Eliot, Lewis, and Sayers: their initial attachment to their particular fields became of relatively "little importance." However, the overall result of their dedication to those individualized callings or "field[s] of action" was not "indifferent" or negligible. Each of them saw their writing, in all spheres, as a divine commission, something of a prophetic calling. Near the conclusion of "Little Gidding," in its fifth movement, Eliot speaks of the communion between the saints of the present and those of the past, all of whom lived under a divine compulsion: "The drawing of this Love and the voice of this Calling" (*Four Quartets* 144–45).

Lewis, Eliot, and Sayers combined creative imagination with spiritual vision. They wrote in a cultural era that they and many others perceived as a spiritual Waste Land, illuminating the age-old redemptive message of the Church. Their contribution was crucial in the mid-twentieth century, and their work continues to illuminate the redemptive message in the twenty-first century, an era that might also be deemed a Waste Land.

2

Prophets in the Wilderness

Imagination versus Apologetics

✠ ✠ ✠

John the Baptist announced himself as "the voice of one crying in the wilderness" (Matt. 3.3). As the last of the prophets who prepared the way for the coming of the Messiah, he was fulfilling the prophecy of Isaiah, who foretold that a voice would cry out in the wilderness, "Prepare ye the way of the Lord; make straight in the desert a highway for our God" (Isa. 40.3). Wilderness, desert, waste land—these are all familiar and appropriate images for the desolate spiritual environment in which the message is proclaimed. And the voices that cry out in the midst of desolation, announcing the coming of redemption and preparing the way for it, are the voices of prophets.

A sense of calling is common in people who choose to devote their lives to creativity rather than to the pursuit of wealth. Such a feeling of calling or vocation was common among poets of the past, and many writers saw themselves as having a divine calling comparable to that of a biblical prophet.[1] It is not surprising that artists of today who believe in the existence of God often believe that their connectedness to the divine infuses their work. Poets and other creative writers who are Christians are even more likely to view their work as divinely ordained and empowered. But does this mean they function as prophets? Do the truths they seek to communicate bear an authority that is in any way comparable to the authority of divinely inspired biblical prophets? I believe they do, though on a lower level. The God who proclaimed, through the prophet Isaiah, "Behold, I will do a new thing; now it shall spring forth; shall ye not know it?

I will even make a way in the wilderness, and rivers in the desert"
(Isa. 43.19), speaks anew in every generation, ordaining prophets to
announce the "way in the wilderness," and water "in the desert."

C. S. Lewis, T. S. Eliot, and Dorothy L. Sayers recognized the absence of spiritual understanding in the world around them, and apprehended their responsibility to respond to it. Although common
usage today connects the word *prophet* with the idea of foretelling
the future, the first meaning given for it in the *Oxford English Dic-
tionary* is "a person regarded as an inspired teacher or proclaimer
of the will of God." This definition implies that the term *prophet*
may refer to any person inspired to proclaim spiritual truths. Sayers's recognition that the word has application to Christian writers
in modern times is apparent in her view of Charles Williams as "a
major prophet" (*Letters of DLS* 4: 143). The term *prophet* can be
applied equally to Sayers herself and to Lewis and Eliot.

The biblical prophets communicated, as preachers, through direct
exhortation, but they also communicated more indirectly through
imagery and figurative language—the tools of poetry. The concept
of the prophet-poet clearly has Old Testament roots, but its application to later poets is not confined solely to writers like Milton
who associated themselves with formal Christianity. Major poets
like William Blake, William Wordsworth, and Percy Bysshe Shelley,
who held less conventional spiritual views, likewise saw their role as
prophetic. They reckoned themselves prophets in that they felt called
to boldly proclaim truths that people of their day needed to hear;
and they wrote with a sense of accountability to that calling.

Biblical prophets were both preachers and poets. As preachers,
they exhorted and admonished; as poets, they accosted the imagination of their audience with flaming words and searing pictures.
Similarly, Christian writers of modern times may function as both
preachers and poets. In their reasoned defense of their faith, Lewis,
Eliot, and Sayers are communicating as apologists, or preachers,
but many of their greatest works are the products of creativity, arising less from the rational functioning of the brain than from the
imagination and the spirit.

We must be careful, however, not to draw too sharp a dividing line between the two prophetic functions. Although preaching is a didactic form of rhetoric, seeking to teach and persuade through reasoned argument, preaching may also employ the imaginative devices of poetry, like metaphorical language and pictorial images. The two functions, preaching and poetic utterance, support one another. Nonetheless, the distinction between them does provide a basis for examining different kinds of Christian writing. Works in which Lewis, Sayers, and Eliot function as preachers, attempting to teach and persuade, are intrinsically different in form from their creative works of fiction and drama, and from their actual poetry. In their persuasive works, reason is dominant; in their creative works, imagination is dominant.

Accepting the Call

Eliot's sense of calling is evident in his first important poem, "The Love Song of J. Alfred Prufrock." Lyndall Gordon points out that, "despite the poem's mannered surface, Eliot is looking beyond [the scene of elegant Bostonian social life] . . . towards a characteristic theme of his own, a prophet's obligation to articulate what he alone knows" (*Imperfect Life* 68–69). And yet the overwhelming need of the poem's persona to "disturb the universe" by asking a profound question is frustrated by his sense of complete inadequacy. The middle-aged Prufrock, who is the speaker in the poem, also gives voice to the insecurities of Eliot himself as a young poet, worrying about whether he can command respect even as a person, much less as a poet-prophet. He would like to "presume" upon the sophisticated complacency of the women that "come and go" in elegant drawing rooms, and startle them by speaking of the lives of the poor, the "lonely men in shirt-sleeves, leaning out of windows." But, though he has "wept and fasted, wept and prayed," the would-be prophet does not have the "strength to force the moment to its crisis." He perceives himself as the object of scornful dismissal before he has even begun to seize the "moment of [his] greatness" as a prophet;

he has already, figuratively, seen his head "brought in upon a plat-
ter." His fearfulness forces the realization: "I am no prophet" (Eliot,
"The Love Song of J. Alfred Prufrock" 6). The reader readily sees
that, indeed, he is not John the Baptist. But we may wonder why the
insecure Prufrock (speaking for the uneasy aspirations of Eliot himself) alludes to that particular prophet. Perhaps it is because John
the Baptist, as the voice "crying out in the wilderness," preached
repentance and thus prepared "the way of the Lord" (John 1.23).
Eliot was not yet ready to be a herald of Christ's kingdom, but he
already saw his world as a bleak place, a wilderness, and already
felt the impetus to cry out something that would be confrontational,
and would perhaps offer hope.

Russell Kirk, in *Eliot and His Age,* describes "The Love Song
of J. Alfred Prufrock" as the "first of Eliot's several poems about
Hell," and proposes that Prufrock is a kind of Everyman: "a modern man surfeited with comforts and embarrassed when he is confronted by revelation—who refuses to bear witness to the truth"
(48). In this respect, the poem suggests that Eliot was aware of the
possibility that he himself was, or might be, called to bear witness
to spiritual truth. As Kirk observes, the poem reflects "the mind of
a young man in search of firm ground" (48).

In *The Waste Land,* his next major work, Eliot affirms his awareness of the spiritual calling that he was taking on. Lyndall Gordon
clarifies the essential religious and prophetic nature of this jarring
poem. She observes that many educated readers of Eliot's era "actually had no idea what the poem was about," whereas readers with
a religious background did, because "they saw through the crust
of erudition to the residue of timeless forms—sermon, soul history,
confession—almost drowned out by the motor-horns, pub talk, and
the beguiling patter of a bogus medium, all that noise of wasted
lives" (*Imperfect Life* 149). Gordon recognizes that the power of the
poem is a religious power: "To reach through *The Waste Land* to the
sermon that haunts it, transforms the reader—any reader. Literacy
is not necessary, for it's a poem best heard. The rhythms of the Bible
beat behind it, speaking to us subliminally with prophetic power: the

lamentation of Jeremiah, 'For my people . . . have forsaken me the fountain of living waters, and hewed them out cisterns, broken cisterns, that can hold no water' [Jer.1.14]; and Ezekiel's warning cry, 'And your altars shall be desolate, and your images shall be broken. . . . In all your dwelling places the cities shall be laid waste . . . ' [Ezek. 6.4–6]" (148–49).

Although *The Waste Land* is religious and prophetic in the sense that Gordon describes, it is not a poem of faith. In *The Art of T. S. Eliot,* Helen Gardner explains the poem's unfulfilled, pre-Christian, quality: "*The Waste Land* moves, if it moves at all, towards some moment which is outside the poem and may never come, which we are still waiting for at the close. It does not so much move toward a solution as make clearer and clearer that a solution is not within our power. We can only wait for the rain to fall" (88). Five years later, in 1927, the "moment" arrived when Eliot embraced the "solution"; he made a confession of faith by being baptized and confirmed into the Church of England.

Ash Wednesday is the poem that expresses Eliot's state of mind at this point in his life—a state of mind marked by contrite repentance and relinquishment of worldly ambition. The submissiveness of the request "Teach us to sit still," in the first movement, suggests Eliot's patient preparedness to assume the role of the prophet. This role becomes more explicit in the second movement, through the reference to Ezekiel's valley of dry bones ("And God said / Shall these bones live?"); through the reference to having acquired a "devoted, concentrated . . . purpose"; and, most of all, through the words of God commanding him, as he did Ezekiel (Ezek. 37.9), to prophesy "to the wind" (Eliot, *Ash Wednesday* 62). Eliot receives the prophetic charge with great humility; he says, at the end of the third movement, "Lord, I am not worthy / but speak the word only" (63).

C. S. Lewis's desire in early adulthood was, like that of Eliot, to become a poet,[2] but unlike Eliot it was not as a poet that he became famous. In his early thirties, Lewis began an academic career, and came to regard his work as a university tutor and lecturer as a vocation. In a letter to Owen Barfield in December 1947, he observed that one often regards "the vocation actually imposed on one [by God]" as an "interruption of one's (self-chosen) vocation" (*Collected Letters of CSL* 2: 818). Although in its immediate context his remark alluded to the draining responsibility of caring for the physical needs of others, the observation may be aptly applied to another more prolonged and important sort of "interruption" to his vocation as an academic.

The interruption started in the fall of 1939, when he was asked by Centenary Press to write a book for a projected Christian Challenge series "intended to introduce the Christian faith to people outside the Church" (*Collected Letters of CSL* 2: 289, note 152). The result was *The Problem of Pain*. When it was published in the fall of 1940, Lewis's gift for this sort of writing was apparent—a gift for explaining the Christian faith. He sent a copy of his book to a friend, who replied that her gratitude to him for giving her a copy was "small compared to [her] gratitude to God for having given it to [him] to write it" (2: 449). *The Problem of Pain* began the chain of events through which Lewis took up his second vocation, one that was nonprofessional. He became an apologist.

In February 1941, the BBC's director of religious broadcasting asked Lewis to do a series of radio talks that would respond to the religious ignorance of the general public by restating Christian doctrine in positive terms and in "lay language" (*Collected Letters of CSL* 2: 469–70). Although he must have realized that it could be professional suicide for an Oxford lecturer to speak on the radio on a subject outside his field of expertise, Lewis agreed to the proposal, and later agreed to do several more broadcast sequences.[3] Scarcely had Lewis made the initial commitment to the BBC than he received another challenging and unusual request. He was asked by the chaplain-in-chief of the Royal Air Force to lecture to members of the RAF on the Christian faith. Again, Lewis accepted.

It is hard for most of us to comprehend the staggering audacity and recklessness that Lewis showed in accepting such invitations. In *C. S. Lewis in a Time of War*,[4] Justin Phillips records that J. R. R.

Tolkien, Lewis's good friend and colleague, said quite bluntly that Oxford University would not forgive a person for speaking on the BBC about a subject in which he was not academically qualified, nor for "writing popular works of theology" (Phillips 222). Although Lewis knew this, he felt compelled to accept the call. The compulsion he felt is explained, at least in part, by something he said in a sermon he preached in 1939: "He who surrenders himself without reservation to the temporal claims of a nation, or a party, or a class is rendering to Caesar that which, of all things, most emphatically belongs to God: himself." Lewis goes on to point out that although one's religion cannot overwhelm and eliminate our ordinary "natural activities," it must, in some sense, "occupy the whole of life." Boldly, he declares that we cannot seek for a compromise between the claim of God and other claims: "God's claim is infinite and inexorable" ("Learning in War-Time" 31).[5]

Academic tasks—lecturing, tutoring, and scholarly writing— were what Lewis would consider the "natural activities" of his life. They were natural in the sense of being part of a routine, and natural in the sense that they came easily to him. His decision to take up the more difficult task of apologetic speaking and writing indicates that he believed, as his sermon had admonished others to believe, that the claims of God are "inexorable." It was a costly choice. The cost to his career was that—though the number and caliber of his academic publications, and his acclaim as a lecturer and tutor, surpassed those of most of his colleagues—Oxford University never gave him the promotion to full professorship that he deserved.

Sayers was much more reluctant to claim being called by God to preach and challenge, yet preach and challenge she did, often with more outspoken vigor than either Eliot or Lewis. Soon after completing her undergraduate studies at Oxford in 1915, she published two small volumes of verse. The title of one, *Catholic Tales and Christian Songs,* and the subject matter of the poems it included indicate that she was drawn to religious themes, even in those early years. Before long, however, the need to make a living became so pressing that Sayers decided to venture into an area of writing that seemed devoid of religious significance, but that promised to be lucrative. The whodunit was in its heyday, and in 1923 Sayers published her first detective story, *Whose Body?* Within a decade she had done more than secure a living; she had made a name for herself. Not only was she financially secure, she had quickly become one of the best-known writers of the genre.

The pampered and uninhibited life style of Sayers's fictional protagonist, Lord Peter Wimsey, gave little indication that his creator held traditional Christian ideas and values. Yet even in this early phase of her writing career Sayers regarded the whodunit as a very respectable—even a spiritual—genre. She believed that such books were much more than escape reading, regarding them as good in the simplest sense of the word. She explained this in her introduction to an anthology of mystery fiction that she had edited, proposing that detective stories are strongly moral and, in fact, religious in an almost archetypal way, because they deal with "the monstrous images of Sin and Death" (Introduction to *Great Short Stories . . . ,* Third Series 11).[6] She observed, in another context, that the detective hero is essentially "a simplified symbolic figure (like a piece in a chess game) representing that which works for order in opposition to chaos" ("Detectives in Fiction").[7] Sayers refused to regard detective fiction as escapist and lowbrow. Indeed, her well-reasoned essays on the subject, and her own twelve full-length whodunits and numerous short stories, published between 1923 and 1937, helped to vindicate the detective genre as a body of writing. Detective fiction was increasingly credited with artistic and intellectual merit.

Sayers's determination to vindicate detective fiction reflected her Christian faith. In her own whodunits, she strove for a deeper treatment of human spirituality than was implicit in the classic detective story as it had been established almost a century earlier by Edgar Allan Poe and Sir Arthur Conan Doyle. Over time her works of detective fiction displayed a growing awareness of universal themes underlying the usual elements of the whodunit: well-plotted clues and puzzling events. By the 1930s she was pushing back the boundaries of the detective story as a literary form and focusing on more profound mysteries—first, the mysteries of human nature, and eventually, those of human spirituality.[8]

In Sayers's 1935 review of Chesterton's *The Scandal of Father Brown*, it is apparent that she saw the mystery of the human spiritual condition to be the basis of all great literature, even mystery stories. She begins with a series of questions about the approach of the detective writer: "Are the crimes to be real sins, or are they to be the mere gestures of animated puppets? Are we to shed blood or only sawdust? . . . and is the detective to figure only as the arm of the law or as the hand of God?" She analyzes the implications of these questions: "If we wipe out God from the problem we are in very real danger of wiping out man as well. . . . We owe Mr. Chesterton a heavy debt in that, with very great courage in a poor and materialistic period, he planted his steps firmly upon the more difficult path, and showed us how to enlarge the boundaries of the detective story by making it deal with real death and real wickedness and real, that is to say, divine judgment" ("Salute to Mr. G. K. Chesterton" 9). In her last works of fiction, Sayers approached this ideal herself, depicting human relationships and the struggle between good and evil in a way that was spiritually probing. By the late 1930s she had turned away from the writing of detective fiction to devote herself to Christian drama and apologetics.

Lewis, the Self-Effacing Apologist

Apologetics—the explanation and defense of the Christian religion— is a special form of persuasive writing.[9] Lewis's *Mere Christianity* is the best-known and most successful work of apologetics by a lay person, and perhaps by *anyone*. Yet Lewis never intended to usurp the prerogative of professional theologians, and was fully aware that (being untrained in systematic theology) he was, in the strictest sense, unqualified to formally defend the Christian faith. Nonetheless, he believed that the trained theologians of the past century and of his own day had *not* succeeded as apologists; he saw a need that he felt he could and should meet. Acknowledging, in one of his essays, that most of his books were "evangelistic," he explains that, when he began writing them, Christianity was being presented "either in the highly emotional form offered by revivalists or in the unintelligible language of highly cultured clergymen." Recognizing that most people would never be reached by either of these extremes, Lewis believed that he needed to become "a *translator.*" He described himself as "turning Christian doctrine, or what [he] hoped to be such, into vernacular, into language that unscholarly people would attend to and could understand." He argued that if the "real theologians" had not neglected their responsibility by failing to engage in "this laborious task of translation," thereby losing touch "with the people (for whom Christ died)," there would have been no need for him to become an apologist (Lewis, "Rejoinder to Dr. Pittenger" 181, 183).

The fact that Lewis spoke as a lay person to other lay people was a definite advantage. He was pronouncing truth, not from a platform elevated high above the people he addressed but from a level closer to theirs. In a letter written in 1953 to Sheldon Vanauken, a friend and former student, he reveals the humility with which he viewed his prophetic vocation. He described his feelings as a mixture of awe and fear; like those a boy might experience the first time he is allowed to fire a gun: "The disproportion between his puny finger on the trigger & the thunder and lightning wh[ich] follow is alarming." Lewis's self-effacing spirit is especially striking when he suggests that his readers should think of him as "a fellow-patient in the same hospital who, having been admitted a little earlier, c[oul]d give some advice" (*Collected Letters of CSL* 3: 325). It is sometimes easier to accept help when the person offering it seems to be only a little beyond the point at which we have arrived. Lewis was therefore determined not to hold himself above others as a spiritual authority—an elevation that might exist if the apologist were a professional theologian.

Sayers, the Reluctant Apologist

Dorothy L. Sayers described the dogma of the church as "a terrifying drama of which God is the victim and the hero" ("The Greatest Drama Ever Staged" 13). Her gift for gripping restatement of basic Christian ideas made her apologetic essays almost as popular and influential as those of Lewis. Both Sayers and Lewis functioned as prophet-preachers working through the public media, laboring tirelessly through the venues of radio and periodicals, especially during the years of World War II. The essays that Sayers wrote for the *Sunday Times* just before and during the war were uncompromisingly theological. She increasingly identified herself with the heroic Christian writers she eloquently praised for speaking with authority of "the soul's development in time" and for depicting the vigorous grappling with evil that transforms it into good ("Strong Meat" 17).[10] This was her own mandate, the platform from which she would preach for the next decade. Yet one of the most striking things about Sayers's preaching was the reluctance, the trepidation, with which she did it. Although her misgivings were not apparent to those she addressed, they are of great significance.

Sayers's numerous apologetic essays are lively and confrontational. Many of them appeared in major newspapers; some took the form of radio talks or public lectures. The tone and nature of their content is often apparent from their titles: "The Dogma is the Drama," "The Greatest Drama Ever Staged," "The Triumph of Easter," "Creed or Chaos?" and "The Execution of God." Ann Loades observes that nothing was "more important for Sayers personally, and for human society, than that Christian doctrine should be both believed and understood," and that Sayers used "all her gifts of intellect and imagination" in explaining God's acts in the world, particularly the Incarnation (iv).[11] Suzanne Bray points out that although C. S, Lewis's radio talks became far more widely known than those of Sayers, the broadcasts by Sayers and Eliot that were commissioned by the BBC's Religious Broadcasting Department preceded those of Lewis.[12] Bray further observes that the success of Sayers and Eliot as radio apologists served to dismiss "the official reticence about the use of lay people in religious broadcasting" (29–30), thus paving the way for the invitation extended to Lewis, and the great success of the radio talks that later became his *Mere Christianity.*

Sayers's apologetic voice sounded out compellingly from the radio, and her assertive personality drew people to her public lectures. In some of these lectures, she was part of a panel of apologists. In 1946, the Society of St. Anne[13] sponsored a Mission—a series of lectures and discussions on the Christian faith to be held during Lent. Sayers was involved in organizing the lecture series, and the lecturers included T. S. Eliot and herself. In a letter that Sayers wrote to the *Daily Sketch* to clarify the nature of the series and to publicize it, she explained that the object of the Mission was "to give intelligent people an opportunity of hearing an orderly exposition of the Christian Faith, and of asking as many questions as they like and having those questions intelligently discussed and answered." She went on to say that these "services, lectures and discussions" would show that "the Christian revelation does 'make sense' of the universe and of the lives of individual men and women" (*Letters of DLS* 3: 203).

In spite of her gifts of argument, her zest for debate, and her obvious success as an apologist, Sayers had serious doubts as to whether such expository Christian writing—such preaching—was what she called her "proper job." Some of her misgivings paralleled Lewis's concern about his lack of formal theological training. Other misgivings arose from her sense of professionalism. She saw herself not as a *Christian writer,* but as a professional writer who happened to be a Christian, and she strongly doubted whether writing that was directly apologetic should occupy a major part of her time and energy. Though she and Lewis shared much in letters about the challenges of such writing, and though they were of one mind theologically, she distinguished her motives as an apologist from those of Lewis by saying that her impetus for explaining the gospel was more a passion for ordering minds than for saving souls.

Yet the challenge was one she could not ignore, because—though she believed she did not have "a pastoral mind or a passion to convert people"—she could not tolerate having her "intellect outraged by imbecile ignorance and by the monstrous distortions of *fact* which the average heathen accepts as being 'Christianity' (and from which he most naturally revolts)" (*Letters of DLS* 2: 310). She made this point in a letter to the editor of the *Catholic Herald*—a letter in which she goes on to emphasize the need for Christians of all denominations to focus on the key doctrines of the faith that they all hold in common. She argued that until Christians "have hammered the Incarnation into the head of the heathen" there is no value in making proclamations on minor doctrinal points and distracting people from the main point. The letter bemoans the tendency of some church leaders to appeal to the "lowest common denominator" by submitting to liberal humanism and suggesting that all that really matters is that we all "believe in God and follow Christ in the spirit of love." Sayers believed such statements to be worthless (*Letters of DLS* 2: 310–11).

Nonetheless, the zeal that Sayers expresses for bipartisan evangelism in this letter of 1941 contrasts sharply with the reluctance to evangelize she expresses in several letters over the next two decades. Her inner turmoil on the issue of to-preach-or-not-to-preach surfaces frequently in her letters to C. S. Lewis. The question of whether she should be an apologist was charged with emotion for her. The love-hate relationship she had with this sort of writing comes out most powerfully in a long letter she wrote to Lewis in 1943 in which she complained about the way circumstances, her own tendencies, and God himself had drawn her—in some ways, against her will—into apologetics.

In this letter she cleverly expresses the complexity of her feelings about being a Christian spokesperson by mimicking Lewis's own style in *The Screwtape Letters*. For part of her letter, the speaker is the demon Sluckdrib (whom she has invented as her personal tempter), who is working diligently to make her go wrong, in both actions and attitudes, in her defense of the faith through writing Christian material. He reports that the effect of writing Christian dramas[14] upon the character of Dorothy L. Sayers is satisfactory, since she now exhibits numerous vices, including "intellectual and spiritual pride, vainglory, self-opinionated dogmatism, irreverence, blasphemous frivolity, . . . impatience of correction[,] . . . shortness of temper, neglect of domestic affairs, lack of charity, egotism." But, Sluckdrib reports, in spite of the badness of the tree from which it comes, the "fruit"—that is, the literary work—that Sayers produces continues to be good: "the fools eat it and it does them good" (*Letters of DLS* 2: 410–11).

Sayers goes on, in the same letter to Lewis, to complain of a letter she had recently received from an atheist that she resents having to reply to. She feels "no missionary zeal" toward this correspondent and blames God for presenting her with the obligation to deal with such a case. She tells Lewis she has recommended that this man read several books, including two by Lewis: *Broadcast Talks* (later *Mere Christianity*) and *The Problem of Pain*. If the atheist is upset by reading these books, she says, she will "hand him on" to Lewis, who (she claims) "like[s] souls" a lot more than she does. She ends the letter by bemoaning the fact that "there aren't any up-to-date books about Miracles," a comment that prompted Lewis to write a book on that very subject (*Letters of DLS* 2: 413).

In a later letter to Lewis written in August 1946, Sayers speaks of another difficulty she experienced in the role of apologist. She is worried by the contradiction she senses between her reputation as an eager expositor of Christian doctrine and her own image of herself as a very unemotional Christian. Her apologetic role is, she believes, somehow at odds with the fact that she does not possess something she feels she can call "my faith" in a personal and emotional sense. She explains to Lewis that because she can apprehend truths only by "imaginative intellect"—a faculty which seems unspiritual and impersonal—she feels pushed into "false situations" by people who regard her religious essays as "personal confessions." Sayers understands that what the Church teaches is truth of the highest order, yet this understanding feels like an assent of the mind, more than of the heart. Intellectually, she finds it easy to expound and defend the Church's position, but she fears that she is sometimes in danger of falling "victim of [her] own propaganda" by talking herself into an acceptance of some truth that she has not truly apprehended on a personal level (*Letters of DLS* 3: 255).

However, Sayers tells Lewis in this same letter that she has "apprehended" some truths on a deep level, and it is these that she knows she can communicate through her creative work without insincerity or falsehood. In other kinds of writing—writing of the 'preaching' sort—she has serious misgivings. She says, "I can never embark on this kind of thing without a strong conviction of guilt, or look on the results without shame." She does, nonetheless, admit that there is a solution to the problem: she does not have to accept writing assignments that she does not feel are appropriate for her. She realizes that when offered a "platform" she needed to ask herself, "is there any truth apprehended by me, which this platform or this medium, gives me a suitable opportunity to communicate?" (*Letters of DLS* 3: 256).

One aspect of Sayers's uneasiness was the fear that the writing of apologetics encouraged her to write in a way that was too spontaneous for the gravity of the topic. Instead of taking pride in her success as an apologist, she judged herself harshly, saying, at one point, that she was lured into producing "lies as serious research." Then she backed down from the severity of this self-accusation, and said that while her assertions were "not actual lies," she believed the points she made in her apologetic essays and talks were weak because they came too spontaneously and lacked unity and sufficient balance of "intellect and imagination." Intellect and imagination were, she said, the faculties by which she personally apprehended things (*Letters of DLS* 3: 257).

Although some of Sayers's misgivings seem extreme, almost irrational, she was right in recognizing that the work of the apologist is treacherous, emotionally and spiritually. In an earlier letter to Sayers, Lewis himself reveals a similar sort of internal spiritual warfare involving complexities of motive, uncertainty about a work's value, and persistent self-doubt. In his own case, he explains, the strength of the impulse to write an apologetic piece had "no constant ratio to the value of the work done." He recognizes that his own occasional misgivings arise from "the fact that apologetic work is so dangerous to one's own faith," and confesses that a Christian truth never seemed dimmer to him than when he had just defended it (*Collected Letters of CSL* 2: 730).

Sayers's fear that her reputation as an apologist was forcing her into a false position as a artist is especially apparent in another of her letters to Lewis.[15] Lewis had requested, on behalf of the publishers, that Sayers contribute to a series of short books intended to be "a sort of library of Christian knowledge for young people in the top forms at school" (*Collected Letters of CSL* 2: 721). Sayers refused, reminding Lewis of his own example, in *The Great Divorce*, of the "corrupt artist . . . [who has] turned from serving the work [to] making the work serve him" (*Letters of DLS* 3: 258). She argues that her creative undertakings, like her dramas *The Man Born to be King* and *The Just Vengeance*, are just as significant as Christian work as her apologetics, perhaps even more so since they are significantly "larger" and (she feels) "more honestly constructed" (*Letters of DLS* 3: 258).

In this instance, and in a number of others, Sayers was adamant in her refusal to make apologetic writing or speaking her first commitment. The archbishop of Melbourne had invited her to speak at a Church congress in Australia, telling her that it would be "a grand opportunity." Sayers expressed her frustration to Lewis, asking, "for what? For missionising—but I am not a missioner."[16] Sayers believed that to accept such an invitation would mean neglecting her duties at home, falling behind in her current work,[17] and exhibiting herself "in a false attitude on a platform!" (*Letters of DLS* 3: 258–59). In spite of the fact that the offer included an all-expense-paid trip (including first-class travel by sea), Sayers refused to go to preach in Australia. She had stood on platforms before and would do so again, but she drew the line at defining herself as a "missioner."

Dorothy L. Sayers was clearly a more reluctant apologist than Lewis. Though she recognized him as an ally and colleague in the field of apologetics, she occasionally had misgivings about what she called Lewis's "fervent missionary zeal," describing him, in a letter to an Anglican monk, as one apt to rush in too hastily to "strike a blow for Christendom, whether or not one is equipped by training and temperament for that particular conflict" (*Letters of DLS* 3: 314). Yet at the same time (and in the same letter), she rejects the suggestion that Lewis was arrogant in defending the faith, and (rather patronizingly) admires his aggressiveness. "Lewis," she says, "is magnificently ruthless with people who do set out to produce what purports to be a logical argument and then fake the premises, or beg the question, . . . or ignorantly confuse efficient causes with final causes and attribute the resulting absurdity to St. Thomas. He is down on the thing like a rat: he is God's terrier, and I wouldn't be without him for the world" (*Letters of DLS* 3: 315).

The trepidation Sayers experienced was relieved from time to time by a renewed conviction that apologetic writing was God's work, not her work or Lewis's work.[18] Her frequent uneasiness was important and valuable, however, because it forced her to examine her own heart and motives ruthlessly, and to admit that the calling to defend the faith did not require that she herself should represent Christian perfection. Sayers saw herself humbly, as a flawed participant in the work of the Kingdom of God, and, even more than Lewis, she was extremely apologetic about being an apologist.

Sayers saw the gospel clearly as "a thing of terror" (*Christ of the Creeds* 83). The terror results from the fearsomeness of the redemptive message—a message that often frightened those who delivered it. When the prophet Isaiah was called by God to proclaim his message, he cried out, "Woe is me! for I am undone; because I am a man of unclean lips, and I dwell in the midst of a people of unclean lips: for mine eyes have seen the King, the LORD of hosts!" (Isa. 6.5). It is a "fearful thing to fall into the hands of the living God" (Heb. 10.31); it is also a fearful thing to set oneself up as his spokesperson.

Eliot on the Futility of Secularism

Eliot, equally awed by the responsibility of communicating the "thing of terror" that was the gospel, believed that an apologist's direct exhortations might be less effective than more indirect presentations of the faith. Eliot's reluctance to speak out as a Christian apologist—a much greater reluctance than that of Lewis or Sayers—reflects his innate preference for subtlety and understatement. He perceived, largely from a distance, the dangers inherent in apologetics. On one of the few occasions when he spoke from an actual pulpit, he made it clear that he laid no claim to the authority that a clergyman would have. In this address, delivered in the Chapel of Magdalene College, Cambridge, in 1948, Eliot begins by admitting his unsuitability for the role of preacher,[19] explaining that he is not giving a sermon as such, but merely speaking "from the layman's point of view." The term *layman,* he says, does not mean merely "a Christian who is not a priest or minister," but also indicates that the individual is a person "who professes his adherence to a definite body of Christian believers . . . a Christian who is also a member of a congregation, meeting regularly for worship in a particular place . . . who recognizes a loyalty to that local congregation and place of worship, and who is willing and eager to serve them" (Eliot, Sermon Preached in Magdalene College Chapel 2).

Having identified himself as a Christian layperson willing to serve the Church, Eliot expresses uncertainty about whether the layperson can, though personal witness, directly bring about the conversion of others. He does not know, he says, whether anything he has ever done or written has "contributed to the conversion of anybody," and states that, if it has, it was not the result of deliberate intention on his part. He believes that Christian laymen like himself will have done as much as they can and should do if they think carefully about their faith, make good use of the intellect God has given them, and "live rather differently because of [their] faith" (3–6).

These were admonitions that T. S. Eliot applied to himself: he lived differently and wrote differently because of his faith. As managing editor of the *Criterion,* the leading literary journal in London during the period between the wars,[20] Eliot demonstrated clarity of thought undergirded by a practical Christian world-view—a worldview that recognized the person of Jesus Christ at the center of the redemptive message. The clarity afforded by such a view allowed him to distinguish between core issues and minor controversies.

In one *Monthly Criterion* review covering several works,[21] he struck an unexpected blow at the ongoing skirmishes in the public press between well-known defenders of the Christian and non-Christian positions, in his comments on the sparring between Catholic journalist Hilaire Belloc and anti-Church writer H. G. Wells. Eliot's *Criterion* discussion of the squabble between Belloc and Wells questions the qualifications of the two men to speak authoritatively on philosophical and scientific matters, and expresses grave doubts about the value of conducting Christian apologetics in this manner. Eliot points out that although the debate between Belloc and Wells is essentially theological, the entertaining style in which it is conducted is probably of more interest to readers than the points being discussed. He calls Belloc and Wells "two highly paid pugilists" who "undertake to show each other up in their knowledge of sciences in which both are amateurs." Yet to the poorly informed reader, both lines of argument may appear fairly successful. Eliot notes that readers simultaneously "distrust them both . . . [and] agree with them both." Eliot regards such debates as useless, because they leave readers continuing to believe what they had already believed. Then, while ceding that Belloc's claim that Wells "has never learned to think" might be accurate, Eliot humorously notes that the same accusation might equally be applied to Belloc himself. Certainly, Eliot feels, the present discussion does not convince us that either of them are good thinkers; their main techniques are, it seems, assertion and bluff ("Popular Theologians" 253–59).

Eliot does, however, reveal his own readiness to strike a blow against secularism when he goes on in the same review to credit Belloc with being "able to 'place' Mr. Wells rather better than Mr. Wells places him," and with being quite right about the inconsistency in contemporary secularism. Eliot agrees with Belloc that atheists are characterized by "muddle-headed emotionalism" and a fear of facing the consequences of their lost faith. He also agrees with Belloc's observation that modern thinkers like Wells "who have ceased to believe that Our Blessed Lord was God, or even that He had Divine authority, cling desperately to the emotions which the old belief aroused—because they find those emotions pleasant." It is, Eliot concurs, a common thing to throw out religious doctrines but cling to religious sentiment ("Popular Theologians" 253–59).

Eliot, in the same literary review, also takes up a subject that is crucial to Christian doctrine as he reviews *The Life of Jesus* by John Middleton Murry.[22] Although Murry was a respected literary critic and had been a friend and collaborator of Eliot's for some time, Eliot's review of this recently published work was incisively negative. Eliot notes the presence of intellectual inconsistency similar to that of H. G. Wells. Although Murry is superior to Wells as a theologian, there are, Eliot observes, serious errors in his reasoning. Murry's line of thought caters to the desire to "have one's cake and eat it too"—that is, to possess a religion of sorts without really having to commit to anything or believe in anything but the most popular current ideas. Eliot skillfully exposes the untenable nature of Murry's depiction of Christ, giving this passage from the book as an example:

> To most of those who would have cared (about His message) the way to understanding has been marred by their belief in Jesus as God, as the Son of God in some peculiar and transcendental sense. This he was not, nor ever claimed to be. He believed he was the son of God, in precisely the same sense as he believed all men to be sons of God. The difference between him and other men, in his eyes, was simply this: that he knew he was the son of God, while they

did not. Therefore he was God's first-born, or first-reborn, son. But even that had no part in his message. His wonderful news was simply this: that all men were God's sons, if they would but become his sons, and that he was sent to show them the way. (Murry 43–44; qtd. in Eliot, "Popular Theologians" 255)[23]

Eliot recognizes in this the "familiar gospel of Rousseau," a view that includes "the denial of Original Sin," and points out that, although this passage attempts to express what Murry believes about Jesus, it fails to indicate what, if anything, Murry believes about God. Eliot demolishes any semblance of scholarship and authority that might have been associated with this *Life of Jesus,* declaring that until the author has thought intelligently about the existence and nature of God, he is not capable of writing an acceptable book on the person of Christ. Eliot concludes, "You cannot be precise about Jesus unless you are precise about God" ("Popular Theologians" 256).

Recognizing Murry's "affinities with Modernism," Eliot goes on to examine other flaws in the book pertaining to the divine nature of Christ, the view of miracles, and the events surrounding the crucifixion. "According to Mr. Murry," Eliot reports, "the whole drama of the betrayal, trial and crucifixion was a frame-up; a political game rigged by Jesus himself. He had an accomplice, and the accomplice was Judas." Judas is portrayed by Murry as the only one who understood Jesus, and more of a man than any other disciple. With such distortion of scriptural material, John Middleton Murry, in Eliot's words, "leads his train of disciples into the wilderness" ("Popular Theologians" 257). Here the word *wilderness* acknowledges that the intellectual landscape of modernism and secularism was a Waste Land, place of spiritual bleakness, where the only redemption possible must begin with a right understanding of Jesus. Eliot's critique of Murry's eccentric view of Jesus served an apologetic function by exposing the kind of fallacies common in contemporary attacks on Christian orthodoxy, particularly on the divinity of Christ.

About nine years later, Eliot reviewed another book by John Middleton Murry, and again used Murry as an example of the wrong-mindedness in modern thinking.[24] This time the subject was Shakespeare, whose work Murry was attempting to read from a secular perspective. Murry proposed that for such "modern" readers as ourselves, Hamlet's question, "For in that sleep of death what dreams may come?" (*Ham.* 3.1.66), can be nothing more than a whimsical speculation, implying that the expectation of consciousness after death was no longer part of anyone's thinking. Eliot sees in such an implication the extreme arrogance of modernism. He admits that many modern readers may share Murry's doubts about the afterlife, but judges that such cavalier dismissiveness of the idea of life after death is nothing less than "perverse" ("Mr. Murry's *Shakespeare*" 710). It would be shocking, Eliot notes, to outstanding Christian and scholarly minds of earlier eras, such as that of the great seventeenth-century critic Samuel Johnson, that so few people would fail to be concerned, and even "terrified," not by death itself, "but by what may come after" (710). Eliot urges respect for the fearsome realities that modernists dismissed so lightly. Yet he elegantly and ironically defers to the author in his closing comment: "But I do not understand Mr. Murry half so well as Mr. Murry understands Shakespeare" (710). Despite this gesture of self-effacement, Eliot *did* have enough incisive understanding of modern secularists to challenge what he saw as the spiritual recklessness and perversion of those who deny the immortality of the soul.

In another *Criterion* review, Eliot exposed the secularism of George Bernard Shaw, a highly esteemed dramatist and a major spokesman for the anti-Church position. Eliot reviewed a book called *Mr. Shaw and "The Maid,"*[25] a critique by John Mackinnon Robertson of Shaw's play *Saint Joan*. In writing a play about Joan of Arc, Shaw was dealing with a subject of which he had minimal knowledge—much less knowledge than John Mackinnon Robertson. Robertson's book reviewing Shaw's play exposed not only Shaw's lack of information, but also his complete disregard for the truth of his subject. Eliot highly approved of Robertson's book, agreeing that a play based on a significant historical character such as Joan of Arc is a piece of writing in which "facts matter." Eliot commends Robertson as a modern, clear-thinking man, a "Rationalist," who uses "his facts with a grim northern wit which operates with the effect of a steam roller," and whose great knowledge of and respect for St. Joan will be appreciated, especially by Christian readers. Robertson makes it very clear, says Eliot, that Shaw is totally unable "to devote himself wholeheartedly to *any* cause," and that to Shaw the ideas of truth and falsehood do not seem to have the same meaning as they do to other people. Eliot identifies the danger inherent in the play *Saint Joan* to be the "deluding of a numberless crowd of sentimentally religious people who are incapable of following any argument to a conclusion," and recognizes that the world has become dense with such quasi-religious and unthinking people. Such people admire Shaw's plays without realizing that the "Life Force" that Shaw presents as the driving force behind Joan's power, is (in Eliot's terms) "a gross superstition." Shaw's depiction of Joan of Arc is, Eliot judges, a travesty of the true nature of the spiritual strength that defined her and an unworthy representation of a remarkable historical character ("Mr. Robertson and Mr. Shaw" 389–90).

The judgment "gross superstition" that Eliot applied to the play *Saint Joan* raises a key point in Eliot's view of secularism. He regarded it as essentially superstitious, a line of thought that had become a kind of religion in itself. Eliot contended that Shaw's dishonest handling of historical material was undergirded as much by his disrespect for the Christian Church as by his disrespect for historical fact. This view is more fully explained in a comment he made on Shaw in connection with H. G. Wells and Bertrand Russell.[26] Eliot observes that although there are great differences between these writers, "they all hold curious amateur religions based apparently upon amateur or second-hand biology," and on distorted views of the religion of the past like that expressed in the novel *The Way of All Flesh*.[27] Eliot sees that all three of these writers (i.e., Shaw, Wells, and Russell) "exhibit intelligence at the mercy of emotion." Rather than hailing them as the rationalists they believed themselves to be, he diminishes their prestige as modernist thinkers by conceding that writers such as these three have a set of beliefs that may be regarded as a "faith," and suggesting that it may be uncharitable to look down on the personal beliefs of those whose lives and experiences are very "different from ours" ("The Idea of a Literary Review" 6).

Eliot's combination of gentle condescension and firm dismissiveness reflects the security of his own religious position. He recognized, however, that his religious position was no longer a popular one and believed that the world had become a spiritual Waste Land in which Christianity had ceased to be viewed as relevant, or even respectable. In the essay "Thoughts after Lambeth,"[28] he argues that the fact that the world is now post-Christian is an advantage in clarifying the true message of the Church. He rejoices that he himself, having announced his Christianity, is now considered by many to be a "lost sheep" who will be, sadly, absent "from the roll-call of the new saints" of secularism. Paradoxically, he considers it "a hopeful sign of the times" that the orthodox Christian faith is "at last relieved from its burden of respectability" ("Thoughts after Lambeth" 368–69), and that the "new religion [of secularism] is continually heard to be 'on the march', . . . [and that those atheists] who would have once been considered intellectual vagrants are now [seen as] pious pilgrims, cheerfully plodding the road from nowhere to nowhere, trolling their hymns" (369).

Eliot's Indirect Preaching

In his literary and social criticism, Eliot's voice was subtly modulated, yet frequently very pointed in the rebuke of secularism. Eliot's defense of Christianity was different in tone and approach from that of apologists like Lewis and Sayers. Ironically, it was both more tolerantly courteous and more incisively dismissive. Sayers particularly respected Eliot's indirect approach to communicating his faith through his *Criterion* reviews and his essays on literary and cultural subjects. She pictured Eliot, the respected editor and critic, carrying "his Christianity in his baggage, as it were," and believed it was clear to Eliot's readers that he was "anti-something"—specifically anti "fashionable psychology" and clearly opposed to other popular things that were, from a Christian point of view, "due to be reacted against" (*Letters of DLS* 3: 314).

Eliot's indirect apologetic approach was appealing to Sayers because it echoed an idea she had raised in a letter to Lewis. She proposed that the appalling religious ignorance of the public could be combated by indirectly introducing Christian ideas into people's minds. She suggested that Christians write books that pretend to be about some currently acceptable subject but are really "Christian Propaganda in disguise." This was, she said, the kind of clever unscrupulousness "for which the unjust steward, of the parable in Luke, chapter 16, was commended" (*Letters of DLS* 3: 181).

Eliot would not have regarded his insertion of Christian ideas in his *Criterion* reviews and other essays as a kind of "Christian Propaganda in disguise," and his upper-class propriety would not allow for open "unscrupulousness." Yet Sayers was perfectly correct in her perception of the Christianity implicit in Eliot's writing and in her recognition that the worldly cleverness commended by Christ, in that rather difficult parable of the unjust steward, could take the form of indirect "Christian Propaganda" in order to penetrate the darkness of religious ignorance. Jesus said, cryptically, that "the sons of this world are more shrewd in dealing with their own generation than the sons of light," and encouraged his followers to learn such shrewdness (Luke 16.8 ESV). Eliot, a son of light, was as shrewd as a son of this world: he intentionally and effectively functioned as a prophet in the Waste Land—but under cover.

Russell Kirk proposes that Eliot's gradual assumption of a prophetic role started from his early poem "The Love Song of J. Alfred Prufrock." He points out that "the literary public of 1917 became aware that Eliot had something of the seer in him. . . . Some people even sensed that the earthly hell of the War was paralleled in this innovating 'Prufrock' by the enduring hell of fallen human nature" (Kirk 49). Lyndall Gordon identifies Eliot's sense of divine calling from the time of his conversion onward:

It seemed to Eliot that Providence had led him from one point to another: he said this to Stead[29] who watched him become "a man with a mission". . . . He looked to the dramatic speech of the prophets, Isaiah and Ezekiel. In his own Bible he marked God's call to Isaiah: "Fear not: for I have redeemed thee, I have called thee by name; thou art mine."

To take up the role of God's spokesman was, of course, daunting in so secular an age. . . . Eliot needed . . . the verbal license of an expansive scenario, like that of *The Rock*[30] to free a prophetic voice. (Gordon, *Eliot's New Life* 39–40)

And again, in her later biography of Eliot, Gordon similarly describes Eliot's understated way of fulfilling his prophetic call: "If he was remote between 1947 and 1957, there is a possibility that he had to be alone as a voice crying in the wilderness. . . . Isaiah's verbal purification is part of his call. . . . [He] offers himself not as a person but as a channel for a message. Eliot's Becket[31] defined his vocation in his Christmas sermon. And this may be the closest we can get to the mission that lies behind the studied neutrality of Eliot's appearance. The unassuming demeanor, the quiet manner, the measured, neutral voice were designed to outlive personality" (*Imperfect Life* 474–75).

Eliot's indirect preaching against the spiritual vacuity of modern culture appeared in scholarly lectures and essays in which he identified the spiritual and religious issues that lay beneath literary issues. In "Religion and Literature" (1935), he recognizes that since the modern world offers no "common agreement on ethical and theological matters," it is all the more "necessary for Christian readers to scrutinize their reading, especially works of imagination, with explicit ethical and moral standards" (388), and to be prepared to apply their religion "to the criticism of any literature" (389). Conforming to his own advice, he applied his religion to the literature and literary figures that he critiqued. In his introductory essay to the *Intimate Journals* of the French poet Baudelaire, Eliot proposes that Baudelaire's suffering "implies the possibility of a positive state of beatitude" and that Baudelaire rejects the natural world because he is either reaching for or actually has a "perception of Heaven and Hell" ("Baudelaire" 423). Eliot's sees in Baudelaire's tortured perspective the "knowledge of Good and Evil" (428–29), observing that "since we are human, what we do must be either evil or good," and that "the glory of man is his capacity for salvation . . . [and] damnation" (429). Eliot adds (as a footnote to the phrase "evil or good") a quotation from St. Paul's letter to the Romans that offers the choice of sin leading to death or obedience leading to righteousness.[32]

Though Eliot did not undertake direct apologetics in the way that Lewis and Sayers did, his voice was strong in challenging the assumptions of secularism. In a personal reminiscence dating from the late 1940s, Kathleen Raine wrote, "Mr. Eliot gave hell back to us. . . . The shallow progressive philosophies both religious and secular of our parents' generation sought to eliminate evil from the world. Mr. Eliot's visions of hell restored a necessary dimension to our universe" (79).

In his essays on eminent writers, Eliot spoke often of spiritual struggles and of the solemnity of ultimate choices. In concluding his essay on Matthew Arnold (a nineteenth-century poet and cultural theorist), Eliot observes that Arnold had the "conservatism which springs from lack of faith," and suspects that he was disturbed by how little he had within him "to support him" and that "looking outward" Arnold was disturbed by the "state of society." Arnold's troubled state of mind anticipated the desolate Waste Land of twentieth-century culture. Eliot identifies the spiritual vacuity that led Arnold to hope that in "Culture" lay the way of salvation, and sums him up as "a representative figure" who probably "cared too much for civilization, forgetting that Heaven and Earth shall pass away, and Mr. Arnold with them, and there is only one stay" ("Matthew Arnold" 112). The "one stay"—so cryptically alluded to—catches the reader. Some will decide it is just a riddle to be passed over, but thoughtful readers will realize what Eliot means. The "one stay," the one solution to the problem of sin and death and to the frightening temporality of this world, is Christ—the Lion in the Waste Land.

In his postconversion poem, *Ash Wednesday,* Eliot identifies Christ, the incarnate Word of God, as "the Word / Within the world and for the world" (*Ash Wednesday* 65). That magnificent phrase speaks of the majesty of God the Son—the Word that came down from heaven, coming into the world to redeem it—but it also points to the reflected light of Christ the living Word, operating through the words of his prophets. Eliot's words were redemptive words, "within the world, and for the world."

Prophet-Poets

C. S. Lewis, Dorothy L. Sayers, and T. S. Eliot had another side to their literary output—a side that was arguably more important than their well-reasoned prose defending the Christian faith. They were not only prophet-preachers; they were also prophet-poets. In their other mode of writing, the creative mode, they functioned poetically in that they did not seek to *explain,* but to *show* through emotionally charged pictures and images. The making of images is a main function of poetry. Even though pictures and images are often used to illustrate points in the expository writing of Lewis, Sayers, and Eliot, it is reason, not imagination, that dominates in their nonfiction prose. But their greatest achievements were not their works of nonfiction, not their works that relied on exposition. The literary power of Eliot, Lewis, and Sayers found its fullest expression in their creative works: their poetry, fiction, and drama. These works resounded in the reader's consciousness and took root in the reader's spirit; they touched hearts more deeply than any essays or lectures could.

The evangelistic potentialities of imaginative writing became apparent to Lewis shortly after the publication of his first novel, *Out of the Silent Planet.* Speaking, in a letter, of the astonishing ignorance of Christianity that he found in his readers' responses to this fantasy work, he said, "I believe this great ignorance might be a help to the evangelization of England: any amount of theology can now be smuggled into people's minds under cover of romance without their knowing it" (*Collected Letters of CSL* 2: 262). As early as 1939, and well before he began to write the Narnia books, Lewis realized that Christian truths are more powerfully conveyed through images—that is, through poetic means—than through direct and reasoned argument.

Sayers was likewise very aware of the great power of images. Part of her frustration over the amount of time she had spent on writing reasoned arguments for the Christian faith arose from the fact that she knew that her strength as a writer lay in her imaginative works. Considering herself a scholar by training, and a writer of stories and plays by vocation, she believed that what she said in her apologetic writing was just a recasting of what the Church said, particularly in the Creeds. What she wanted most was to be able to express such truth through her own medium. By creating dramas, she was making pictures that would be the image of truth—"not the Creeds, but the substance of what is in the Creeds" (*Letters of DLS* 4: 136–40).

During the 1940s, when the volume of her apologetic writing and speaking was greatest, Dorothy L. Sayers became more convinced than ever that her gifts as a writer and her true power lay in a more creative sort of writing, particularly drama. She lectured and wrote frequently on the subject of Christian drama.[33] She understood the close connection between religion and drama, stemming from the ritual origins of theater in ancient times. She understood that this connection is reflected in the fact that the celebration of the Eucharist involves worship that is interactive, and that the rituals of Christian worship are essentially dramatic.

Sayers also recognized drama's immense spiritual potential. She appealed to the Church to reclaim drama as its own territory— territory lost at the end of the Middle Ages. She herself became a leading participant in the great flowering of Church drama in England in the next few decades. *The Zeal of Thy House*, written for the Canterbury Cathedral Festival of 1937, was the first of Sayers's religious dramas. This was followed in 1939 by *The Devil to Pay*, and in 1940 and 1941 by her series of twelve radio plays for the BBC on the life of Christ—*The Man Born to Be King*.

Again, as she had done with the whodunit, Sayers identified—in a seemingly secular literary genre—the potentially rich spiritual dimension of drama. She argued passionately that theater could be and should be a means of communicating spiritual truth. She observed that when there is any strong natural human urge that the Church fails to incorporate into its own life, that urge will not just fade away; it will just continue on, "becoming increasingly secularized," and eventually will be put to "the service of any rival religion, which is ready to make use of it." Sayers bluntly identifies what this loss will mean for the church: "The Church itself will become impoverished for lack of that natural power and vivacity. During the last four or five centuries, this has certainly been happening to European drama, and it is becoming fairly obvious that the Church has got to do something about it. She has vacated a particularly dominating pulpit and has no right to appear pained and surprised if she finds it occupied by other preachers with powerful lungs. . . . Our Lord had occasion to speak sharply about the superior enterprise of the children of this world, who do not miss their opportunities" ("Sacred Plays" 1: 21).

Sayers responded to her own challenge; through her drama she reoccupied that "particularly dominating pulpit." It is in her plays that we find her most profound treatment of the emotional and spiritual problems of her day, and it is in functioning imaginatively and creatively as a dramatist that she speaks most powerfully as a poet-prophet.

Eliot expressed a similar view of the spiritual potential of creative literature that indirectly communicates the Christian message. Although he admitted that he "admires and enjoys . . . delightful fiction" that is explicitly Christian, like Chesterton's *The Man Who Was Thursday,* he was unhappy about the fact that such works do not force people into "the serious consideration of the relation of Religion and Literature" because they are too consciously religious. What he wanted was a literature that is "*un*consciously, rather than deliberately and defiantly Christian" ("Religion and Literature" 391–92; italics mine).

There is always an unconscious element in imaginative writing. In creative works of fiction, drama, and poetry, the Christian message emerges without the conscious and deliberate intention of authors when that message is so much a part of the writer's inner being that it has become one with what he or she is. This chapter has shown how vital and integral the message of redemption was to Eliot, Lewis, and Sayers. It was part of their consciousness. That Christian consciousness flows through the poetry and plays of Eliot, the fiction and poetry of Lewis, and the plays and poetry of Sayers. The subjects covered in my remaining chapters will be explored primarily by examining these creative works.

Lewis, Eliot, and Sayers functioned as both prophet-preachers and prophet-poets. Their apologetic effectiveness was the greatest the modern world had seen; yet, as Sayers recognized, their own true medium—the medium in which they communicated most powerfully—was not expository, it was creative. To point people to Christ through pictures, symbols, and stories was their highest calling.

3

Christ

The Unsafe Savior

✠ ✠ ✠

The trouble with the modern age, Eliot said, "is not merely the inability to believe certain things about God and man which our forefathers believed, but the inability to *feel* towards God and man as they did" ("The Social Function of Poetry" 15). He explains this "decline of religious sensibility," pointing out that the spiritual Waste Land of modern times is largely the result of the disappearance of "religious feeling," and that the terms that people used in the past to express religious ideas have now become "meaningless" (15). Eliot believed that the rhetoric of apologetics had become virtually incomprehensible to many people; their brains were unreceptive because their hearts were numb. Eliot's diagnosis of a state of emotional numbness is tied to his view that appealing to the heart, or the emotional sensibilities, is the key to reaching people with the Christian message. Lewis and Sayers agreed with Eliot that creative works that appeal to the imagination and spirit will be more powerful than well-reasoned expositions in restoring religious feeling and renewing spiritual responsiveness in an era blighted by modernism.

Modernism was a movement that had widespread influence on thought and culture in the late nineteenth and early twentieth centuries.[1] It grew out of the convergence of several historical and cultural shifts: industrialism, the rejection of realism, and the rejection of traditional forms in art, literature, and faith. It was especially apparent by the time Lewis, Sayers, and Eliot began writing. With its emphasis on making an abrupt break with the past and its naïve view of "progress" (the assumption that things are steadily getting better and better), modernism dominated other modes of thought, including formal philosophy, the sciences, social organization, and even the activities of daily life. The modernism that Lewis, Sayers, and Eliot confronted was characterized by a general disillusionment arising from the absence of any basis for certainty about anything. The rejection of traditional religious modes of thought left a huge vacuum, intellectually and emotionally.

The Demand for a Response

The loss of religious feeling—even among religious people—that Lewis, Sayers, and Eliot observed includes, most markedly, a loss of connection with the person of Christ. The question "What think ye of Christ?" (Matt. 22:42) points to the central issue of the gospel and implies more than an opinion based on factual information. Over and over throughout the New Testament, the appeal goes out to "believe on the Lord Jesus Christ" (Acts 16.31), "believe in his name" (John 3:23), "believe in your heart" (Rom. 10:9), receive him (John 1:12; Col. 2:6). This believing in the heart, this receiving, speaks more of emotional assent than rational acceptance, and it is on the level of feeling that the deepest faith takes root.

For centuries, it was imagery of the Crucifixion that most shaped people's conception of Christ and their emotional response to him. Christ on the Cross was the dominant subject of European art, and the atoning death of Christ was the central doctrine of the faith. Artists were obsessed, almost mesmerized, by visions of the Passion. In painting, in sculpture, and in literature, the subject was treated over and over. Medieval Christendom understood that it was necessary to see Christ imaginatively—and to see him as the suffering Savior.

Yet medieval literature presented Christ in terms of both humiliation and authority. An early medieval poem called *The Dream of the Rood* moved Lewis deeply, even before he became a Christian

(*Surprised by Joy* 166). It describes Christ as "the Hero young" and "the righteous King, the Lord of heaven" suffering, "stretched out grievously" on the Cross (3), and describes "all creation" weeping and wailing over "the slaughter of its King" (3).[2] Lyric poems of the eleventh and twelfth centuries similarly encourage strong emotion toward the person of Christ by depicting the pathos of the Crucifixion along with a didactic challenge. They urged accountability to the divine purpose of the Crucifixion, and the meaning of it in their own lives.

Other medieval poems make the same appeal. In the short poem "Ye That Pasen by the Weye," Christ speaks from the Cross and challenges the passersby to recognize the uniqueness and intensity of his suffering. In "Vox Ultima Crucis" [The Voice from the Cross], Christ urges people to set their eyes on the heavenly home he had made possible for them by his sacrificial death. In another short poem, "I Have Labored Sore," the suffering Christ, having completed the work of atonement, announces that he will return very soon and call heaven and earth and hell to judgment. And then, he says, "shall know both devil and man / What I was and what I am."

The image of Christ as the suffering Redeemer and final judge continued to dominate Christian thought from the Middle Ages into the Renaissance. In the metaphysical poetry of the seventeenth century, Christ is depicted in the context of his suffering, and the image of his brokenness clearly defines the demands he makes — demands based on his identity as Savior and Lord. John Donne describes a confrontational encounter with the crucified Christ in "Good Friday, 1613. Riding Westward." The poem has a fearsome quality, in that Donne is subjected to the demands of the suffering Savior, who is both the submissive sacrificial Lamb of God and the terrifying Lion of the tribe of Judah. Like the medieval poets and artists, Donne depicts the person of Christ in a way that evokes the right responses of anguish and remorse. The initial feelings may be almost horror and revulsion, but they become a deep personal grief — the *good* grief that draws one toward, rather than pushing one away: the grief that leads to repentance. This is part of the right feeling toward God that Eliot found lacking in the modern world, but it is a feeling he believed could be restored if the image of Christ as the suffering Redeemer is restored.

Dorothy L. Sayers shared Eliot's belief that the "trouble of the modern age [was] the inability to *feel* towards God" as early generations did (Eliot, "The Social Function of Poetry" 15). She directly confronts the lack of religious feeling and prevailing disinterest in Christ through the depiction of Christ in her radio plays based on the gospel narratives. Lewis similarly challenges the apathy toward the person of Christ through imaginative tales in which Christ is represented by a lion. Eliot challenges the absence of a right feeling toward God through his poetry, in which Christ appears sometimes in gentleness, sometimes with violence. All three writers portray the duality of Christ: his suffering and brokenness on the one hand, and his frightening authority and supremacy on the other. The two dimensions of their Christology are not, however, set up as contrasts that balance each other out. The self-sacrificing love and compassion of the Lamb of God operates within the terrifying majesty of the Lion of Judah.

The Depiction of Christ in Sayers's Plays

In June 1943, Sayers received a letter from a young man who, in response to her radio plays on the life of Christ, expressed his struggle with the spiritual dilemmas that plagued his generation. Sayers, in a very long and compassionate letter, addressed every question and every problem the young man had raised, placing them in the context of the person and redemptive work of Christ. She counters the young man's account of the lack of direction of his generation by pointing out that all roads to truth lead ultimately to the same place: to Calvary (*Christ of the Creeds* 76–83).[3] Sayers assures her correspondent that the Christian story is not a "soothing syrup": its message is one of confrontation, and everyone is, in the final analysis, accountable to God. Everyone must choose to accept or reject the atonement made available by Christ's work at Calvary. She ends her letter with a poignant image of Christ appearing in atoning power in the midst of the modern Waste Land: "He is in the desert, walking to his death" (83).

In making it possible for people look again at the person of Christ, through the twelve radio plays of the series *The Man Born to Be King*,[4] Sayers restored the possibility both of attaining an imaginative grasp of who Jesus was and of regaining a right feeling toward God. The powerful depiction of Christ in these radio plays grew out of Sayers's disgust at the failure of the contemporary Church to show the truly terrifying nature of the Lion of Judah. Christ is presented, she says, as totally unthreatening; his "shattering personality" has been "muffled" and surrounded with "an atmosphere of tedium." She goes on, "We have very efficiently pared the claws of the Lion of Judah, certified him 'meek and mild,' and recommended him as a fitting household pet for pale curates and pious old ladies" (Sayers, "The Greatest Drama Ever Staged" 6).

In her introduction to the published version of *The Man Born to Be King*, Sayers discusses the challenge of retelling the story of Jesus for a modern audience. She was determined that it be presented not liturgically or symbolically, but realistically and historically, so that people would get the point that "this is a thing that actually happened" (17). Sayers depicts Christ as overpowering and irresistible; he is one who does, when lifted up, draw all men to himself. He was a hero, Sayers declares, whose goodness was not static: "He was a lively person. He excited people. Wherever He went He brought not peace but a sword, and fire in the earth; that is why they killed Him. He said surprising things, in language ranging from the loftiest poetry to the most lucid narrative and the raciest repartee" (26). She points out that no one in Jesus's day could accuse him of "insipidity." That insult, she observes has been inflicted by "pious hands" of later eras. "To make of [Christ's] story something that could neither startle, nor shock, nor terrify, nor excite, nor inspire a living soul," she asserts, "is to crucify the Son of God afresh and put him to an open shame" (37).

The play series aroused much controversy—controversy that pertained to the very issue that Sayers had recognized as crucial to the project: the depiction of Christ. Sayers was right about the widespread addiction to what she regarded as the wrong sort of image of Christ. But what the controversy represented was a greater evil than the addiction of many churchmen and churchgoers to insipid religion. She was convinced that the widespread desire to maintain a watered-down image of Christ, a pared-claws version of the Lion of Judah, was fueled by the determination of what Lewis's Screwtape would call "Our Father Below" to prevent the real Lion from coming into view and dominating the landscape.

The Man Born to be King was produced and broadcast over a ten-month period under the supervision of the Rev. J. W. Welch, who was the BBC's director of religious broadcasting. Dr. Welch had commissioned Sayers to write the plays and had had the faith and vision necessary to carry the project through, even when Sayers herself became so frustrated by misunderstandings with the producers that she almost resigned. Welch's foreword to the published text of the plays expresses the great need for this kind of presentation of Christ. Welch explains that the BBC had realized that their listeners comprised three groups: "those who approved of religious broadcasts, those who were indifferent but not unfriendly, and those who were positively hostile" (12). The producers were most concerned about the second and third groups—people from whose lives a sense of God had vanished, people who found the language of religion meaningless and who had little knowledge of the basic tenets of the Christian faith. Such people were experiencing, Welch believed, "dissatisfaction with materialism," and a need for a "spiritual interpretation of life" (12). Though these people seemed to have rejected formal religion, Welch believed that there was "a unanimous consensus of opinion that in the man Jesus lay the key to many of the riddles of life" (12). Welch's conclusion was that it was the duty of religious broadcasting to present the truth about the world and life and humanity in such a way that people would listen. He pointed out that the message had to be Christ-focused, observing, "Now it is a fact of history that every Christian revival during the past nineteen hundred years has come, at least in part, from a fresh study of the life and teachings of the Christ. . . . Now the task of the church in any age is to *reveal* Christ" (12). Rev. Welch believed that Christ no longer seemed relevant to many people because of the "huge barricade of unreality" that surrounded his image, causing people to associate him with "the teaching of a remote childhood or to bad stained glass and effeminate pictures" (12). Welch believed that "much ruthless stripping away" was needed if the true nature of Christ was to be perceived, but wondered if that was even possible. "To chisel away the unreality which, for the majority, surrounds his person," he said, "might hurt some of the minority; yet the task was to destroy only the unnecessary and false, and so to release the true" (12).

Welch saw the challenge inherent in Sayers's realistic depiction of Christ in *The Man Born to Be King* and understood that it aggressively confronted both religious people and nonreligious people. By stripping away the religiosity and sentiment that had become part of the Christian package, Sayers's plays allowed people to *see* Christ and experience his "coercive" power. Letters from listeners poured in by the hundreds—letters that told, not of engagement with a set of religious ideas, but of encounters with a person:

> "Your play *The Man Born to be King* is quite changing the atmosphere in our house . . . resentment and criticism [are] dying away in the presence of Christ."
>
> "[Children] don't want Christ as somebody in a book—gentle, kind and charming as Cinderella, but a real being who can give them strength and courage to love God and be themselves, forming their own opinions from Christ's teaching."
>
> "The plays [helped] thousands to realise for the first time what the Gospel story means . . . [as it was] expressed in a manner which would make it more intelligible to [many] who never read their New Testament."
>
> "For myself the last broadcast convicted me deeply. It was a living scene, and I was part of it. God spoke to me through it."

"The inspiration of [the plays] will remain with me until my life's end." (Qtd. in Welch 14)

Some letters commented on the incongruity of the strong protests against *The Man Born to Be King* that came from ostensibly Christian sources. One listener observed, "It is amazing to me that people who conceive themselves to be defending the Christian use of Sunday should spend tons of money in trying to prevent an effort like this, which seems to me more likely to bring home to the ordinary British public who and what Our Lord Jesus Christ is than anything else that has been done in our time" (qtd. in Welch 14). But the experience was too much for many, perhaps because the sequence of twelve plays builds up to and climaxes in the Crucifixion. What listeners got was more than a credible depiction of Jesus as a real living person—it was an encounter with the crucified Christ. It was demanding, and for some too frightening.

In his foreword to the plays, Welch attempts to account for the opposition that the broadcasts received from some quarters. "Some listeners," he says, "were quite incapable of believing that Christ . . . was in any sense fully *human;* and even supporters of the plays flinched and shrank away from the glimpse of the Crucifixion we were given in the eleventh play." The images and impressions that most people had stored in their minds, Welch argued, had made many of them incapable of listening to the true story. They were afraid to truly "behold the Man"; they preferred their "easy and comfortable version of him." Welch was right in asserting that the gospel story, as people knew it or thought they knew it, had failed to convey the redemptive message because it did not "arrest, convict, attract, compel men to a decision" (16).

The presentation of the gospel in *The Man Born to Be King* did "arrest, convict, attract, [and] compel." The Christ in these plays is, Welch affirms, "a veritable Hound of Heaven." The eleventh play, the one depicting the Crucifixion, was the most convicting: "Though it only hinted at the physical horror . . . [it] was almost unbearable because the stupidity and brutality of the ordinary man and woman in the crowd convicted *us*. *We don't want to believe* that the Crucifixion was like *that*" (16).

Sayers's stage dramas similarly focused on the theme of fearsome redemption. Most of her nonradio plays were commissioned by churches to be performed at special anniversaries and festivals. In the first of these, *The Zeal of Thy House,* written for the Canterbury Festival of 1937, the protagonist is a historical character—the architect William of Sens, who rebuilt the choir of Canterbury Cathedral after it had been destroyed by fire in 1174. William's spiritual arrogance is confronted and defeated by an encounter with the suffering of Christ. He is told, "when God came to test of mortal time . . . / He made no reservation of Himself / Nor of the godlike stamp that franked His gold, / But in good time let time supplant Him too" (Sayers, *Zeal of Thy House* 97). He is told how, in a climax accompanied by earthquake and darkened sun, Christ triumphantly cried, "It is finished!" and completed the plan of redemption (97). This revelation of the isolation, despair, and anguish of Christ's triumphant suffering is the pivot of the play. William encounters the unsafe Savior and is broken and remade.

Sayers's dramatic depiction of the terror of the gospel rises to a peak in *The Just Vengeance,* written for the 750th anniversary of Lichfield Cathedral in 1945. At the pivotal point of the action, Christ, the victim and the victor, cries out:

Say that the guilt is Mine; give it to Me
And I will take it away to be crucified.
It is all so very much simpler than you think:
Give Me the greedy heart and the little creeping treasons.
Give Me the proud heart and the blind, obstinate eyes . . .
Give Me the confused self that you can do nothing with;
I can do something. (339)

Near the end of the play, the risen Christ appears in terrifying splendor, standing before the Cross, which is now a "Cross of glory," and declares his majesty, saying "I [am] the Image of the Godhead bodily / In whom the Godhead and the Manhood are one, / . . . I the end, and I the beginning of all things" (349–50). All roads to salvation lead to Calvary, where Christ is, simultaneously, the sacrificed victim, like the Lamb of Old Testament ritual, and the glorious victor, the Lion of the tribe of Judah.

The Depiction of Christ in Lewis's Fiction

The lion Aslan in C. S. Lewis's *Chronicles of Narnia* belongs to the long tradition of myths and children's stories in which animals function like human beings. Lewis's poem "Impenitence" proclaims his delight in the use of animals in children's stories to represent personality types. He speaks of "the man-like beasts of the earthy stories" like *The Wind in the Willows,* and the "true" beasts that "cry out to be used as symbols . . . parodies by Nature" that reveal human nature and become true archetypes (*Poems* 2). The reflection of human nature by representative animals is easy to accept, but divine nature is a very different matter: Lewis's sustained and consistent depiction of the nature and redemptive role of Christ through a fictional character who is an animal—a lion—is unprecedented.

Imaginative literature gives a solid and familiar shape to abstract ideas and allows things that seem remote to become congenial and accessible. Lewis had steeped himself in myths and other fanciful tales from earliest childhood, and his imagination was saturated with images in which inanimate objects or lower forms of life represent higher realities. The lion Aslan is an imaginative depiction through which the complex nature of the incarnate God is given a form that is congenial and accessible to the fictional children who visit the land of Narnia and to the real children and adults who read the books.

Scripture itself uses similar symbolism. The lion image is used in reference to God by a number of Old Testament prophets, in Genesis.[5] The lamb image, suggesting an offering for the atonement of sin, is used of the promised Messiah in the Old Testament and of Christ himself in the New Testament, most notably in John the Baptist's proclamation, "Behold the Lamb of God, which taketh away the sin of the world" (John 1.29). The most striking use of such imagery to depict the redeeming and triumphant nature of Christ is found in the Revelation of St. John, chapter 5, when Christ is seen as both a lion and a lamb. In verse 5 of that chapter, it is revealed to John that "the Lion of the tribe of Judah" has conquered, but in verse 6, it is as a lamb that Christ appears as victor—"a Lamb" standing as though it had been slain.

If one considered how Christ might be presented in an imaginative story in a nonhuman form, the image of a lion would seem reasonable. Yet Lewis's account of how he came to depict Christ as a lion shows that the idea emerged without any reasoning process or conscious choice. In a short article written in 1960 for the *Radio Times,* Lewis explains that it is difficult to be accurate about how he came to write *The Lion, the Witch, and the Wardrobe* because "a man writing a story is too excited about the story itself to sit back and notice how he is doing it." One thing he is certain of is that his Narnia books, and the three books of his space trilogy, began with him "seeing pictures" in his head. Initially they were not even ideas for plots, "just pictures." The first Narnia book began, he says, "with a picture of a Faun carrying an umbrella and parcels in a snowy wood." This picture had been in his mind for more than twenty years, until one day he decided to "try to make a story about it" without having much idea of how it would go. "But then," he says, "suddenly Aslan came bounding into it. I think I had been having a good many dreams of lions about that time. I don't know where the Lion came from or why He came. But once He was there He pulled the whole story together, and soon He pulled the other six Narnian stories in after Him" ("It All Began with a Picture" 53). While Lewis's capitalization of the pronouns *he* and *him* indicates that Aslan represents Christ, this account of the origin of the series makes it clear that using a lion as an image for Christ was not something Lewis deliberately decided to do. It was, he believed, something given to him.

The lion is an awesome, but unifying, presence in the seven Narnia books. After the first book, his appearances are briefer and unexpected, and usually unsettling. Even though he unmistakably stands for goodness, his goodness is far from meek and mild. From the first mention of him in *The Lion, the Witch and the Wardrobe*, it is clear that he is a creature who roars and bares his teeth, and who is definitely not safe. Nonetheless, to free the boy Edmund from the consequences of his sin of treachery, the powerful, majestic Lion allows himself to be demeaned, abused, and killed. He chooses to become the victim of evil, succumbing to the Lamb's role, so that the power of evil can be reversed. He is bound, shorn of his mane, and mocked. As he lies on the Stone Table, waiting for the blow of the White Witch that will kill him, he fulfills the role of the Lamb of God. His face is "braver, and more beautiful, and more patient than ever" (*The Lion, the Witch, and the Wardrobe* 151). But his victimization and defeat are not the end of the story: what the White Witch and the grieving children do not know is that "when an innocent and willing victim is killed in a traitor's stead," the Stone Table (that represents the law and the consequences for sin) will crack, "and death itself would start working backward" (160). In the climactic battle of chapter 16, the resurrected Aslan descends on the scene as a roaring lion. As he flings himself on the White Witch, her face is full of terror and her destruction assured (174). When peace is restored and Aslan quietly slips away, Mr. Beaver echoes his earlier description of Aslan as not safe, but good, explaining to the children, "He's wild, you know. Not like a *tame* lion" (180).

In *Prince Caspian,* the next book of the series, the first clear sighting of Aslan by all four children inspires both love and fear: "Aslan had stopped and turned and stood facing them, looking so majestic that they felt as glad as anyone can who feels afraid, and as afraid as anyone can who feels glad" (148).

In *The Voyage of the Dawn Treader,* in a scene near the end of voyage, Aslan appears as both a Lamb and a Lion. First the children see a Lamb who is so white they can hardly bear to look at it, who invites them to come and have breakfast. When they ask him if they can find the way to Aslan's country from where they are, he tells them that, for them, the door to Aslan's country will be from their own world. Their surprise at this revelation is followed by another surprising revelation: "'There is a way into my country from all the worlds,' said the Lamb; but as he spoke his snowy white flushed into tawny gold and his size changed and he was Aslan himself, towering above them and scattering light from his mane" (214–15). This magnificent shape-shifting shows the unthreatening, loving nature of Aslan (the lamblike aspect) dramatically intersecting with his frightening majesty.

In *The Silver Chair,* a girl name Jill, visiting Narnia for the first time, encounters Aslan without forewarning, having no idea who or what he is. The huge lion is sitting by the only stream from which she can drink, and she is close to dying of thirst. Though he invites her to come and drink, Jill is too terrified to do so. He will not move aside to allow her to drink in comfort; nor will he promise not to "do anything" to her if she does come to the stream to drink. Instead of calming her fear that he might devour her, the Lion tells her that he has "swallowed up girls and boys, women and men, kings and emperors, cities and realms." Desperately thirsty, but terrified, Jill cannot bring herself to accept his invitation to come and drink, and says she will go and look for another stream. "There is no other stream," says the Lion. Suddenly, in spite of the Lion's fearsomeness, Jill finds that her mind has "suddenly made itself up." She goes forward toward the stream, sensing that this action is "the worst thing she had ever had to do" (17).

In *The Horse and His Boy,* two children traveling through treacherous terrain on horseback are terrorized, several times, by lions. Yet the boy, Shasta, is finally told that there is only one lion. When he asks the identity of the lion, the answer he receives causes both terror and joy: "Myself," said the Voice, very deep and low so that the earth shook. . . . Shasta was no longer afraid that the Voice belonged to something that would eat him. . . . But a new and different sort of trembling came over him. Yet he felt glad too" (159). All around him is "shining whiteness" and "golden light." Turning, he sees that, moving along beside him and taller than his horse, there is "a Lion. . . . It was from the Lion that the light came. No one ever saw anything more terrible or beautiful" (160). The fear that such scenes inspire is good fear—the right feeling toward God that Eliot spoke of as absent from the Waste Land of modernity. It is the godly fear that stands in direct opposition to the insipid religiosity that "efficiently pared the claws of the Lion of Judah" (Sayers, "The Greatest Drama Ever Staged" 6).

The Depiction of Christ in Eliot's Poetry

The first allusion to Christ in T. S. Eliot's poetry occurs in an early sequence of four short poems called *Preludes,* first published in 1915. Eliot expresses a wistful premonition of what might lie beyond the sordid, and seemingly futile, reality of human life. The speaker is "moved by fancies" and, despite the images of desolation that curl around him, is aware of something transcendent and infinite: "some infinitely gentle / Infinitely suffering thing" (*Preludes* 4. 25). This momentary glimpse of the compassionate gentleness and suffering that presides over all things alludes to the Lamb of God. The "infinitely suffering thing" Eliot speaks of is Christ, "the Lamb slain from the foundation of the world" (Rev. 13:8).

Such gentleness does not prepare us for the drastically different image of Christ that Eliot introduces just a few years later in "Gerontion."[6] In this poem, written well before his own formal submission to the violence of salvation, Eliot describes Christ as a devourer, a tiger. The poem is named for a character called Gerontion, who provides the main consciousness in the poem. Early in the poem, he describes himself and his shabby, lethargic existence: "an old man in a dry month, / . . . waiting for rain. . . . / My house is a decayed house, . . . / I an old man, / A dull head among windy spaces." Then the poem takes an unexpected turn. Though the speaker may still be the old man, he seems to speak more for a group, saying, "Signs are taken for wonders. 'We would see a sign!'/ The word within a word, unable to speak a word, / Swaddled with darkness. In the juvescence of the year / Came Christ the tiger" (Eliot, "Gerontion" 21).

The request for "a sign" alludes to several New Testament texts. In Matthew, chapter 12, Jesus rebukes the Pharisees for their unbelief when they ask him to vindicate his ministry and authority by showing them "a sign." They had already seen many miraculous signs; Christ himself, the Word of God incarnate, was word enough, sign enough. Jesus calls them "an evil and adulterous generation," and indicates they will receive no further sign but the sign of his own death and resurrection (Matt. 12.38–42). Later, just before his crucifixion, Jesus disappoints Herod's wish to see some "sign" for his personal diversion (Luke 23.8–9). In both these incidents, the desire to see a sign does not come from a sincere search for truth, but instead from a rejection of truth. Such unbelief is the spiritual state Eliot depicts in the poem "Gerontion."

The line "The word within a word, unable to speak a word," together with several other phrases in the following lines, alludes to the beginning of John's gospel, where Christ is presented as the Word of God, God Incarnate, coming into the world: "In the beginning was the Word, and the Word was with God, and the Word was God. The same was in the beginning with God. All things were made by him; and without him was not any thing made that was made. In him was life; and the life was the light of men. And the light shineth in darkness; and the darkness comprehended it not. . . . He was in the world, and the world was made by him, and the world knew him not. He came unto his own, and his own received him not" (John 1.1–5, and 1.10–11). The phrase "swaddled with darkness" is a reference to Christ's nativity—*swaddled* suggesting the swaddling clothes of the Christ child, and *darkness* suggesting the obscurity into which he was born. But *darkness* also alludes to the darkness mentioned in the passage from John's gospel quoted above.

In these densely packed lines—"Signs are taken for wonders. 'We would see a sign!'/ The word within a word, unable to speak a word, / Swaddled with darkness. In the juvescence of the year / Came Christ the tiger" ("Gerontion" 21)—Eliot is alluding to three seemingly disconnected things: the unbelief inherent in the request for "a sign," the nativity of Christ (who is, in infancy, the unspeaking "Word"), and the image of Christ as a dangerous and uncontrollable entity: a "tiger." The connection Eliot is making between these three things becomes clearer if we look at another text that he is working from in this passage—a sermon on the Nativity by Bishop Lancelot Andrewes,[7] whom Eliot considered one of the greatest preachers of the English Church. In "Lancelot Andrewes," an essay Eliot wrote on the preacher in 1926 (339), Eliot indicates his fondness for this passage in Andrewes's Christmas Sermon of 1618: "Signs are taken for wonders. 'Master, we would fain see a sign', (Matt. xii. 38), that is a miracle. And in this sense it is a sign to wonder at. Indeed every word here is a wonder. . . . the Word without a word; the eternal Word not able to speak a word; a wonder sure. And . . . swaddled, and that a wonder too. 'He,' that (as in the thirty-eighth of Job (v. 9) He saith), 'taketh the vast body of the main sea, turns it to and fro, and rolls it about with the swaddling bands of darkness;'—He to come thus into clouts [baby clothes], Himself!" (Andrewes 133).

This is the passage alluded to in "Gerontion." Eliot's depiction of Christ as a tiger is also derived from Andrewes, specifically from his Nativity sermon of 1622, that describes slothful "seekers" who mistakenly believe that they need not feel any urgency since they naïvely assume Christ will pose no danger to them, thinking "Christ is no wild-cat" (Andrewes 167). Such foolish and complacent people contrast drastically with the magi's intense focus in their seeking of the Christ child. Andrewes affirms that Christ is quite the reverse of what such nonchalant people assume, and is well represented by the image of a fearsome and relentless pursuer, the "wild-cat."

In "Gerontion," when Eliot speaks of "The word within a word, unable to speak a word, / Swaddled with darkness," he is presenting the infant incarnate Christ as meek and vulnerable. Yet he immediately shifts to a completely contrasting image: "In the juvescence of the year / Came Christ the tiger," meaning that in spring, the energizing time of year associated with the Resurrection, Christ enters as an overwhelming force. There is an immense paradox set up in these four lines: Christ, the God-Man, is both mutely helpless and dangerously powerful, and yet those of the "evil and adulterous generation" keep asking for some additional sign, some entertaining wonder (Eliot, "Gerontion" 21).

The sign they will receive is the atonement itself and the wonder of its representation in Holy Communion. We learn that "Christ the tiger" comes not to eat, but "To be eaten, to be divided, to be drunk"—comes not as a life-destroying predator that will devour us but as a life-restoring Eucharistic sacrifice. The poem exposes what Eliot sees as the travesty of unbelief as it depicts the bread and the wine of this holy ceremony being consumed by various unholy communicants. But it is not eaten by the speaker, the little old man Gerontion, who sees the Eucharistic ritual as a kind of futility, like "Vacant shuttles [that]/ Weave the wind." The character Gerontion, very aware of his own sinfulness, asks, "After such knowledge what forgiveness?" When the tiger is mentioned again later in the poem he is associated not with the atonement, but with judgment: "The tiger springs in the new year. Us he devours" (Eliot, "Gerontion" 22).

In *Mastery and Escape: T. S. Eliot and the Dialectic of Modernism*, Jewel Spears Brooker points out that in "Gerontion" Eliot focuses on the sinfulness of the "state of mind that permanently precludes affirmation or belief" (103). She comments on the significance of the tiger image, pointing out that "'Came Christ the tiger' . . . is extremely startling as a reference" to the Incarnation of Christ, and that the later reference to Christ suggests that he comes as the tiger in his Crucifixion (104). The idea is startling: in his death we associate Christ, not with ferocity, but with the image of the meek "Lamb of God." Brooker explains, "Eliot is capitalizing on the biblical teaching that whereas Christ came first in meekness as the Lamb of God, submitting to his enemies without a whimper, he will come again in power as the Lion of Judah, slaying his enemies with the breath (wind) of his mouth" (104–5). Brooker goes on to show that the tiger image culminates at the start of stanza six with the lines, "The tiger springs in the new year. Us he devours." This, she says, reverses the situation of devouring we saw in stanza three; "Instead of the tiger being eaten . . . , he springs and devours those who are devouring him" (105).

Brooker sees in this poem many sorts of "flagrant rejections of Christ" as God (106). The Pharisees (alluded to in the request for a sign) were ostensibly asking for a "sign" of his divinity, but were in fact refusing the signs already given them because of their determined unbelief. Participants in the Mass (of the sort described in the poem) reject him too, by their sinful, and therefore blasphemous, partaking of the emblems of his death. Brooker identifies the tiger image as a broad indictment of those "who are learned but blind," in which "the image of a ferocious, powerful, devouring presence [becomes] an extraordinary conceit for . . . the absence of god, of belief, in the modern world" (106).

George Williamson's discussion of "Gerontion" observes that the rejection of Christ depicted in this poem occurs on an individual level as well. Though the speaker, the "old man in a dry month" (Eliot, "Gerontion" 21), seeks to explain or justify himself to a "you" that is not clearly identified, it is reasonable to conclude that this listener is "Christ, the sign of life" connected with the juvescence of springtime (Williamson 111). The dryness of the speaker indicates his spiritual neediness. Earlier in his life, the speaker suggests, there had been a kind of nearness to what he calls "your heart"—which was a thing of beauty, but he has since been "removed therefrom / To lose beauty in terror." A tiger-like presence *is* terrifying, but the terror is not what finally estranges Gerontion from the beauty. The terror, he says, is lost "in inquisition," in the endless questioning that has destroyed the passion he felt earlier. He says, "I have lost my passion . . . / I have lost my sight, smell, hearing, taste and touch: / How should I use them for your closer contact?" The poem ends with the speaker permanently separated from belief and from passion, and the poem's final lines show him driven by the random winds of life to "a sleepy corner," and defined by his "Thoughts of a dry brain in a dry season" (Eliot, "Gerontion" 23). Eliot's depiction of Christ in this 1920 poem, with its aggressive, devouring imagery, anticipates the many allusions to Christ in Eliot's better-known works, his major works of the ensuing years. The allusions are sometimes subtle, but nearly always startling.

Part 1 of *The Waste Land* uses the term "Son of man" (a phrase sometimes used of biblical prophets and one that Christ applied often to himself) as a term of direct address. The passage in which it occurs is full of the imagery of wastedness and barrenness: "stony rubbish," "broken images," "dead tree," "no relief," "dry stone," and "no sound of water." It is as though the presence of the "Son of man" (Christ himself or some prophetic figure) is invited into the depleted landscape of the Waste Land. In the very next lines, the "shadow" of a "red rock" is twice mentioned, and an invitation is offered to "come in under" this shadow, possibly as a way of sheltering from the harsh desert sun (Eliot, *The Waste Land* 38). Isaiah 32.2 speaks of a hiding place in the desert under "the shadow of a great rock in a weary land"—a passage that has often been interpreted as a reference to Christ.

Later in part 1, the image of a "Hanged Man" appears on one of the tarot cards of the clairvoyant. This tarot figure, shown hanging on a T-shaped cross, is understood by interpreters of the tarot cards to represent the mythic fertility god, who is killed but rises again, restoring fertility to the land and his people. Eliot's own "Notes on 'The Waste Land'" tell us that he associates the Hanged Man with both this mythic restorative figure and "the hooded figure in the passage of the disciples [going] to Emmaus in Part V" (*The Waste Land* 51). The "hooded figure," as his notes to part 5 make clear, is Christ.

In part 5, the unrecognized "hooded figure" of the journey to Emmaus is in the background from the start. In this section of the poem, the first few lines seem to be spoken by the disciples of Jesus. They convey their response to Jesus's agony in Gethsemane, followed by his trial and crucifixion, and how they feel after "the torchlight," "the frosty silence in the gardens," "the agony in stony places," and the "prison and palace." They contemplate what has happened to Christ: "He who was living is now dead"; and what is happening to them: "We who were living are now dying." The next voice we hear describes "a road winding" among "mountains of rock without water," and the imagery of dryness and longing for water rises to a crescendo in which the sound of water becomes an agonized nightmare: "drip, drop, drip, drop, drop, drop, drop," but, as we soon discover, "there is no water" (Eliot, *The Waste Land* 47–48).

The next scene focuses on the hooded figure. The narrative voice asks of his companion, "Who is the third who walks always beside you?" The uncanniness of the situation, as it is recreated by Eliot, is frightening because the third figure is both there and not there. The speaker says that when he counts, as he is walking beside his companion, there are only the two of them. But the speaker also conveys another, almost out-of-body, perspective, in which he can "look ahead up the white road" and observe himself and the other walker. When he steps outside his body, and drops behind, and looks ahead at himself and his companion, he sees that there are not two in the group, but three: "There is always another one walking beside you / Gliding wrapt in a brown mantle, hooded." He cannot tell whether the mysterious figure is "a man or a woman," but he hopes his fellow traveler can tell him who it is, and asks again, "But who is that on the other side of you?" (*The Waste Land* 48).

Eliot's notes to the poem mention two scenarios that contributed to this mysterious figure. One is the desperate struggle for survival of Shackleton's companions during one of his Antarctic expeditions, when the men sensed that there was a mysterious extra person with them (*The Waste Land* 54). The other scenario that Eliot says was behind the unexplained, ubiquitous "third" figure is the appearance of Christ to the two disciples on the road to Emmaus (53), recounted in Luke 24.13–35. This event took place soon after the Resurrection, when strange things were unfolding before the blurred vision of the disciples. Eliot's unidentified third figure in the final movement of *The Waste Land* is more disconcerting than comforting, and seems to represent—more explicitly than in Shackleton's account and more tensely than in Luke's narrative—the numinous quality of a presence that is ultimately benevolent. It also shows the fearsome dimension of redemptive encounters that were anticipated in the tiger image of "Gerontion."

In *Ash-Wednesday,* the first poem published after Eliot's baptism, the redemptive work of Christ is brought into clearer focus. The beginning of part 5 stresses Christ's identity and supremacy as the incarnate Word. This passage intricately intertwines two meanings of *word:* that of "word" as communication generally and that of "the Word" to designate Christ, the living, incarnate Word, the ultimate communication of God to man. In this passage, Eliot is again building on the opening of John's gospel: "In the beginning was the Word, and the Word was with God, and the Word was God" (John 1.1). But the first four lines of part 5 of *Ash-Wednesday* also include another idea originating in the first chapter of John—that of the Word being refused: "He came unto his own, and his own received him not" (John 1.11). Eliot's lines play off the idea of the word of God (or the Word of God) not being received and therefore, potentially, lost or wasted: "If the lost word is lost, if the spent word is spent / If the unheard, unspoken / Word is unspoken, unheard; / Still is the unspoken word, the Word unheard" (Eliot, *Ash Wednesday* 65).

The point of this intricate passage is both general and specific. In a general sense, any form of communication, any intended "word," may remain unspoken or be ignored and hence seem to be lost. More specifically, Christ, the Incarnate Word—God's most direct communication of himself—may be refused, may be "unheard," and may appear to be "lost" or wasted. Yet the intrinsic nature and worth of the spoken "word" or the Incarnate "Word" is not in the least diminished. The communication of God to man, through Christ, is an absolute. The fact that it may be refused, may be "unheard," does not alter what it is. With the mention of the Word being "unspoken," Eliot alludes to Christ refusing to speak a word at the time of his trial (Matt. 27.14), and at the same time he continues the line of thought in John, chapter 1, that speaks of Christ coming into the world for its benefit—to be "the true Light, which lighteth every man" (John 1.9)—and yet not being received.

Part 5 of *Ash-Wednesday* continues to explore the paradox, playing on the similar sound of word and world and continuing to place imagery of silence in contrast with imagery of speech. Christ is described as "The Word without a word, [and] the Word within /

The world and for the world." The next line, "And the light shone in darkness . . ." again parallels the passage in John: "And the light shineth in darkness; and the darkness comprehended it not" (John 1.5).[8] Eliot, like John's gospel, affirms that Christ, who is the living Word and the Light of the World, cannot be made less than what he is, even when who he is and what he offers is not received. The nine-line passage concludes cryptically, "Against the Word the unstilled world still whirled / About the centre of the silent Word" (Eliot, *Ash Wednesday* 65).[9] Christ is the center or axis of all reality—"By him all things consist" (Col. 1.17)—and the troubled or "unstilled" world continues to rotate about that center. Christ is its creator, savior, and sustainer.

Northrop Frye speaks of this passage in his discussion of Eliot's insight into the role of the poet and the power of language. Frye points out that "in Christianity Logos means, not word, reason, or universal wisdom, but the person of Christ" (44). Frye recognizes that Christianity underlies Eliot's view of poetry, and observes that Eliot starts out with "the word within the word, unable to speak a word," ends with the Word as "the circumference of reality, containing within itself time, space, and poetry" (46). Eliot, in this one brief passage depicting the nature of Christ, moves from the helplessness of "*unable* to" to depict the mighty reality that is *able* to do anything, the Tiger that can devour us or redeem us.

Ten years later, in 1940, Eliot more fully portrayed the redemptive role of Christ in movement 4 of "East Coker."[10] This movement, composed of five stanzas of five lines each, depicts the compassion of Christ side by side with his severity. Christ is depicted as a "wounded surgeon" performing an operation. The fact that the surgeon is wounded and has bleeding hands identifies him as the suffering Savior and ultimate healer: "Beneath the bleeding hands we feel / The sharp compassion of the healer's art" (Eliot, *Four Quartets* 127). Helen Gardner observes that this section of "East Coker" can be better understood through reading Isaiah 53 on the "suffering servant"[11] and Philippians 2 on the idea of Christ "emptying himself" (Gardner 66).

The second stanza of movement 4 introduces the first person plural: "we" are the patients, the recipients of severe medical treatment, treatment that shows little interest in what pleases us and makes us comfortable. We are reminded of the gravity of our illness—it is our innate sinful nature that is the result of "Adam's curse"—and warned that "our sickness" must become even worse, if we are to be finally restored. Stanza 3 reveals that the best outcome we can hope for from this medical care is death. The shocking paradox is that "we shall / Die of the absolute paternal care / That will not leave us, but prevents us everywhere." This "absolute paternal care" refers to the force of redemption, which seeks to restore us in spite of ourselves and refuses to abandon us. It "prevents us"—hedges us around—on every side. There is no escape (*Four Quartets* 128).

In the fourth stanza of movement 4, a feeling of intense cold travels from the patient's feet to his knees, and yet at the same time he experiences the heat of fever. The intensities of frigidity and fire move through the body. Paradoxically the frigidity is connected with "purgatorial fires." But, like the fire of Purgatory that Dante depicts, these fires are not punitive but redemptive. Eliot tells us that "the flame is roses, and the smoke is briars." The flame and smoke (representing suffering) are transformed into something beautiful ("roses") and redemptive ("briars" suggesting the crown of thorns). The tortuous and loving beauty—the "flame [that] is roses"—is the warmth that ends the chill and brings health (*Four Quartets* 128).

Imagery of the crucifixion dominates the last stanza of movement 4, where we learn that only by partaking of the flesh and blood of Christ can we be restored. "The dripping blood our only drink / The bloody flesh our only food: / In spite of which we like to think / That we are sound, substantial flesh and blood— / Again, in spite of that, we call this Friday good" (*Four Quartets* 128). The imagery is both horrific and glorious. Christ is both the sacrificial Lamb that takes away the sin of the world and the terrifying divine surgeon who is ruthlessly determined to bring us down to death in order to heal us. We prefer to believe ("we like to think") that we are in good health ("sound" and "substantial") and have no need of the healing represented by the bread and wine of the Eucharist. The appalling truth is that we are desperately diseased and that the surgery must destroy us before it can help us. This is the fearsome good news of Good Friday.

Vision Precedes Redemption

The gospel narratives of the life of Jesus were written by "eyewitnesses" (Luke 1.2)—people who had literally *seen* him. "The Word became flesh . . . and we beheld his glory" (John 1.14). Throughout the centuries of the church-age, people were able to vicariously *see* Christ with the eyes of faith. The loss of religious emotion that Eliot observed in the twentieth century occurred, he believed, largely because of the loss of a valid perception of Christ. Eliot, Lewis, and Sayers strove to help people perceive Christ imaginatively, so that they might believe and be redeemed.

In an essay called "What Are We to Make of Jesus Christ?" Lewis sums up the challenge, even danger, inherent in an encounter with Christ. Jesus was never, Lewis points out, "regarded as a mere moral teacher." The effects he had on people varied widely; he produced strong reactions like "Hatred—Terror—Adoration. There was no trace of people expressing mild approval." When Jesus said "I am the way, the truth, and the life," he meant, Lewis explains, that no one could reach absolute reality except through him. Lewis asserts that the demands of Christ are ruthless: he is telling us, "'Try to retain your old life and you will be inevitably ruined. Give yourself away and you will be saved.'" Lewis affirms that Jesus tells us that he is the only way to life, saying, "'Eat Me, drink Me, I am your Food. And finally, do not be afraid, I have overcome the whole Universe'" ("What Are We to Make of Jesus Christ?" 79, 81, 84).

Lewis, Eliot, and Sayers, in their depictions of Christ, were doing what the medieval poets had done, what John Donne had done, and what the Church has been mandated to do. In portraying Christ as they did, they were providing something that was virtually absent from organized Christianity in their day: a renewed vision of Christ and renewed vitality for the message of redemption. They were also drawing attention to the Church's failure. Sayers alludes to this in a 1943 letter to the Rev. James Welch:

> I admire the Archbishops for their gallant attempt to cope with the social and economic situation; but really if it's *Christianity* they are concerned about the best thing they could do would be to instruct their clergy that for the next twelve months, Sundays and week-days, in season and out of season, they should preach God incarnate and Christ crucified . . . and leave the Sermon on the Mount and the reformation of banking and even kindness to animals until they had made people aware that Christianity was about *Christ*: not primarily about what he said about behavior, but WHO He was and What He DID. (*Christ of the Creeds* 73)

Eliot believed that the spiritual dilemma of his day was the inability to *feel* rightly toward God, and recognized that many people were clinging to a professed belief in which they, in truth, "no longer believe" ("The Social Function of Poetry" 15). He feared that religious knowledge could become so fragmented and contaminated that it would provide no basis for genuine personal faith. People who express themselves through Christian terminology are not necessarily people of faith. "When religious feeling disappears," Eliot observed, "the words in which men have struggled to express it become meaningless" (15). Eliot, like Lewis and Sayers, connected the disappearance of religious feeling with the absence of a true perception of Christ, and believed that the solution to the dilemma lay in helping people to vicariously see who and what Christ is. Jesus said, "He that hath seen me hath seen the Father" (John 14.9). Eliot, Lewis, and Sayers believed that an imaginative vision of the Lamb of God who is also the Lion of Judah can restore a right feeling toward God and reconnect us with Christ, the Unsafe Savior.

4

Choosing to Be the Chosen of God

✠ ✠ ✠

The depiction of Christ as Lamb and Lion is not a static image; it invites connection to the divine and introduces the possibility of redemption. Redemption is not a certainty until a choice has been made. It is a free choice, but it is made in response to spiritual drawing, the drawing of Christ himself, and it requires the acceptance of momentous changes, and the transition from one spiritual state to another.

The term *conversion,* as it is now used by Christians, is relatively new. It came into wide use through the great evangelical revival movements, such as those in England in the eighteenth century, and those in the United States in the nineteenth century.[1] The term is not based as directly on scripture, as many assume. In the New Testament, *epistrophe,* the Greek word for "conversion," also means "returning," "turning," or "turning again." Similarly, in the Old Testament, Hebrew words for "conversion" also suggest "returning," "recovery," or "restoration." "The law of the Lord is perfect, converting the soul" (Psalm 19.7) from the King James Version becomes "The law of the Lord is perfect, restoring the soul" in several modern translations.[2]

The Christian use of the term *conversion* has been often connected with the action of *man*—the acts of choosing and turning—more than with the action of *God.* Although repentance is an action and the exercise of faith in Christ requires choice, the movement toward faith operates under the influence and by the power of the divine agency. Modes of conversion, or ways of coming to Christian faith, range from a sudden personal crisis to a gradual growth into a new mode of thinking and living. In the latter case, conversion is often the consummation of a process toward greater understanding, assimilation, and yielding to truths that have been introduced and cultivated by familiarity with scripture or Christian teaching. Although there are unconscious elements, the process eventually becomes a conscious acknowledgment of Christ as Savior and a conscious commitment to live in accountability to him. In some cases, there is a particular moment of choice and change, but for many people, particular moments do not stand out, and the experience is perceived, in retrospect, as a gradual process. The main components of this process are repentance and faith. Repentance involves what one turns *from,* which is the former life; faith points to what one turns *toward,* which is God. Although the will of man plays a part, conversion occurs through the operation of God, to which man consciously responds.

Responding to God's Drawing

In Sayers's play *The Just Vengeance,* the response to the drawing of God's spirit is depicted as choosing to be the chosen of God. Christ promises the sinners that he will bear their sin and carry their sorrow, and also that he will redeem evil into good. There is, however, one requirement: a choice must be made. Christ says, "But all this / Still at your choice, and only as you choose / Save as you choose to let me choose in you. / Who then will choose to be the chosen of God?" (Sayers, *The Just Vengeance* 319).

The accounts of people's encounters with Christ in the New Testament include both ideas: being chosen and choosing. Most of the incidents are, in some sense, partial accounts because, although we see individuals transformed by their contact with Christ, we are not told of earlier instances of the divine working in their lives. These people, so drastically changed by meeting Jesus, had earlier stages of spiritual awareness and had perhaps even recognized their spiritual neediness before the crucial interaction with Jesus that was the climax of their conversion. We are not shown Christ gradually leading these people to recognize their sin. For many, the preaching of repentance by John the Baptist (who was, very literally, the one who prepared the way for Christ) would have been the experience that initially confronted them with the fact of sin and the need for repentance. Most of those we see changed by direct contact with Christ already had a contrite spirit. What is most striking in the Gospel accounts of what we would today call "conversion" is that Christ leads each person to the crucial step, asking each to radically relinquish everything: "Forsake all," he says. "Take up your cross." "Be born again."

Helen Gardner, in *The Art of T. S. Eliot,* describes Eliot's spiritual transition, making astute observations about the nature of religious conversion generally:

> Nobody can underrate the momentousness for any mature person of acceptance of all that membership in the Christian Church entails. . . . Behind any such act of choice and affirmation of belief lie obscure experiences which the conscious mind has translated into a decisive step. . . . What is found is what is looked for, and since to look for anything is to act on the hypothesis that it exists, faith precedes faith in a regressive series. But the finding . . . is profoundly mysterious. Nobody can explain why what seems at one time unbelievable . . . comes to seem truth itself and the ground and test of all other truths. The Christian only gives the mystery a name when he speaks of grace; and must assent as he thinks of his choice to the words of the Lord, 'Ye have not chosen me but I have chosen you.' To Christian and non-Christian conversion is incomprehensible. (103–4)

Gardner here identifies the key aspects of conversion. It involves an "act of choice"—a decision that is an "affirmation of belief" and an act of the will in which faith is exercised. With that choice of belief, there is a turning in a new direction, a change of life that involves what Gardner calls a "decisive step." Initially, the simultaneous choice and turning may appear to form a point of time experience, but they are, in fact, part of an ongoing process, as, in Gardner's words, "faith precedes faith in a regressive series." By "regressive series," she suggests that we can best perceive the sequence of events by looking back in time from a later period in the process. Once this notion of process is grasped, we better understand that conversion is not the result of man's search for truth, but the result of God's initiative. Afterward one can look back and see that God was there all along, and had been prompting the many small steps of faith that led to this point. We perceive the truth of Christ's words, "I have chosen you," but, as Gardner points out, we cannot explain it. Conversion is ultimately "incomprehensible"—a spiritual mystery. But it is a mystery that may be represented through pictures.

Approaching the Mystery

In the fifth movement of "The Dry Salvages," Eliot speaks of godliness as the ability to perceive "The point of intersection of the timeless / With time," while in the fifth movement of "Little Gidding," he speaks of the shape of history and the shape of an individual life as comprised of "a pattern / Of timeless moments" (*Four Quartets* 136, 144). Identifiable points of time in a conversion experience may be spiritually charged moments when contact is made with the divine. Other key moments are simply points in time when a solemn decision is made. Some such moments may be barely distinguishable within the complex process, but others are luminous and unforgettable, not because of elevated emotion but because a choice is made that has eternal consequences.

In *Surprised by Joy,* Lewis describes his experience of coming to faith. He recounts both gradual changes and identifiable moments, tracing a series of stages and events throughout his early life that reflect the process Gardner identified as "faith preceding faith." By 1929, Lewis had ceased to doubt the existence of God and was moving toward faith in Christ. In a January 1930 letter to his friend Arthur Greeves, he spoke of increased awareness of his own sinfulness, especially of pride, and of the ludicrousness of his habitual "posturing" and desire to appear "frightfully clever" (*Collected Letters of CSL* 1: 878). "Closely connected with this," he said, "is the difficulty I find in making even the faintest approach to giving up my own will" (*Collected Letters of CSL* 1: 878–79). In early February of the same year, he wrote to Owen Barfield, "Terrible things are happening to me. The 'Spirit' or 'Real I' is showing an alarming tendency to become much more personal and is taking the offensive, and behaving just like God" (*Collected Letters of CSL* 1: 882–83). Six months later, disappointed regarding his hopes of literary recognition, he was beginning to experience the relief and joy that relinquishment can bring. He wrote to Greeves: "If we can take the pain well and truly now, and by it *forever* get over the wish to be distinguished beyond our fellows, well. . . . And honestly, the being cured, with all the pain, has pleasure too: one creeps home, tired and bruised, into a state of mind that is really restful, when all one's ambitions have been given up. Then one can really for the first time say 'Thy Kingdom come': for in that Kingdom there will be no pre-eminences and a man must have reached the stage of not caring two straws about his own status before he can enter it" (*Collected Letters of CSL* 1: 926). The process of surrender was for Lewis a very gradual one. More than a year later, in September 1931, he reached the culminating moment he describes in his autobiography when, at a particular hour, he came to the point of believing "that Jesus Christ is the Son of God" and entered the Kingdom (*Surprised by Joy* 237).

Dorothy L. Sayers grew up in the Christian faith, and had no consciousness of entering the Kingdom of God at a particular point in time. She identified herself as Christian from childhood. Although her Christianity is almost imperceptible in her popular detective fiction of the 1920s and early 1930s, Christian themes were emerging by the mid-1930s in both her fiction and nonfiction. The very vocal Christianity that characterized her work of the 1940s and 1950s suggests that some distinct change may have occurred just prior to World War II. Yet Sayers (who was well able to distinguish between the nominal and the real in religious experiences) could not look back and identify a specific time at which she *became* a Christian.

Sayers found some disadvantages in being a cradle-Christian. In a letter to the Rev. Gilbert Shaw, chaplain of St. Anne's House, Soho, Sayers recounted a disagreement she had with C. S. Lewis about the Austrian philosopher Rudolph Steiner, who originated anthroposophy. Lewis perceived Steiner as a "good pagan" who had influenced his own conversion. Sayers had a more negative opinion of Steiner, but, intimidated by Lewis's reference to his conversion, she told Shaw, "I didn't argue [with Lewis]. I can always be silenced and browbeaten by people who have been converted, because I have not myself had any such momentous experience and it seems to put them straight away into the same category with St. Paul—far above the criticism of the likes of us" (*Letters of DLS* 3: 264). There is wry humor in this comment, but there is also a note of regret over the absence of a "momentous experience." Many Christians, like Sayers, cannot pinpoint an identifiable point of turning, a clearly defined crossing of a threshold. But even for Lewis, who did identify crossing more than one threshold (crossing over first into theism, and later into faith in Christ), the points of time were part of a gradual process.

T. S. Eliot's movement toward Christian faith was not so well documented, but it certainly began many years before the point at which he formally associated himself with the Church. He was baptized into the Church of England in June 1927,[3] after a period of repentance and turning even more gradual than that of Lewis. In the fall of 1928, he publicly proclaimed himself to be a "classicist in literature, royalist in politics, and anglo-catholic in religion" (*For Lancelot Andrewes* 11). It was a disconcerting announcement, partly because he made it indirectly—almost as an aside—in the midst of the introduction to a volume of essays dedicated to Andrewes,[4] and partly because of the implication that the three commitments (literary, political, and religious) were inseparable. He later explained that his Christian faith was his highest commitment, saying that his earlier statement was "a sort of summary declaration of faith in matters religious, political, and literary," and was "injudicious," in that it suggested that the three matters were of equal importance to him. Although there were interconnections between his beliefs in these three areas, Eliot regretted the implication that his religious faith was on the same level as "a political principle or a literary fashion" and recognized that combining them was "a dramatic posture" (*After Strange Gods* 27–28).

The step-by-step changes in Eliot's spiritual state are less apparent than those of Lewis. Lyndall Gordon suggests that in the last part of his 1925 poem "The Hollow Men" we are allowed to overhear something that sounds like an act of conversion as it begins in the utmost privacy of the mind. "A potential convert, still hollow of belief, tries to make the Lord's Prayer ('*For Thine is the Kingdom*') his own prayer. . . . The shadow of doubt and fear draws him back" (Gordon, *Imperfect Life* 211). Since 1917, Eliot had been visiting Anglican churches when he needed to be quiet and think, and he was drawn to the act of kneeling, a bodily position associated with worship, and with emotional brokenness and repentance (211–12). Since adolescence, he had been drawn to stories of Christian martyrdom and mystical spirituality. In *Anglo-Catholic in Religion*, Barry Spurr records that Eliot's note cards from his Harvard years reveal his great interest in "orthodox Christian mysticism" and his familiarity with the most influential early mystics, like Juliana of Norwich and St. John of the Cross (Spurr 23), but Eliot "sharply differentiated Christian mysticism from what he regarded as the charlatanism of the occult," which sought to be connected with supernatural power "divorced from religion and theology" (Spurr 24).[5] In the years prior to 1927 particularly, Eliot was drawn to the beauty of London churches and Italian churches, and later recalled his emotional assent to the validity of worship, as he witnessed people in those churches bowing their heads in reverence and kneeling in prayer (Spurr 34–41). There were many such "moments"—moments that Eliot would later identify as "timeless" in that they allowed a person to feel connected to the eternal. He experienced what he called, in movement 5 of "Little Gidding," "the drawing of this Love and the voice of this Calling." By 1927 he had passed through the "unknown, remembered gate"[6] into the Kingdom (*Four Quartets* 145).

The pictures of conversion created by Eliot, Lewis, and Sayers are rooted in their own redemption and in their own choice to be the chosen of God. Lewis and Eliot both had moments of significance in their movement toward faith, while Sayers was unable to recall specific luminous points of encounter or change in her own religious experience. Nonetheless, the change in the focus of Sayers's writing during the 1930s shows that spiritual development was occurring, and the depictions of conversion in her work show that she had *intuitively* experienced a turning toward God. Particular points in time can be "timeless moments" of great spiritual significance, but the experiences of these writers suggest that they are not as significant as the gradual drawing, the steady movement toward redemption.

The Place of Repentance

The first movement of "Little Gidding" speaks of the reader's hypothetical arrival at a place of prayer and repentance: "If you came this way / Taking the route you would be likely to take / . . . If you came at night . . . / If you came by day." No matter where we have come from or the route we have taken, the essential aspects of our religious experience in such a place as Little Gidding are "always . . . the same." We are told that we have not come to this place "to verify, / Instruct [ourselves], or inform curiosity / Or carry report." We are not here to continue our pattern of self-aggrandizement. Instead, we "are here to kneel"—a physical position indicative of repentance. Repentance includes mourning over sin and turning away from certain things and toward others. All Christian conversions may be seen, in this sense, as "always . . . the same" (*Four Quartets* 138–39).

Yet, as Sayers observes in her review of Lewis's autobiographical *Surprised by Joy,* "Conversions are not all of one kind. Some are ecstatic, emotional, and to all appearance sudden. But there is another pattern of spiritual history which, being less spectacular, attracts less attention. This [pattern] shows a Christian beginning—sometimes purely formal, sometimes pursued with sincere endeavor—followed

by a vigorous apostasy. . . . Next comes a period of unbelief, leading to a slow reconversion, stubbornly resisted, at the intellectual
level, and ending, with no ecstasy at all, in the reluctant submission
and reorientation of the will" ("Christianity Regained" 1263–64).
Here Sayers is speaking, not just of Lewis's conversion, but of conversion generally, and perhaps also alluding to her own spiritual
journey. Her experience included an acute awareness of sin, a turning from the world and toward God—that, though not an actual
event—was a very distinct reality. Although she had no memory
of a distinct change of status, or change of state, presumed to accompany a conversion event, she knew that her identity as a Christian made her essentially different from those with no allegiance
to Christ. She said that her faith was based on reason, and by her
very temperament felt unable to approach God through intuition
or religious emotion. Yet the one sort of "inner light" she could
identify in herself was an awareness of "judgement and conviction
of sin" (*Letters of DLS* 4: 137).

Similarly, Lewis's autobiographical *Surprised by Joy* (written
more than twenty years after his conversion) and his earlier, allegorical work *The Pilgrim's Regress* described the movement from
unbelief to faith as primarily an intellectual process. Nonetheless, he
was very conscious of the way the emotions were involved. In letter
23 of *The Screwtape Letters,* he said that conversion, for the earliest
converts to Christianity, resulted when the fact of the Resurrection
and the doctrine of redemption operated on "a sense of sin" which
is already present (119). There is, Lewis observed, an ongoing consciousness of sin that is often more intense than what was perceived
at the time of conversion: "The true Christian's nostril is to be continually attentive to the inner cesspool" (*Letters to Malcolm* 98).

In his poem "After Prayers, Lie Cold," Lewis speaks of the
Christian's daily confession of sin and the daily cleansing he receives. Rising from his evening prayers in which he confesses his
sins, he gets into bed. He knows that his soul has been made "White
as the bed-clothes . . . , and cold as snow, . . . / Emptied and clean,
a garment washed and folded up, / Faded in colour, thinned almost

to raggedness / By dirt and by the washing of that dirtiness" (*Poems* 130). The depletion depicted here is the emptying that is part of the redemptive process. The poem's point, made clear in the second line, is that God "is merciful" and "we are forgiven" (130).

In the movement toward redemption, there may be no decisive moments of turning (as was the case for Sayers). The early stages of the process may be characterized by a mood as bleak as that of *The Waste Land,* an uneasiness as common as the "sense of sin" Lewis described, or an impulse as simple as Eliot's desire to kneel when he visited a church. Each case involves, however, the humble recognition of sinfulness, and the decision to repent. All must come in a way that is — as Eliot said in the first movement of "Little Gidding" — "always the same" (*Four Quartets* 139).

Relinquishment

Movement 1 of "Little Gidding" depicts coming to the end of oneself — to the "world's end." It pulls the readers into a scene in which we arrive at a specific place of prayer, and kneel. This is why we have been brought here: to kneel "where prayer has been valid." The prayerful kneeling prescribed in "Little Gidding" requires intentional relinquishment through "put[ting] off / Sense and notion" (*Four Quartets* 139). In this context, *sense* refers to reliance on what we know from our sense experiences of the external world, and *notion* refers to reliance on the internal world of our own thinking processes, what we can reason out and fully understand. The spiritual changes experienced at Little Gidding require us to relinquish reliance both on sensory experiences of the physical world and on our own mental processes. Notions are put off, sense experiences are superseded, the penitent recognizes that the initiative lies completely with God, and comes to the end of himself — comes to the point of total relinquishment.

Movement 1 of "Little Gidding" addresses the reader directly, using "you," placing him at the point of arrival at this specific location, and telling him what is expected of him, and what is not. "If you came this way, / Taking the route you would be likely to take / From the place you would be likely to come from" (*Four Quartets* 138). In this passage Eliot draws his reader, imaginatively, to a place where he will have a life-changing experience. "From the place you would be likely to come from" recognizes that each traveler will come from a different direction. But though you might be taking "any route, starting from anywhere" and coming at "any time or at any season," several requirements will "always be the same" (139). One of them, as we saw above, is repentance; another is relinquishment.

It is significant that Eliot says we must "*put off* / Sense and notion" [italics added]. There must be a total putting off before there can be a putting on. This extreme self-surrender at Little Gidding, or at any place that represents "the world's end," means abdication of our own volition and intentionality. We are described as "not knowing what [we] came for," and either we "had no purpose" or we find that the purpose is "far beyond the end [that we] figured," and "altered in fulfillment" according to the purposes of God (*Four Quartets* 139).

Lewis described a similar experience of relinquishment and expressed a similar awareness of the initiative of God. In *Surprised by Joy,* he recounted having to abandon, one after another, various philosophical positions with which he had been enamored, as deeply rooted intellectual prejudices were slowly undermined. He describes God's steady pursuit of him and his sense of having to make a choice that seems devoid of words, and almost devoid of images. Yet he is aware that he is "holding something at bay, or shutting something out" (224). There is a choice involved: he feels that he can choose between opening the door or holding it shut. He says, "I knew that to open the door . . . meant the incalculable. The choice appeared to be momentous but it was also strangely unemotional. . . . I chose to open. . . . I say 'I chose,' yet it did not really seem possible to do the opposite" (224). He was not aware of his own motives and desires affecting the decision. The paradox of free will operating within the will of God is apparent when Lewis says, "You could argue that I was not a free agent, but I am more inclined to think that this came nearer to being a perfectly free act than most I have ever done" (224).

Lewis came to the end of himself, and knew he had to turn his life in a new direction: "I felt as if I were a man of snow at long last beginning to melt. . . . An attempt at complete virtue must be made. . . . For the first time I examined myself with a seriously practical purpose. And there I found what appalled me; a zoo of lusts, a bedlam of ambitions, a nursery of fears, a harem of fondled hatreds. My name was legion. . . . I was to be allowed to play at philosophy no longer" (*Surprised by Joy* 225–27).

Breaking with the past and relinquishing things we have long valued is painful. Dante depicted the growth in godliness and virtue as a steady ascent, in which the different aspects of the old nature are purged one by one on the mountain called Purgatory. Similarly, Lewis shows the process of redemption continuing in the Christian life, as God's spirit within us works inexorably to purge the lingering sins that "so easily beset us" (Heb. 12.1). In *Mere Christianity*, Lewis creates a powerful metaphor for the ongoing process of salvation: "Imagine yourself as a living house. God comes in to rebuild that house. At first, perhaps, you can understand what He is doing. . . . But presently He starts knocking the house about in a way that hurts abominably and does not seem to make sense. . . . The explanation is that He is building quite a different house from the one you thought of—throwing out a new wing here, putting on an extra floor there, running up towers, making courtyards. You thought you were going to be made into a decent little cottage: but He is building a palace. He intends to come and live in it Himself" (205).

The Christian life requires accepting God's initiative and giving up our attempt to control our own lives. Christ demanded that the disciples abandon their former way of life and follow him. Lewis commented wryly on the ruthlessness of divine demands, demands that terrified him before he became a Christian: "Amiable agnostics will talk cheerfully about 'man's search for God.' To me, as I then was, they might as well have talked about the mouse's search for the cat" (*Surprised by Joy* 227). In *Mere Christianity*, Lewis described salvation as relinquishment of our intentionality, "the change from being confident about our own efforts to the state in which we despair of doing anything for ourselves and leave it to God" (146).

Sayers's most poignant account of relinquishment comes in a poem included in her early volume of poetry, *Catholic Tales and Christian Songs* (published in 1918). The Greek title, ΠΑΝΤΑΣ ΕΛΚΥΣΩ means "I will draw all," as in the words of Christ recorded in Matthew 5.28: "And I, if I be lifted up from the earth, will draw all men unto me." The first five stanzas of the eight-stanza poem portray Christ as a heroic figure from medieval romance literature, bewitching and tyrannical, whose claims on the soul are angrily rejected (*Poetry of Dorothy L. Sayers* 84). The "glories" to which Christ calls the soul appear to be a "cruel pretense" and an "unattainable lie" (84). Yet the call of Christ proves irresistible; it is a call that will not allow the soul to find satisfaction in any other place. In the last stanza the speaker arrives at a point of complete acquiescence:

> O King, O Captain, wasted, wan with scourging,
> Strong beyond speech and wonderful with woe,
> Whither, relentless, wilt thou still be urging
> Thy maimed and halt that have not strength to go?...
> Peace, peace I follow. Why must we love Thee so? (85)

We witness complete spiritual and physical helplessness being, paradoxically, countered and overruled by the strength of the wasted, wan, and woeful Christ. His relentless claims are compelling. The speaker in the poem, bereft of personal resources of strength and momentum, has come completely to the end of herself. In relinquishment she finds a basis for a new beginning because she encounters the suffering Savior who is also the triumphant hero. The encounter leads to submission and obedience.

The speaker in the poem represents, at least in part, Sayers herself. The poem allows us to imagine her as a young woman, submitting and following, not in the spirit of grudging acceptance depicted in the first part of the poem, but in the spirit of intense love depicted at the end. Surprisingly, this account of powerful religious emotion seems to be exactly the sort of experience Sayers, in later life, could not recall ever having had. Perhaps she never did have such an experience herself, but simply created a conversion scenario for this early poem. We cannot be certain, but what is clear and important is that as a young Christian she imaginatively perceived, and depicted in poetry, the intellectual and emotional components of the relinquishment that accompanies conversion.

The call to the relinquishment of worldly hopes is already apparent in Eliot's early work. In *The Waste Land,* Eliot was already approaching what he would later call "the world's end," and developing a language of longing and prayer. As Lyndall Gordon observes, the poem uses "biblical images of thirst and journey [to represent] a Modern pilgrimage away from the sterile site of urban despair" (*Imperfect Life* 213). Helen Gardner's account of Eliot's conversion observes that before his 1928 announcement of his affiliation with Christianity a distinct threshold had been crossed: "The author of *Ash-Wednesday* [1930] is a Christian while the author of *The Waste Land* is not" (103). His conversion was both a distinct event and a process; it was both an active choice and a kind of ceasing to act, as he acquiesced to the will of God. Helen Gardner explains how choice is involved: "Behind any such act of choice and affirmation of belief lie obscure experiences which the conscious mind has translated into a decisive step. . . . Any such act, which makes an apparent break with the past, is itself a result of the past, and when it occurs makes the past assume a pattern not visible before" (103).

T. S. Eliot's most personal and poignant account of relinquishment is in the poem *Ash Wednesday* (which we considered briefly in chapter 3). It is a poem full of extreme and puzzling images, but very clearly a poem of brokenness. There are six movements; the first three reveal that Eliot's conversion was not accompanied by feelings of joy and expectations of personal fulfillment. He deliberately turns away from such idealistic expectations—expectations associated with the kind of cozy religion that he hated. Lyndall Gordon says he despised "a watered-down Christianity of sweet promises" (*Imperfect Life* 361). The first movements of *Ash Wednesday* bear this out, in that they reflect, not joy and gratification, but submission to the annihilating power of Christ the Tiger. The operation of redeeming grace depicted in the first movements shows us Eliot having come fully to the end of himself.

The poem's title confirms that it is a work concerned with repentance.[7] The ashes rubbed on the foreheads of penitents on Ash Wednesday represent grieving over sin, and this grieving is the spiritual state depicted in the poem's first movement, through its emphasis on renunciation and self-abandonment. The speaker, arguably Eliot himself, sees himself as no longer striving. His earlier strengths are now "vanished powers," and he defines himself by what he does not know, what he cannot do, and what he is leaving behind. As the last lines of movement 1 reveal, the speaker's submission to the power that has overwhelmed him has produced brokenness, contrition, and meekness. He prays for God's mercy, and prays that he might forget the matters that he dwells on too excessively and too introspectively: "These matters that with myself I too much discuss / Too much explain." In this request Eliot relinquishes the habit of introspection. The repeated variations on the phrase "Because I do not hope to turn again" suggest a larger sort of relinquishment—relinquishment of the past and the achievements associated with it. In the lines, "Because these wings are no longer wings to fly / But merely vans to beat the air," Eliot relinquishes his fame and views his prestige as the most eminent poet and critic of the era as essentially futile. The next lines, "The air which is now thoroughly small and dry/ Smaller and dryer than the will," suggest the relinquishment of personal agendas. As the prayer that makes up the first movement moves toward conclusion, Eliot makes two requests to be taught something. The first, "Teach us to care and not to care," is a profound paradox; we must learn to care *more* about the things that really matter and care *less* about the things that do not matter eternally. The second request is that we learn to abandon self-generated momentum: "Teach us to sit still" (*Ash Wednesday* 60–61).

In movement 2 of *Ash Wednesday,* the speaker reports, quite peacefully, that he has been consumed and reduced to bones, which are the bare essentials of his selfhood. Three white leopards are sitting under a juniper-tree, having just devoured his legs, heart, liver, and brain. But his bones are lying there, and the voice of God is heard asking, "Shall these bones live?" Finding himself thus "dissembled" or broken down, the speaker can do nothing but let go of everything he has been and done, allowing the achievements of the past to be obliterated (*Ash Wednesday* 61–62). The dominant feeling is not one of energy and new momentum; instead it is one of peaceful self-abdication. Helen Gardner points out that in these lines "there is no feeling of resentment, but rather a feeling of finality," and observes that the word *dissemble* is used "to describe the falling apart of those elements that made up the personality" (115). The speaker considers it a blessing to be "dissembled" and self-forgetful. The whiteness of the bare bones suggests that a kind of cleansing has occurred, and the speaker is content to be forgotten, and to forget.

The bones, however, are not inert. The question "Shall these bones live?" is an allusion to Ezekiel 37.3, when the prophet is shown a valley of dry bones, and asked by God, "Son of Man, shall these bones live?" In Ezekiel's case, God breathes new life into the bones and they become a great army. In *Ash Wednesday,* the bones are those of the speaker, representing all that remains of Eliot himself after the relinquishment accompanying conversion. The question is whether such unpromising remnants of his former self can be revitalized. The feeling is optimistic: it is a good thing to be so deconstructed and "scattered." There is a parallel here to the biblical image of a piece of pottery that must be unmade, broken in the potter's hands, in order to be remade. By the end of movement 2 there is an increase of joy and peace. The bones are shining and singing and anticipating that they will be "united." The desert imagery at the end of the movement is not desolate, as in *The Waste Land:* the "quiet of the desert" brings tranquility and restoration. The speaker has indeed learned "not to care" about certain things—things that would make him anxious. He is waiting quietly.

The prayer of movement 1 has been answered: he has learned to "sit still." There is promise of a fruitful future in the lines "This is the land which ye / Shall divide by lot." The fact that the self has been divided, to be later reunified, does not really matter. God has provided a space in which the redeemed soul can thrive: "This is the land. We have our inheritance" (*Ash Wednesday* 61–63).

Movement 3 of *Ash Wednesday* proposes that although hope and despair are equally "deceitful," a "strength [that is] beyond hope and despair" overrules the "stops and steps of the mind." The penitent is pictured in this movement as steadily ascending, but he also feels himself "fading, fading." The relinquishment of pride and personal dignity is accompanied by complete faith in Christ, evident in the closing lines of the movement: "Lord, I am not worthy / Lord, I am not worthy / but speak the word only" (*Ash Wednesday* 63).[8] The spiritual state depicted is one of self-abdication and absolute trust in the sufficiency of Christ.

In the last three movements of *Ash Wednesday* peace and hope become stronger because the relinquishment is complete. The emphasis in the fourth movement is on the process of "restoring" that is part of redemption, and on the need to "redeem the time." Movement 5 affirms that Christ, the Incarnate Word, is—as we saw in chapter 3—the axis of all things. He is the still center that provides the only source of peace. Movement 5 also affirms that, in spite of the existence of hypocrisy and denial, the redeemed soul arrives at a "place of grace," a place that is a "garden in the desert" (*Ash Wednesday* 65–66).

Movement 6 of *Ash Wednesday* reaffirms the theme of relinquishment with the threefold repetition of the line from the first movement" — "I do not hope to turn again." The speaker finds himself wavering between "the profit and the loss / In this brief transit where the dreams cross." Thus poised between a sense of profit and a sense of loss, he is calm and glad because the sense of loss is no longer accompanied by mournfulness. New life is embraced and, as we see a few lines farther on, "the lost heart stiffens and rejoices" as "the weak spirit quickens," and as all the "savour" of life is renewed. He can taste again, and it is good; even though it is a "time of tension between dying and birth"—dying to the old and being born into the new. The calm assurance of the redeemed souls in Dante's *Paradiso* is echoed in the line "Our peace [is] in His will."[9] The last two lines of the poem are lines that must be understood, not as an expression of uncertainty, but as an expression of calm assurance: "Suffer me not to be separated / And let my cry come unto Thee" (*Ash Wednesday* 66–67). This is spoken as a child would speak to a loving parent, and it is reminiscent of Jesus's words, "Suffer the little children to come to me" (Mark 10.14). The request is made to a God the speaker has now come to know and trust. His hope rests in God alone because all else has dropped away.

Lewis's and Eliot's Depictions of the Initiative of God

Several of Lewis's poems show the momentousness of choice—even the small choices that are part of the larger process. "Nearly They Stood"—a poem from *The Pilgrim's Regress*—reveals that although individual choices may seem small, the final consequences are enormous: "The choice of ways so small, the event so great" (*Poems* 102–3). God prompts us, but we must choose for ourselves—choose to turn Godward. And yet, as Lewis beautifully depicts in another poem, we are constantly hemmed about by God:

> You rest upon me all my days
> The inevitable Eye,
> Dreadful and undeflected as the blaze
> Of some Arabian sky;
> . . . .
>
> Oh, for but one cool breath in seven,
> One air from northern climes,
> The changing and the castle-clouded heaven
> Of my old Pagan times!
>
> But you have seized all in your rage
> Of Oneness. Round about,

Beating my wings, all ways, within your cage,
I flutter, but not out. (*Poems* 115–16)

God's intentionality—like the blazing of the sun—rests upon us all our days. We may sometimes think fondly of the cooler air of a more pagan period, but the God who seeks to draw all things to himself, has "seized" and taken possession of us. In the final lines, the speaker pictures himself as a bird who beats his wings in the cage—the cage of God's ownership—but he has chosen, and will continue to choose, to remain there.

In Lewis's fiction, God's initiative in the process of conversion is presented most powerfully in *The Voyage of the Dawn Treader*. A spoiled and nasty boy named Eustace Scrubb is transformed, because of no desire or merit of his own. Eustace has come to the end of himself—a despicable self that reaches the zenith of its meanness when he turns into a dragon. The miserable, suffering boy, trapped in this bestial facsimile of his own nature, is wondering what will become of him when a huge lion appears, surrounded by light, and terrifying. The lion comes close to Eustace, looks straight into his eyes, and compels the boy-turned-dragon to follow him to the top of a mountain where there is a pool. The lion tells him he can bathe and ease his pain, but first the dragon skin must be removed. Eustace tries three times to remove the dragon skin from his body, but only the lion can do this. Eustace's permission is all that is required. Eustace submits to the redemptive initiative of Aslan, the dragon skin is painfully peeled off by the lion's claws, and he is seized and thrown into the restorative water. He has become a boy again, and the lion takes him out of the water and dresses him in new clothes (88–91). The episode is one of Lewis's most moving depictions of redemption, and in it we see Christ as the Lion-Lamb, simultaneously merciless and merciful.

Another picture of redemptive violence occurs in Lewis's novel *That Hideous Strength*. Jane Studdock and her husband Mark are growing apart, moving in seemingly opposite directions, and at the same time both are similarly resistant to anything connected with Christianity. But they are both drawn by Christ, each through very different means, and transformed. Jane is initially repelled by the uncompromising authority that controls the Christian enclave called St. Anne's. Yet she realizes that her only true friends are there, and that it is the only place where she can be safe. The uncompromising authority resides in the director of St. Anne's, whose name is Ransom. As his name suggests, Ransom is a Christ figure who radiates "the bright solar blend of king and lover and magician," and who calls up all the ancient associations of kingship, "battle, marriage, priesthood, mercy, and power." Meeting him face to face, all Jane's power to resist vanishes and her "world [is] unmade." So important is this *unmaking* of Jane's world that the phrase "her world was unmade" is used three times in the space of two pages. She is completely vulnerable, "left without protection" (142–43).

Lewis's embodiment, in his fiction, of the redemptive aggressiveness of God is paralleled in Eliot's plays. The plays subsequent to *Murder in the Cathedral* were of an unusual sort in that they were essentially religious plays, but written for secular audiences—plays that, without using religious language, show the spiritual lostness of modern people and the extremities that must be reached if they are to be restored to spiritual health. In *The Family Reunion*,[10] the protagonist, Harry, is pursued by supernatural beings resembling the avenging Furies of Greek myth and drama. However, Harry's repentance, turning, and restoration are facilitated by these pursuers, and it becomes increasingly apparent that the force Harry was trying to evade is far from malevolent. It transpires that he has been fleeing from God himself, the Hound of Heaven.

Eliot's next play, *The Cocktail Party,* similarly depicts the insistence of God without using language and symbols that are overtly religious. It traces several very different redemptive processes that require a distinct turning from futile pursuits and selfish egotism. Lavinia and Edward, a married couple on the brink of divorce, are released, in stages, from the imprisonment of their old patterns of life and empowered to live together and love one another with humility and kindness. In the same play, the character Celia is redeemed more drastically, for she is offered, and chooses, a journey that is full of terror but also—finally—ecstasy. When the play opens, all three are unhappy and disoriented, yet they themselves do not instigate the conversion process. In the first scene of act 1, they are confronted by aggressive statements, such as, "It will do you no harm to find yourself ridiculous. / Resign yourself to be the fool you are" (*The Cocktail Party* 308). Later, they are told they are about to become the prey of "devils who [will] arrive at their plenitude of power" when they finally have these particular mortals "to themselves" (356).[11] The unhappy characters feel there is a trap closing in on them (346); they realize that they are "not free" but that it is up to an outside force to give them freedom (350–51). By the conclusion of the play, they have accepted their place in the supreme design. By accepting the past, they have been able to "alter its meaning," and turn their lives into "something new" (385). Lavinia and Edward have a new life in which "every moment is a fresh beginning" (387), while Celia has moved into the other of the "two worlds of life and death" that Shelley wrote of in *Prometheus Unbound*[12]—the one that is "underneath the grave" and in which the shadows and contradictions of this world are triumphantly reconciled (Shelley I.195–96).

Fearsome Redemption in Sayers's Plays

Sayers's plays similarly depict the reconciliation of contradictions through the violence of redemption. Drastic changes occur when a person allows himself to become the chosen of God. The protagonists of Sayers's plays are coerced with lion-like ruthlessness, yet they also make a choice in response to the mercy of God.

The protagonist in Sayers's play *The Zeal of Thy House* is an actual historical character: the twelfth-century architect William of Sens. A master of the new Gothic style in architecture, William was responsible for rebuilding the eastern part of Canterbury Cathedral, the portion known as the quire or choir. While, figuratively speaking, the structures of Western Christianity were being formed during the Middle Ages, literally speaking, the structures of the greatest Christian edifices were being built during the same period. The architects who designed and erected the magnificent cathedrals were among the greatest artists who ever lived. Working from the little that is known about the historical William of Sens, Sayers shapes a credible character of enormous intellectual and artistic ability. The character embodies the superiority of intellect and creativity that such medieval builders possessed, but William of Sens, as Sayers develops him in this play, is more complex. Without being a follower of Christ, he is a man integrally involved in the Church and the affairs of God's Kingdom on earth. An arrogant man, he is oblivious to the true nature of his own sinfulness, shockingly ignorant of the immensity of God's holiness, and pitifully blind to the sacrificial love of Christ.

William's arrogance and spiritual stupidity are challenged by a divinely appointed accident. Yet even after his body has been broken by a fall from the scaffolding and he is no longer physically fit to continue to direct the building of the quire, his pride is unbroken, and he refuses to resign from his position. He is aware only of his more external, mundane flaws, and makes a formal confession to the prior, acknowledging his "fleshly faults" of "lust, wrath, and greed' (Sayers, *The Zeal of Thy House* 90–92). Though the prior pronounces absolution for these confessed sins, William is not permitted to experience the restful sleep of a man who is at peace with God. As the Choir's versicle expresses it, "The ministers of God are sons of thunder" (92). The angels are uncompromising ministers, agents of God, who relentlessly push the arrogant man toward self-knowledge and true conversion.

Complaining that he cannot sleep while the choir voices "wail through aisle and cloister / Howling on judgment," William argues that he deserves to be able to rest, since he is "confessed [and] absolved [with no need to] think of judgment" (Sayers, *The Zeal of Thy House* 93). Then he suddenly becomes aware of the presence of angels. The archangel Gabriel lays his hand on William's spiritually blind eyes, saying, "Let there be light!" William argues that his sins can no longer "show black" because he is "shriven" and "washed . . . white" (93). He has, in principle, understood the doctrine of sin and grasped the ideas of confession and restoration. However, the confession he made was invalid; it was just a shallow mimicry of repentance. He has confessed only the outward failings, fleshly faults, easily "sloughed off" (94), and has not even recognized his deep inward sinfulness. Another archangel confronts him, saying, "I am Michael, / The sword of God. The edge is turned toward thee / . . . [Because of t]he sin that is so much a part of thee / Thou know'st it not for sin" (94). In blindness, audacity, and pride William challenges the angel, pointing confidently to his lack of envy and sloth (94). Michael replies, "There where thy treasure is / Thy heart is also. Sin is of the heart" (95). William refuses to accept this judgment, arguing that his heart was in his work, and that it was good work. He blasphemously suggests that God wants to slay him because he is jealous of the grandeur of his work. He cries, "Let Him destroy me, since He has the power / To slay the thing He envies—but while I have breath / My work is mine; He shall not take it from me" (95).

The insult to the holiness of God makes the audience shudder. We expect that the architect will receive—at the very least—the severest of rebukes. Yet, astonishingly, loving mercy is poured out to him. As the architect raves and challenges God to heap on "more torments" and strike him helpless in hands and feet, the angel Michael begins to tell him of the anguish endured by Christ, and of the helplessness of *his* hands and feet on the Cross. He hears of Christ's sufferings one after the other: "blindfolded and scourged and smitten . . . Whose sweat, like blood / Watered the garden in Gethsemane," and he begins to realize how much more profound Christ's sufferings were than any he had suffered or could envision suffering. The angel draws a further parallel to William's own curtailed career as a builder when he tells him that Christ, the "Master Architect," had to say, "It is finished," and remove himself from the scene at a point when his work in the world seemed to have scarcely begun. He had to "depart and leave / the work to others" (Sayers, *The Zeal of Thy House* 95–97). Suddenly, William is able to envision Christ the suffering Savior, *his* suffering savior, and is able to see his own sin for what it is. He cries out,

O, I have sinned. The eldest sin of all,
Pride, that struck down the morning star from Heaven
. . . .
Smite only me and spare my handiwork.
Jesu, the carpenter's Son, the Master-builder,
Architect, poet, maker—by those hands
That Thine own nails have wounded—by the wood
Whence Thou didst carve Thy Cross—let not the Church
Be lost through me. Let me lie deep in hell,
Death gnaw upon me, purge my bones with fire,
But let my work, all that was good in me,
All that was God, stand up and live and grow.
The work is sound, Lord God, no rottenness there—
Only in me. Wipe out my name from men
But not my work; to other men the glory
And to Thy Name alone. (Sayers, *The Zeal of Thy House* 98–99)

Now, truly turning from all that had defined him in the past, he relinquishes everything that he had valued as a workman, everything that had contributed to his glory as an artist. He acknowledges that he is worthy of damnation and is prepared to accept that fate. He lets go of the belief that the buildings he constructed were monuments to himself, reflecting his glory as an architect and builder. The choice has produced a drastic change. What he now values is God's glory, and God's alone. He asks that what he has produced will survive only as a means of glorifying God, and asks that after a period of punishment, he may have "one glimpse, one only, of the Church of Christ, / The perfect work, finished, though not by me" (Sayers, *The Zeal of Thy House* 99). With redeemed eyes, he is able to envision the stupendous glory and perfection of the Church Invisible, of which earthly cathedrals are only shoddy symbols (99). Encountering the terror at the core of the gospel, William of Sens responds to the invitation implicit in the brokenness and triumph of Christ, and chooses to become the chosen of God. The angels praise God that "the race is run" and proceed to "lead homeward . . . the sheep that strayed," pronouncing that he has by "sharp, thorny ways" entered the "strait gate at last" (100).

Sayers's last drama, *The Emperor Constantine,* depicts another historical character who experiences redemption through the initiative of God. The play traces the complex progress and gradual conversion of the great Constantine himself—the pivotal figure in the official Christianization of Western Europe in the fourth century AD. Constantine subdued the entire civilized world under the banner of Christ, yet it was not until he was on his deathbed that he himself was truly converted. Although this is a creative work and partially fictionalized, Sayers is faithful to the facts of history and to Church tradition. She retells the story of Constantine in a way that clarifies the main issues underlying his military and political triumph in the name of Christ, and his final coming to a genuine personal faith. She explains, in her Introduction to the play, Constantine's complex connection with the 'Christ' under whose banner he triumphed:

> It seems possible to trace, running through the recorded acts, words, and writings of Constantine, a consistently developing apprehension of Christ. There is the Christ known to the pagan world, one god among many, worshipped by an increasingly numerous sect whose sober and disciplined life made it a valuable element in the state; there is Christ the Lord of Hosts, the powerful patron-deity of His Imperial Vicar; there is, later on, the Christ of the theologians, True God, the Holy and the One; there is, perhaps, in the end of it all, Christ the Redeemer, sacrificed upon the wood of the Cross for the sins of man—and of Constantine. (7–8).

In this huge chronicle-play, Sayers interprets what she calls "the enigma of history"—and, at the same time, the enigma of conversion.

As Sayers tells the story, Constantine initially knew something of Christianity through his mother, Helena, who was the daughter of King Cole of Britain.[13] Early in his military career, Constantine had a vision of the cross, made it his emblem, and came to believe that he triumphed through the help of a vaguely defined deity—the "One Great God" (Sayers, *Emperor Constantine* 55). By the time he gains control of Rome, he has clearly associated himself with Christ. He tells the Senate, and the people of Rome generally, "I have won this victory by favour of the gods, and in particular the God of the Christians, whose sign you see on my helmet" (64). Yet more than a decade later, his faith in Christ is still political and strategic rather than personal, and the true Christians who surround him are well aware of this. An old servant of his mother observes, "Forgive us our trespasses and God be merciful to me a sinner—that's what he needs to learn. He never thinks of the blessed Lord that died to save us, except as an ally to win his battles for him." Helena partially defends her son, saying that Constantine has been called by God to win battles for him. She agrees, however, that Constantine will not know the true love of God until he faces his own sinfulness (101). He reaches this point several years later, after the tumultuous Council of Nicaea and after he has been betrayed by his own family and has unjustly killed his son. In excruciating pain, he tells his mother, "You told me once that until I understood sin I should never understand God. Now I know sin—I *am* sin, and understand nothing at all. . . . I and mine are so knit together in evil that no one can tell where the guilt begins or ends. And I who called myself God's emperor—I find now that all my justice is sin and all my mercy bloodshed" (181). Helena explains that the price of sin is always paid by "the blood of the innocent," and that "there is no redemption except in the cross of Christ [who is] true God and true Man, wholly innocent and wholly wronged, and we shed His blood every day" (182–83).

Constantine's brokenness at this point is part of the process of repentance, a process that does not reach its climax until just before his death, some eleven years later, when he—finally—is baptized and "received into the fold of Christ's Church." To put on the white robes of baptism, he lays aside the purple robes of emperor, indicating his relinquishment of the worldly achievement that has defined him. He says, "Put away the purple—I shall never wear it again. Christ's robe alone, white and unspotted . . . ," and prepares for baptism with the words, "Let us now put off all dissimulation, stripped naked to the cleansing waters" (Sayers, *Emperor Constantine* 187–88). Constantine's slow process of conversion occurs according to the plan of God, who has reached out to him over many years through his mother, through visions, through victories, through Christian bishops, and through personal tragedy. Although his journey to faith is much more gradual than it initially appears, the turning is finally complete.

There are many kinds of conversion. The disciples are called by Jesus to forsake their nets; Bunyan's pilgrim presses toward the only place where the burden can be taken off his back; the reader who is pulled into *Four Quartets* arrives at Little Gidding "not knowing what [he] came for"; Eustace Scrubb is un-dragoned by Aslan; William of Sens's stubborn pride is finally broken when he is shown Christ's brokenness; and the Emperor Constantine conquers the world as "Christ's champion" long years before he truly recognizes Christ as Lord. Yet each character must finally come the same way: in repentance, brokenness, and humility. In each case a choice is made to be the chosen of God.

5

Angelic Interference

✠ ✠ ✠

Many conversions involve unexpected and unexplainable encounters, and although the divine agents in these encounters are occasionally identified as angels, their identification is not important. The presence of angels is elusive, and their forms may be deceptive, but their work is central to the redemptive operation of God's spirit.

Angels, like devils, are creatures of myth in the broadest sense, but they are also part of what Lewis explains as the true myth that is Christianity.[1] The modern infatuation with angels is far removed from the definition of them in Psalm 103 as "mighty ones who do [God's] bidding" (103.20 *NIV*). The loss of knowledge of and respect for scripture has led to a greatly diminished understanding of biblical concepts, particularly those associated with supernatural occurrences. Angels, in the scriptural sense, have become an endangered species.[2] The subject of angels, though rooted in scripture, has lost credibility—even among people who hold scripture in high esteem. And the idea of "guardian angels" has become whimsical rather than theological. Popular culture has become so enthralled with the concept of angels that serious theologians prefer to avoid the subject.

The Terrifying Nature of Angels

In his article "Kindred Spirit," Kenneth Gangel coined the word *angelmania* for the excessive interest in angels that had developed by the last decades of the twentieth century (5–7). The response

among serious Christians has been to shy away from the thought of
angels, and the fact that their existence and importance are affirmed
by scripture. Angels have been virtually expelled from the Church
and yet are vigorously acclaimed by the masses. They are depicted
in a plethora of angel lore, most of which drastically conflicts with
the way they are presented in scripture. To some Christians, the angels of many inspirational books and kitschy décor are more than
embarrassing; they are blasphemous.

In the work of Lewis, Eliot, and Sayers, angels are indispensable
to the operation of the divine will. Their depiction of angels is both
scriptural and imaginatively original. Angels appear in expected
contexts—like the gospel narratives of Christ's birth and resurrection—and in unexpected contexts, infiltrating social gatherings and
presiding over planets. Sometimes they are seen by humans; sometimes they are not. Sometimes they are gentle and reassuring, but
more often they are ruthless.

Writing of devils in his 1941 preface to *The Screwtape Letters,*
Lewis contended that the human race falls into two equally serious
errors concerning them: disbelief in them and an "excessive and unhealthy interest in them" (Preface [1941] xi–xix). The imaginative
and theological cunning he brought to *The Screwtape Letters* made
Lewis famous as a spokesperson for the demonic point of view—a
point of view that was, by his own confession, a very oppressive
one. *The Screwtape Letters* may be entertaining to read, but writing about devils was not pleasant, as Lewis often admitted to those
who praised the book (Sayer 274). However, Lewis did take much
delight in writing about their spiritual opposites—angels—in his fiction, nonfiction, and poetry.

Lewis believed that having a wrong conception of angels was
far more dangerous than being oblivious to them. In a new 1962
preface to a later edition of *The Screwtape Letters,* Lewis speaks of
the discrepancy between a right view of angels, and a view based on
the picturesque mental images, derived from art and literature, that
most people have of them. The details of the visual representations
are valid only for what they represent. Lewis points out that angels

are depicted with wings "to suggest the swiftness of unimpeded intellectual energy," and that they are given human form "because man is the only rational creature we know." Asserting that creatures "higher in the natural order than ourselves, either incorporeal or animating bodies of a sort we cannot experience, must be represented symbolically if they are to be represented at all" (Preface [1962] xxiii), he then explains the changes in the way angels have been symbolically depicted by artists throughout the centuries:

> In the [visual] arts these symbols have steadily degenerated. Fra Angelico's angels carry in their face and gesture the peace and authority of Heaven. Later come the chubby infantile nudes of Raphael; finally the soft, slim, girlish, and consolatory angels of nineteenth-century art, shapes so feminine that they avoid being voluptuous only by their total insipidity—the frigid houris[3] of a tea-table paradise. They are a pernicious symbol. In Scripture the visitation of an angel is always alarming; it has to begin by saying "Fear not." The Victorian angel looks as if it were going to say "There, there." (xxiii–xxiv)

Lewis would probably say of angels, as he said of demons, that it is a mistake to think too little of them or too much of them; he certainly would say that a sentimental and unscriptural preoccupation with angels is worse than not thinking of them at all.

Angels are depicted in scripture as "ministering spirits, sent out to serve for the sake of those who are to inherit salvation" (Heb. 1.14 *ESV*), but who, as Matthew 18 tells us, reside in heaven beholding God's face, and who are depicted in Revelation 8.2–4 as standing before God's throne. Terrestrial appearances of angels recounted in scripture are typically brief, usually involving the delivery of a message. But sometimes the visitations are longer, as when the angels function as guardians of people groups, such as in the escorting of the children of Israel in the wilderness described in Exodus 14.19.

Less benevolently, it is an angel who administers the pestilence that is the judgment on Jerusalem for King David's sin in numbering the people: "And when the angel stretched out his hand toward

Jerusalem to destroy it, the LORD relented from the calamity and said to the angel who was working destruction among the people, 'It is enough; now stay your hand.' And the angel of the LORD was by the threshing floor of Araunah the Jebusite. Then David spoke to the LORD when he saw the angel who was striking the people" (2 Sam. 24.16–17 *ESV*). Angelic presence can, however, be as gentle and unobtrusive as the sound of movement in the trees (2 Sam. 5.23–24; 1 Chron. 14.14–15).

In the Old Testament, the activity of angels often merged with natural phenomena, and their visitations had an impersonal quality. This blurring of the agent's nature indicates that who and what these forces were was of much less importance than the message they bore or the function they performed. In the New Testament, the frequency of references to angels is greater than in the Old,[4] and Christ spoke of angels frequently, indicating his intimate knowledge of their operation and the sphere they inhabit. Their appearance at his birth and resurrection set the span of his earthly life within the parameters of their vigilance.

Angels in Sayers's Plays

The *Te Deum Laudamus*, an ancient hymn of praise,[5] opens with a depiction of angelic worship: "To thee all Angels cry aloud: the Heavens, and all the Powers therein. / To thee Cherubim, and Seraphim continually do cry, / Holy, Holy, Holy: Lord God of Sabaoth" (*1928 BCP* 42). Similarly, the *Benedicite*, a *Book of Common Prayer* canticle often used in the Anglican service of Morning Prayer, speaks of angels in its second sentence, setting them in place as the first of a series of "Works," or forces that are called on to praise the Lord. The *Benedicite* commands that praise be offered to God by a long series of things, mainly natural phenomena. The list seems almost random, and many of the things mentioned overlap: dews and frosts, frost and cold, ice and snow, nights and days, light and darkness, lightnings and clouds, mountains and hills, green things, wells, seas and floods, whales, fowls, beasts and cattle, and, lastly, children of men. In liturgical rhythms that are hypnotic and powerful, the *Benedicite* depicts the vast and varied works of God as a great interlocking matrix, in which even the severities of frosts, snow, lightning, and floods represent supernal grandeur. Mankind is mentioned last, and we see ourselves humbly positioned in this great chorus of praise ascending from all created things. Like everything else—ascending from the dew to the stars to the angels—we are called upon to praise the Lord, and "magnify him for ever" (*1928 BCP* 44–46).

In this canticle, the angels, the highest order of all creation, are at the pinnacle, yet they are intimately connected with all the other things that God's bounty has provided. There is no significant separation here between the heavenly and the earthly, or between the supernatural and the natural. In a sense, there is no structured hierarchy in the *Benedicite* list. Though angels are clearly the highest and come first, there is no implication that the "Children of Men," mentioned last, are in a lower position than the "Beasts and Cattle," mentioned second to last. The whole of God's creation is shown as a harmonious totality sending up a chorus of praise.

Influenced by such liturgical material, Sayers's depiction of angels in her drama both elevates them and makes them accessible by connecting them to the rhythms of human life. In *The Zeal of Thy House* (discussed in chapter 4), the central character is the twelfth-century architect William of Sens. The other characters that are important to the plot include the prior of the monastic community at Canterbury, the monks, the cathedral workers, and Ursula, a wealthy woman who becomes the architect's lover. There are also nonhuman characters—four archangels. The concluding lines of the anthem that opens the play describe the majesty of these heavenly beings, who will dominate the play's action even though they are unseen by the other characters: "Like clouds are they borne to do Thy great will, / And swift as the wind about the world they go; / All full of Thy Godhead while earth lieth still, / They thunder, they lighten, the waters o'erflow" (*The Zeal of Thy House* 9). The grand imagery of this opening choral performance is reflected in the subsequent liturgical lines from Psalm 104.4: "He maketh His angels spirits. / And His ministers a flaming fire."

The first characters to speak are the archangels. Michael speaks first, and identifies himself as a warrior whose function is to fight with and for the church militant: "I am God's servant Michael the Archangel; / I walk in the world of men invisible, / Bearing the sword that Christ bequeathed to His Church / To sunder and to save" (*The Zeal of Thy House* 10). The work of Raphael, who speaks next, is to receive prayers "spoken and unspoken" and offer them up before God's throne (10). His role is to facilitate and channel communication between humanity and the divine.[6] Gabriel is the next to announce his role: he is the "heavenly runner between God and Man" (10), differing from Raphael in that his work is the bearing of messages from God to men, rather than supporting the flow of prayer from men to God. The fourth angel, Cassiel, is the keeper of accounts for the Courts of Heaven. Though Sayers initially presents him as saying little because he is preoccupied with recording data and making calculations, his role is much more than clerical: he represents the relentlessness of divine judgment.

Significant scriptural precedents for Cassiel's judgmental role occur in Old Testament passages in which angels meticulously observe, evaluate, and record. When the prophet Ezekiel is given a vision of the temple that will be built in Jerusalem, a large portion of the spectacle that unfolds depicts an angel with a rod meticulously measuring off length after length and announcing the precise stipulations for every dimension of the house of God (Ezek. 40–47). The prophet Zechariah had a similar vision of an angel whose assignment was the literal measuring of Jerusalem. In both passages, the angels' painstaking verification of physical dimensions indicates God's familiarity with minute details. The Old Testament is dense with divine instructions that are precise and numerically based, yet the numbers themselves are not the point. The significance lies in their depiction of God's intimate knowledge of his creation; this detailed knowledge is also emphasized in the New Testament in

Jesus's observation that even the hairs of our head are numbered (Matt. 10.30 and Luke 12.7).

The avenging angel (represented in this play as Michael) and the recording angel (represented in this play as Cassiel) have much in common, but also have significant differences. In scriptural and traditional contexts, avenging angels appear more frequently than recording angels, and their fearsomeness usually makes a far greater impression than the positive aspect of what they represent: the justice and holiness of God. The recording function of angels in scripture involves evaluation and judgment. The man "clothed with linen, with a writer's inkhorn by his side" mentioned three times in Ezekiel (9) and the watchmen on the walls of Jerusalem in Isaiah (62.6, 7) are angels who serve as recorders and sentinels — supernatural presences that watch, remind, and record. In fact, in Isaiah 62, biblical scholars see the "you" near the end of verse 6 as a reference to the angelic watchmen themselves, beings who "take no rest" as they plead with God to establish Jerusalem. Angelic recording and judging are, ultimately, benevolent functions because the justice of God is undergirded by his mercy. The books the angels keep are records of goodness as well as of iniquity. In Malachi 3.16, the "book of remembrance" that is written before the Lord is a careful recording of those "who feared the Lord and thought upon his name"; and in the book of Revelation, the various books opened in heaven by the angels, though associated with judgment in a negative sense, also represent the glorious culmination of God's redemptive purposes.

In Sayers's play, the angel Michael, who bears the sword, is most directly connected with judgment, and his words and actions support his punitive role.[7] That ostensibly negative function is, nonetheless, harmonized with the roles of the other three angels — Cassiel's meticulous keeping of accounts, Raphael's facilitation of prayer and worship, and Gabriel's channeling of God's intentions. The juxtaposition of judgment and grace is most striking in the third and fourth acts. In act 3, the increasing tension in the plot follows the trajectory of the increasing hubris of William the architect. Shortly before God's judgment falls, Michael (who will wield the sword of judgment) makes it clear that the dire consequences arise directly from the sin itself. The "sword in the making" (*The Zeal of Thy House* 64) is not made in heaven; William has forged it himself, through his own sins of lust and pride. The angels prepare to make use of it as the architect is about to be raised to inspect the great arch of the choir in a machine he has designed himself—a basket raised and lowered by a pulley system. The machine will be safe only if there is no flaw in the rope. But there is a flaw—a flaw that is undetected by the two people, a workman and a monk, assigned to inspect the rope. Instead of checking carefully, they are distracted. William is at that moment standing in open conversation with a beautiful woman, with whom—as is well known—he is having an affair. The workman's distraction is caused by his amusement at William's irreverent nonchalance, while the monk's distraction is caused by his anger at William's brazen sinfulness. The breaking of the rope and the resulting fall that maims William are caused by a physical reality—the rope's imperfection—and by a spiritual reality—the psychological effect, on others, of William's sin. Yet the steady movement of the action toward the deserved judgment is intersected by God's mercy when the angels Gabriel and Raphael warn the men who are checking the rope that there is a weak spot. However, the warning is unheard, and the flaw is unnoticed and unreported.

The architect, having just boasted of being a master builder comparable to God himself, goes off stage to prepare to be hoisted in the machine. Michael follows him out, the sword of judgment drawn in his hand. Only one person in the watching crowd sees the angel standing poised above the (off-stage) point where the architect will examine the great arch. A small boy cries out, "Oh, look! look at the angel—the terrible angel! . . . High on the scaffold, with the drawn sword in his hand!" (*The Zeal of Thy House* 73). As the great fall occurs, off stage, the play's spectators and readers are faced with the question of whether the fall of William from the peak of the cathedral is caused by the snapping of a flawed rope or by the slash of an angelic sword. We come to realize that it is both, simultaneously. Divine ordering of events through angelic interference frequently operates through physical means; the forces involved are natural as well as supernatural.

In the fourth and final act of the play, when the physically broken architect is lying at night in the cathedral, the angels speak to him, and he hears them. It is Michael, usually the avenging angel, who slowly and patiently (as we saw in chapter 4) leads the broken and suffering man to an encounter with the brokenness and suffering of Christ himself. Instead of rebuking William, the angel of judgment becomes the angel of mercy. Yet he is uncompromising and relentless as he forces the reality of the Crucifixion on William's consciousness, and brings about the play's victorious climax: the miracle of redemption in which angels rejoice, though they cannot fully fathom it. The four angels speak sequentially, addressing each other and confirming the magnitude of what they have witnessed and been part of: "Sheathe thy sword, Michael; the fight is won. . . . Close the book, Cassiel; the score is paid. . . . Give glory, Raphael; the race is run. . . . Lead homeward, Gabriel, the sheep that strayed" (*The Zeal of Thy House* 99–100).

This play, the first of four that Sayers was commissioned to write in the late 1930s and the 1940s, contains her most complete and magnificent depiction of angels. Angelic presence continues, though on a smaller scale, in Sayers's subsequent dramas. In *He That Should Come,* a radio play broadcast on Christmas Day, 1938, the shepherds see the angelic appearance first as "a ring of fire, all about the earth, and the hills and trees glowing like copper in a furnace." Then, "out of the fire, out of the sky, there came an angel, great and terrible and shining" (269). In *The Devil to Pay* (a retelling of the Faustus story, first produced at the Canterbury Festival in 1939), the angel Azrael appears as the intimidating adversary of the fallen angel Mephistopheles, and a chorus of angels utter the last speech in the play, speaking of God's authority and mercy and triumphantly attributing honor, glory, and power to "him that sitteth upon the throne" (212). In *The Just Vengeance,* first produced at the

Lichfield Cathedral Festival in 1946, the whole of the play's action is presided over by "The Recorder," who is the "Angel of the City" (278). The Recorder tells the protagonist, a World War II airman, that he has come to "the place of images . . . the eternal moment" and that he must make his answer "now to the city, / And to me, that am the Recorder of the city" (294).

In the radio series *The Man Born to Be King*, first broadcast between December 1941 and October 1942, Sayers depicts the life of Christ in twelve short plays. Angels appear, as they do in scripture, in the plays on the birth of Christ and the resurrection. In the first play, "Kings in Judea," the focus is on Herod and the Wise Men, retelling the story of their visit to Jerusalem and Bethlehem recorded in Matthew's gospel. The dream warning them not to return to Herod comes in the voice of an angel calling them by name, and speaking of "a horror or great darkness" and "a sword in the path on the road to Jerusalem." They awake terrified and certain of the authority behind the message (*Man Born to Be King* 60–61). In the final play, "The King Comes to His Own," the frightened guards who fled from the tomb describe their encounter with a being who was not human, but whose appearance was something like that of a tall young man: "His skin and garments were whiter than the moonlight, and his face was beardless, very fresh and smiling. In all my life I never saw anything so terrible as that smiling face. . . . The moon was behind it, but it cast no shadow on the face of the rock. Then as though the great stone had weighed no more than a bubble, it rolled it back with one hand and sat upon it, smiling still. And the moonlight and the torchlight shone through the open door. And the tomb was empty" (*Man Born to Be King* 329). In this account, Sayers captures something of the terror and awe evoked by angelic interference.

The angels that appear throughout Sayers's dramas are frightening and inscrutable beings, instruments of God's redemptive purpose who unwaveringly perform his bidding. They are also glorious, as when, at the opening of *The Zeal of Thy House*, the Choir praises the God who makes his angelic ministers "a flaming fire" (15). Their fearsomeness is integrally tied to the fearsomeness of redemption.

Angels in Lewis's Poetry

The angels in Sayers's plays, based closely on scriptural models, enhance our understanding of the nature of God. The angels in Lewis's poems, based more loosely on scriptural material, enhance our understanding of the nature of human beings in contrast to the nature of angels.

Lewis wrote a number of poems about angels, some of which focus on the limitations of these heavenly beings. The last poem that appears in *The Pilgrim's Regress* is about the inability of angels to understand human experience (*Poems* 107). The voice speaking in the poem is that of an angel, but the poem's focus is on human sorrow over the ravages of time and over the loss of beloved places and beloved people. This is sorrow that an angel can never experience. The angel says he has no knowledge of the grief caused by the death of a loved one, the passing away of youth, and the unrelieved ache for a native land that cannot be revisited. He does not understand why a person would stand at one particular grave, and long to recall "one voice and face." There is a parenthetical expression of angelic regret—"Woe's me!"—in the second to last line. This phrase reveals the poem's main point: the experience of sorrow is the poignant essence of what it means to be human, and bereavement is, paradoxically, a precious gift from God that angels cannot receive. It is sorrow, Lewis is saying, that links our souls to God himself. Wordsworth makes a similar point in his verse play *The Borderers,* when he speaks of suffering as connecting men to what is permanent, and having "the nature of infinity" (3.5. 65; version published in 1797).

Another of Lewis's poems on this theme, "Scazons," points out that God has given man a mixed blessing that angels have not received—something that allows man to reflect the divine nature in a way that angels cannot. Man has been given the "tether and pang of the particular," that is, the attachment to what is familiar by which each of us defines his individual soul. Because we are more than spirits, because we are also *souls,* we feel the pain that arises from the loss of things through time. Angels are quite different in the way they

love things; with their "angelic indifferencies" they feel no preference
for one person or place over another, and have the capacity to love
"universally." Though we are more lowly than angels, this capacity
for particularity in our loves is something that God has planned for a
purpose. He intends, "that we, though small, might quiver with Fire's
same / Substantial form as [Him]." We do not merely reflect God's
glory back to him, as the "lunar angels" do. We are made in God's
image, in a sense that they are not, and we "pay dearly" for it (*Poems*
118). It is painful emotional experiences—the fiery trials of life—that
connect us most with the fire that is God himself. It is a high price to
pay, but not *too* high, since it brings us into vital contact with that
which is priceless.

In a letter to his father written in March 1948, Lewis describes
man as "a creature whom the Angels—were they capable of envy—
would envy" (*Collected Letters of CSL* 2. 844). "On Being Human" builds on this idea, making a case for the sheer joy of being
a human rather than an angel. Yet the lofty superiority of angelic
beings is apparent from the first stanza. Angels have a pure "intelligence" that allows them to "discern" the ultimate forms of nature,
the "Archetypes," and directly grasp the "verities" (absolute truths)
that are accessible to mortal minds only indirectly and in limited
forms. Because they have access to "primordial truth," angels can
perceive the essentials like the Treeness of each tree, "pure Earth-
ness and right Stonehood," and see the "huge principles" that un-
derlie everything. Angels know the realities of the natural world as
God knows them, perceiving the essential meaning of every created
thing, and the holiness of it. Yet Angels cannot know the intensity
of the world as perceived through human senses. The blessed cool-
ness of shade on a hot day cannot be experienced by beings with
"no skin." Angels cannot know the pleasure of summer smells, sea
smells, fire smells, because "an angel has no nose"; angels cannot
enjoy the glorious flavors of food and drink because "an angel has
no nerves" for taste (*Poems* 34–35). Having thus depicted the am-
biguity of the angels' superiority, the poem moves to a more pro-

found point, observing that the limitation of what we humans can perceive is in fact a refuge from phenomena far too great for us to apprehend. We are protected, guarded, by our senses, from the vast and glorious sphere the angels inhabit:

Far richer they! I know the senses' witchery
Guards us, like air, from heavens too big to see;
Imminent death to man that barb'd sublimity
And dazzling edge of beauty unsheathed would be. (*Poems* 33–36)

The divine beauty in which angels dwell, Lewis asserts, would be fatal to mere mortals; we are not equipped to confront the dangerousness of that "sublimity"; we could not endure it were the swordlike "dazzling edge of beauty"—the divine reality as they know it—to be "unsheathed." Yet the poem concludes with a startling, and even more profound, insight about the sort of intimacy with the divine that is exclusive to human beings. Here, in the "charm'd interior" of our human selfhood, the creator God, "Maker" of both angels and men, shares with us "secrets in a privacy / Forever ours, not theirs." In this homey space of our human consciousness, we have, through redemption, a point of connection with God himself that angels cannot share. Because God became man and experienced our human and sense-bound existence, there is the secret of salvation that is "Forever ours, not theirs." This intimacy is something so wonderful that, as we are told in 1 Peter (1.12), angels long to understand it.

The Background of Lewis's Eldila

Lewis's poems reflecting the intrinsic differences between angels and mortals provide a preface to his portrayal, in the novels known as the Space Trilogy, of the consciousness and personalities of angels. These angels are representatives of the inscrutable realities of eternity, and their depiction is one of the remarkable aspects of the three books. Lewis's portrayal of angels in these works of science fiction will be best appreciated, however, if it is prefaced by an examination of his thought on angels in several contexts that are expository rather than imaginative.

In *The Discarded Image: An Introduction to Medieval and Renaissance Literature,* Lewis speaks of the ancient idea that creatures existed who were of "a middle nature between gods and men" (40) through whom mortals may communicate with the gods (41). These creatures, or "daemons," were considered the "highest created spirits" (41). Plato associated such higher beings with the stars, and regarded them as "true gods" (42)—in contrast, presumably, to the false or degraded forms that sometimes appeared in mythology—and he believed them to have some sort of material form (41). Medieval theologians, following scriptural terminology, called such ethereal creatures "angels" and saw them as "pure or naked spirits" without material forms (42). In a letter dated Oct. 24, 1940, Lewis writes, "About angels' bodies: as far as I have seen incorporeality is the normal medieval view (appearances being explained by the temporary manufacture of a body of air)" (*Collected Letters of CSL* 2: 450). In *The Discarded Image,* he points out that, despite the late medieval view that angels were intrinsically bodiless, during the Renaissance, the Florentine Platonists preferred the older, more Platonic view (i.e., that angels have a material form).[8] Lewis observes that in this time period, substantial angelic bodies reappeared, quite visibly, in art. But even then, he notes, artists' representations of these "immortal, celestial, and stellar creatures" were best understood as symbolic (*Discarded Image* 56). Lewis observes that "educated people in the Middle Ages never believed the winged men who represent angels in painting and sculpture to be more than symbols" (71).

Unless we understand the visual and verbal representations of angels to be symbolic, there is, Lewis warns, great negative potential in the presentation of angels in art and literature. When the imaginative depictions of angels are not recognized as symbolic, or when they are theologically irresponsible, they can be dangerously misleading. The best example of a theologically responsible representation of angels is, of course, in the work of Dante. Lewis observes that the "unrivalled majesty" of the angels in Dante's work is derived not only from his "individual genius," but also from the medieval hierarchical view of the universe from which he worked (*Discarded Image* 75).

The hierarchical view of created reality contrasts sharply with the modern view, in which, Lewis notes, man is viewed "at the top of a stair whose foot is lost in obscurity" (*Discarded Image* 74). In the medieval hierarchical model, man "stands at the bottom of a stair whose top is invisible with light" (74–75). In that blinding light are the unfallen angels, beings that stand in glaring contrast to the demonic fallen angels to whom Lewis gave voice in *The Screwtape Letters*. In his 1962 preface to that work, Lewis expresses the wish that he could have portrayed an angelic viewpoint as a balance to that of Screwtape and Wormwood: "Ideally, Screwtape's advice to Wormwood should have been balanced by archangelical advice to the patient's guardian angel." Without this, Lewis says, the picture of a human being's spiritual life given in *The Screwtape Letters* is lopsided. "But," he goes on, "who could supply the deficiency? Even if a man—and he would have to be a far better man than I— could scale the spiritual heights required, what 'answerable style' could he use? For the style would really be part of the content. Mere advice would be no good; every sentence would have to smell of Heaven" (Preface to *The Screwtape Letters* [1962] xvii). Lewis's reluctance to take up this challenge reflects his awareness of the danger inherent in the literary presentation of angels. He knew that modern readers would not necessarily understand that the images presented to them were symbolic:

> These [artistic forms of nonhuman creatures] are not only symbolical but were always [i.e., in the classical and medieval periods] known to be symbolical by reflective people. The Greeks did not believe that the gods were really like the beautiful human shapes their sculptors gave them. In their poetry a god who wishes to "appear" to a mortal temporarily assumes the likeness of a man. Christian theology has nearly always explained the "appearance" of an angel in the same

way. It is only the ignorant, said Dionysius in the fifth century, who dream that spirits are really winged men. . . .

The literary symbols are more dangerous because they are not so easily recognised as symbolical. Those of Dante are the best. Before his angels we sink in awe. (Preface to *The Screwtape Letters* [1962] viii–ix).

As Lewis was himself awed by Dante's angels, we find ourselves awed by the literary depiction of angels that Lewis *did* attempt and succeed in. Though Lewis did not risk depicting unfallen angels as letter-writing counterparts of Screwtape and Wormwood, he did find a literary context in which to portray them.

Angelic Beings in Out of the Silent Planet *and* Perelandra

In a letter written in August 1957, Lewis makes it clear that in *Out of the Silent Plant, Perelandra,* and *That Hideous Strength* he was working from the medieval view of angelic bodies he spoke of in *The Discarded Image.* He explains his depiction of angels in the trilogy as incorporating both the older view (of the early Middle Ages), that angels "had bodies of aether as we have bodies of gross matter," and the later view of the "great scholastics" like Thomas Aquinas, who said that although there is "no composition of matter and form in an angel, yet there is act and potentiality" (qtd. in *Collected Letters of CSL* 3: 873).[9] The idea Lewis derived from the early theologians was that the absence of matter does not mean the absence of form. He imagines angels as having form based on their power and potentiality, a form that need not be, but *may* be, expressed in a material way. In the same letter, Lewis observes that from a religious or theological point of view the question of the bodily manifestation of angels has little importance. He adds, "And anyway what do we mean by 'matter'?" (*Collected Letters of CSL* 3: 873). This question triggers his depiction of the nature of angels in the first two books of the Space Trilogy, books that explore the fearsome nature of these divine emissaries and their redemptive role.

In *Out of the Silent Planet*, the protagonist, Ransom, has been kidnapped and brought by evil men to Malacandra (Mars) to serve as an offering to the authority who rules the planet. He escapes from these men and finds protection and friendship with the Malacandrian creatures called *hrossa*. They are comfortable beings, but there is much on the planet that is discomforting. Ransom's sense of what is matter and what is not is challenged when he first encounters the *eldila*, the spiritual beings who preside over the planet. *Eldila* [sing., *eldil*] are first described to Ransom by his *hrossa* friend Hyoi as a kind of *hnau*—or rational being—but one that is hard to see: "Light goes right through them. You must be looking in the right place at the right time; and that is not likely to come about unless the *eldil* wishes to be seen. Sometimes you can mistake them for a sunbeam or even a moving of the leaves; but when you look again you see that it was an *eldil* and that it is gone" (*Silent Planet* 76). Later, when they are in a boat, Hyoi realizes that an *eldil* is coming to them over the water. He addresses it, asking, "What is it, sky-born?" When it replies, Ransom hears a voice that seems to come out of the air, about a yard above his head, and realizes that a slight difference in the structure of his ear would have made the *eldil* as inaudible to him as it was invisible (79). The message the voice delivers is that Ransom must go immediately to the presiding *eldil*, the Oyarsa, who rules the planet (79).

Ransom is terrified at the thought of encountering this unknown power, yet the terror he feels is not like the fear of the supernatural that a person might have in seeing a ghost. He knows that the Oyarsa is "a real person" (*Silent Planet* 86). He is summoned to appear before him and he must go. The fact that he will not be able to really see these spiritual creatures called *eldila* contributes to the fear. Ransom asks, "Why can I not see them? Have they no bodies?" Hyoi's answer to this question begins with the point that there are a great many kinds of bodies that we cannot see because bodies are not so much matter as "movement." So the issue of perception has to do more with speed than with mass. One speed creates smell; another sound; another sight. But at some even faster speed we may not be able to perceive the body at all. Ransom's Malacandrian friend continues to explain the way our sensory perception is dependent on the movement of light, saying, "The swiftest thing that touches our senses is light, . . . we only see slower things by it, so that for us light is on the edge—the last thing we know before things become too swift for us" (94). Hyoi's explanation then turns more specifically to the difficulty Ransom has in perceiving the *eldila*:

> But the body of an *eldil* is a movement swift as light; you may say its body is made of light, but not of that which is light for the *eldil*. His "light" is a swifter movement which for us is nothing at all: and what we call light is for him a thing like water, a visible thing, a thing he can touch and bathe in—even a dark thing when not illumined by the swifter. And what we call firm things—flesh and earth—seem to him thinner, and harder to see, than our light, and more like clouds and nearly nothing. To us the *eldil* is a thin half-real body that can go through walls and rocks: to himself he goes through them because he is solid and firm and they are like a cloud. (Lewis, *Silent Planet* 94–95)

This explanation of the nature of an *eldil*'s body arises out of Lewis's understanding of angelic bodies, and reflects his interest in the question, raised earlier, of what we mean by matter. The passage has special significance for several reasons. First, it shows (perhaps better than any other passage in the three books) Lewis's grasp of scientific concepts and application of them in these works of *science* fiction. Second, it shows Lewis's ability to weave scientific concepts with spiritual concepts, breaking down the barrier between them. Third, and with immediate application to the plotline of this novel, this scientific explanation of the nature of angelic beings provides a rational context within which Ransom can begin to overcome his terror and regard the *eldila* with a little understanding and much respect.

Eventually Ransom reaches Melidorn, the place where the ruling *eldil* (called the Oyarsa) manifests himself to the other creatures. As he enters his presence, Ransom feels "a tingling of his blood and a pricking on his fingers as if lightning were near him; and his heart and body seemed . . . to be made of water" (*Silent Planet* 119). The angelic ruler recognizes that the real reason for Ransom's fear of him is not, as Ransom claims, the fact that his form is so unlike Ransom's and so difficult to see with human eyes. It is something much deeper. Ransom is forced to identify the root of his fear: the sinfulness of his own planet where "false *eldila*" (fallen angels) destroy men. This is what has caused human beings to assume that if there is any rational "life beyond [their] own air it is evil" (121).

Yet it is redemptive goodness, not evil, that is the most magnificent characteristic of this *eldil*. The Oyarsa deals out justice tempered with mercy to the two other earthlings and to Ransom. Indeed, goodness is the defining characteristic of all the angelic beings we encounter in the trilogy—a goodness that is both serene and energized.

The ensuing conversation shows the magnificence of angelic beings, enhanced by their lofty position in space and in time. When Ransom asks about the age of the planet Malacandra (Mars) in relation to the age of his own planet Earth (called Thulcandra by Malacandrians), his questions are graciously deflected. The Oyarsa knows that Ransom's mind cannot conceive of time in a way that would allow him to grasp any accurate answer. He says, "My people have a law never to speak much of sizes or numbers to you others. . . . You do not understand, and it makes you do reverence to nothings and pass by what is really great" (*Silent Planet* 124).

In *Perelandra,* the second book of the trilogy, Ranson is brought to Perelandra (Venus) by the will of Maleldil (God) himself, and through the operation of *eldila* assigned to assist him. He does not, however, encounter any *eldila* on the planet until the closing episode. Having climbed to the top of the great mountain where culminating ceremonial events will take place, Ransom perceives (dimly at first) the presence of the Oyarsa of Perelandra and the (visiting) Oyarsa of Malacandra. They are enormous in power and authority, and they are speaking of him, and of the redemption afforded him by the mercy of God: "The small one from Thulcandra is already here," [said one *eldil*]. "Look on him, beloved, and love him," said the [other], "he is . . . but breathing dust and a careless touch would unmake him. And in his best thoughts there are such things mingled as, if we thought them, our light would perish. But he is in the body of Maleldil and his sins are forgiven" (*Perelandra* 195).

Their perception of Ransom is benevolent, but almost patronizing. Though he has just endured a complex spiritual conflict and come through it battered but victorious, the angelic beings speak of him and to him as if he were a frail child; they discuss his heroic thwarting of an evil plan in a way that is gently deprecating: "Be comforted," said [the Oyarsa of] Malacandra. "It is no doing of yours. You are not great, though you could have prevented a thing so great that Deep Heaven sees it with amazement. Be comforted, small one in your smallness. He lays no merit on you. Receive and be glad. Have no fear, lest your shoulders be bearing this world" (*Perelandra* 197).

The combination of belittlement and kindness in these words would be incongruous and unconvincing were the speakers not divine emissaries. The angelic beings speak as representatives of a gracious and loving God who values each person for who he is, not what he has done or will do. The heavenly perspective is liberating for Ransom, for it frees him from a prideful sense of his own importance, and from an impossible weight of responsibility. It is the gospel, and only the gospel, that allows such a message to be given with kindness and received with joy. We are to take comfort in our smallness, and in the fact that we are intrinsically without much merit, knowing that any victory and all glory belong to God alone.

In this scene in which Ransom speaks with the two angelic rulers, Lewis depicts the way angelic presence permeates the entire universe. The presiding archangel of Perelandra tells how she created the planet: "I rounded this ball when it first rose from Arbol. I spun the air about it and wove the roof. I built the Fixed Island and this, the holy mountain, as Maleldil taught me" (*Perelandra* 196). Lewis reworks our perceptions of the nature of the universe, breaking down the notion of outer space as a terrifying and inhospitable void. The universe is not empty and dark, but full of mighty and holy beings carrying out the purposes of God. The angels call it Deep Heaven.

In this scene, Lewis further explores the interplay between the scientific and the spiritual, in relation to the forms in which angelic beings may choose to manifest themselves. Ransom initially experiences the *eldila* presence by hearing only; he is aware of a "clear voice like a chime of remote bells, a voice with no blood in it" that seems to come out of thin air and sends "a tingling through his frame" (*Perelandra* 195). But the *eldila* wish to appear in a visible form for this special occasion, in order to honor the young King and Queen who, having come through their trial, are to assume the rule of the planet on this great "morning day" (196–97). The angelic beings can control and choose what form they will take, and yet they do not know what form will be most meaningful to human eyes. They practice on Ransom, trying three different appearances.

The first two forms in which they appear to Ransom are unsuitable, but each has an interesting scriptural precedent. In the first attempt, their appearance is horrifically powerful but inscrutable: "A tornado of sheer monstrosities seemed to be pouring over Ransom. Darting pillars filled with eyes, lightning pulsations of flame, talons and beaks and billowy masses of what suggested snow, volleyed through cubes and heptagons into an infinite black void" (*Perelandra* 197). Lewis is reflecting here the imagery in Ezekiel of complex bird-like creatures emitting fire (Ezek. 1.6–14), and also a scene in the book of Revelation involving birds with multiple eyes (Rev. 4.7–8). The imagery conveys the intense energy and emphasis on movement that occur in biblical depictions of heavenly creatures, but it also juxtaposes allusions to natural forces—storms, fire, and snow—with more mathematical and abstract images of "cubes and heptagons." When Ransom screams in horror at the sensory overload created by this manifestation, the *eldila* realize that this kind of appearance, though reflective of their true nature, cannot be processed by human senses.

They try something else: "'Look then on this,' said the voices again. And he looked with some reluctance, and far off between the peaks on the other side of the little valley there came rolling wheels. There was nothing but that—concentric wheels moving with a rather sickening slowness one inside the other. There was nothing terrible about them if you could get used to their appalling size, but there was also nothing significant" (*Perelandra* 198). This is also a failed attempt. Ransom finds this wheels-within-wheels representation of angelic presence inscrutable, and the angels realize that such a depiction of their nature is not appropriate for this celebratory occasion on the planet Venus.

Finally the angels try a manifestation that works. In it, Lewis conveys more about the nature of angels than he has done in any fictional scene up to this point. Here the archangels Mars and Venus succeed in revealing something of their nature that is meaningful and impressive to human eyes and human minds. As scripture and tradition affirm, angels are best perceived when we recognize something like ourselves, so these mighty beings deign to appear in a form that resembles the bodily form of humans, but that are enormous— about thirty feet high. They are burningly white, and the outline of their form is rather blurred, and "swiftly undulating as though the permanence of their shape, like that of waterfalls or flames, co-existed with a rushing movement of the matter it contained" (*Perelandra* 198). As Ransom tries to focus on them, they seem to be moving toward him at enormous speed, but his awareness of their surroundings indicate that they are in fact stationary. The illusion of movement is caused by the fact that "their long and sparkling hair stood out straight behind them as if in a great wind" (198). Ransom suddenly realizes that there is a sense in which the angelic beings *are* moving, "though not moving in relation to him." He recognizes that this planet, Venus, on which he has encountered them "was to them a thing moving through the heavens," and that "in relation to their own celestial frame of reference they were rushing forward to keep abreast of the mountain valley" (198). The cosmic context these angelic powers inhabit is emphasized as it dawns on Ransom that if they had stood still "they would have flashed past him too quickly for him to see, doubly dropped behind by the planet's spin on its own axis and by its onward march around the Sun" (199).

Again, as in *Out of the Silent Planet,* the absolute *goodness* of angelic beings is juxtaposed with their terrifying reality. The changeless expression of their faces is charity—archetypal charity—arising from "pure, spiritual, intellectual love" (*Perelandra* 199). Yet simultaneously these archangels are the true embodiments of the mythic Mars and Venus, part of the "celestial commonwealth" (201). Ransom recognizes, in awe, that our "mythology [i.e., the tales of gods and goddesses in classical mythology] is based on a solider reality than we dream" (201)—a mythology that, though contaminated by "filth and imbecility," retains its gleams of "celestial strength and beauty" (201). The "solider reality" that is uncontaminated by the Fall belongs to the "true myth" that is the gospel, the story of redemption, in which the contamination caused by sin is undone.

Wheels and Angels

Before we consider the appearance of angels in the third book of Lewis's Space Trilogy, we should look more closely at the mysterious, biblically based, wheel imagery that he introduces in the second book. Although the implications of this imagery cannot be fully comprehended, its significance should not be underestimated or misinterpreted.

The vision of the prophet Ezekiel inspires the *Perelandra* scene in which the archangels appear to Ransom in several different forms. Ezekiel's term for the angelic beings in his wheel vision is "living creatures," and each of the four beings seen by the prophet is associated with a single huge wheel, but at the same time, "their appearance and construction [is] as it were a wheel within a wheel" (Ezek. 1.16). Lewis especially stresses size, and huge size is a main feature of what Ezekiel sees: "their rims were tall and awesome" (Ezek. 1.18). Ezekiel twice says that "the spirit of the living creature was in the wheels" (Ezek. 1.20 and 1.21), thus indicating that he perceives these "wheels within wheels" as expressions of the essential nature of the supernatural beings that surround the throne of God.

Ezekiel's wheels are among the most haunting and mysterious images in scripture. What are we to make of the "wheels within wheels" in themselves, and what is significant about Lewis's allusion to them? Scholarly attempts to interpret Ezekiel's wheel imagery have suggested connections with such things as space ships and the physical complexities of modern multiwheeled vehicles. The *IVP Bible Background Commentary* is more cautious in speculating on the implications of the passage. Noting that, logically, "a chariot with wheels facing in every direction could not travel effectively in any direction," it proposes that the wheels call attention to "God's omnipresence" in all the corners of the globe, and that as the chariot flies through the air "there is a sense of motion implicit in having the wheels in place" (690). The commentators go on to suggest that the "wheel within a wheel" aspect may represent greater stability for a vehicle, as in the case of multiple tires on modern trucks, and that the eyes within the wheels may have their origin in the Babylonian use of the word *eyes* for oval gems.

This attempt to explain the "wheels within wheels" leaves us cold, incredulous, and perhaps even depressed. There is surely more profundity than this in Ezekiel's vision. Even the implication of the phrase "wheels within wheels" in casual conversation suggests a more helpful interpretation than spaceships, multiwheeled transport trucks, and the bejeweled Babylonian statues suggested in the *IVP Commentary*. When people use the idiom "wheels within wheels," they mean that there are invisible and inscrutable forces underlying a situation and controlling it in complex ways that may never be fully grasped or analyzed. The fact that the puzzling Ezekiel passage gave rise to so useful a colloquial expression indicates that people have been generally on the right track all along in their intuitive understanding of the "wheels within wheels" image.

Lewis responded to Ezekiel's image on an imaginative level. He did not attempt to explain it, but he knew how to use it. The use of multiple eyes in the first angelic appearance to Ransom and the use of rolling concentric wheels in the second convey the mysterious grandeur of what angels are and how they function. A passage in the next book of the trilogy, *That Hideous Strength,* affirms the significance Lewis attaches to Ezekiel's imagery of eyes and wheels as indicators of supernatural presence. In this passage, Jane is starting to recognize the unearthly nature of these forces: "The vision of the universe which she had begun to see . . . had a curiously stormy quality about it. It was bright, darting, and overpowering. Old Testament imagery of eyes and wheels for the first time in her life took on some possibility of meaning" (*Hideous Strength* 316).

Lewis's assimilation of wheel imagery to suggest supernatural mysteries probably owes something to Dante's use of concentric circles and wheels in the third canto of *Paradiso.* In the medieval view, based on Ptolemy, the universe was perceived to be made up of nine concentric spheres. Lewis explains in chapter 5 of *The Discarded Image* how Dante's depiction of the heavens in this last section of *The Divine Comedy* was structured on such a view of the universe. In the first canto of *Paradiso,* Beatrice stands transfixed on the peak of the Earthly Paradise, her eyes riveted on "the eternal wheels" (1.65) that are the heavenly spheres. A few lines later the desire for God, that is innate in every created thing, is connected with the eternal "wheel" (1.76).[10] In the last lines of *Paradiso,* the "will and desire" of the human heart that are turned toward God by the operation of divine love are depicted as a rotating movement, smooth and steady, as when a "wheel moves smoothly, free from jars" (*Paradiso* 33.143).

Eliot's use of wheel imagery in *Murder in the Cathedral* is also tied to the providential purposes of God, and hence indirectly to the function of angels. In an important passage early in the play (that is ironically echoed later), Archbishop Thomas Becket speaks of human will in relation to the purposes of God. A human being, whether he is accepting a passive suffering role or taking up an active role, operates within the wheel-like movement of God's eternal purpose. Becket has the sense of being drawn into such a pattern of movement, in which God-ordained suffering and God-ordained action are both beautifully coordinated with the divine will. Both the passive and active roles are described as being fixed "in an eternal action, an eternal patience." He explains that the "action" (the active role) and the "suffering" (the passive role) are both part of the divine "pattern"—a pattern reflected in the turning of the outer rim of a wheel while the center remains fixed and still: "that the wheel may turn and still / Be forever still" (*Murder in the Cathedral* 22).

The majestic, orbit-like sweep of God's sovereign purposes in the universe, and in the lives of men, is like a great wheel, at the center of which is the axis, Christ.[11] There at the center is the perfect stillness and peace on which the movement is based. Eliot's wheel imagery harmonizes with the imagery of Lewis and Ezekiel, in which wheels represent the relentless and inscrutable purposes of God. Angels are the agents through whom those purposes are worked out. The "wheels within wheels" of Ezekiel can never be deconstructed, but they are, as interpreted by Lewis and Eliot, part of the stupendous reality in which angelic beings function.

Angels in That Hideous Strength

Lewis points out, in a letter written in December 1958, that the depiction of angels in the three books of the Space Trilogy arose out of his serious belief in the existence of such creatures. He says: "If the angels (who I believe to be real beings in the actual universe) have that relation to the Pagan gods which they are assumed to have in *Perelandra*, they might *really* manifest themselves in real form as they did to Ransom" (*Collected Letters of CSL* 3: 1005).

That Hideous Strength, the third book of the Space Trilogy, further develops the connection between the classical idea of superior spiritual beings—that is, the gods and goddesses of mythology—and the idea of angels in Christian thought. This is best understood by looking once again at what Lewis says in *The Discarded Image* about the intelligences that inhabit the heavens. According to the great thinkers of antiquity and the Middle Ages, Lewis explains, "each sphere, or something resident in each sphere, is a conscious and intellectual being, moved by 'intellectual love' of God. . . . These lofty creatures are called Intelligences" (*Discarded Image* 115). Lewis goes on to explain that such planetary Intelligences constitute a very small percentage of the vast angelic population (119). In the closing episodes of *That Hideous Strength,* Lewis depicts such planetary Intelligences visiting a particular group of people on Earth.

In a December 1944 letter to his eleven-year-old godson—a lively letter embellished with drawings of Magdalene College's tower and bridge, and of himself, in heavy warm trousers, eating venison— Lewis speaks of the book he is currently working on, *That Hideous Strength.* He says, "I am writing a story with a Bear in it. . . . There are also Angels" (*Collected Letters of CSL* 2: 624). Of all the things Lewis could have said to a child about this complex novel—sub-titled "A Modern Fairy-Tale for Grown-Ups"—it is significant that he mentions the bear (obviously of interest to a young boy); says nothing about Merlin resurrected or the courageous battle against an evil regime. And yet he mentions something that, though it oc-cupies only a small part of the book's mass, seemed to him a key part of its substance: the angels. Because this visitation occurs in a confined and recognizable physical space, the angelic presence is more overpowering than in the earlier books. This time there are not two but five angels who appear near the end of the story.

Unlike that of the two preceding books, the action of *That Hid-eous Strength* is not set on another planet, but in a university town in England, in the mid-1940s. This book is as fantastical as the two earlier books, but in more subtle ways. It is a dystopian story[12] in which an evil regime takes control, or almost takes control, of a whole society. In this classic power struggle, of the weak against the strong, victory is achieved by a small group of good people living in a conclave called St. Anne's, under Ransom's leadership. These people are helped by supernatural forces, including the magician Merlin of Arthurian myth (recently resurrected), when no power that is "merely earthly" can succeed in pushing back the "Hideous Strength" of this adversary (*Hideous Strength* 289).

The heavenly creatures who come to their aid are "celestial pow-ers: created powers . . . [who reside] in the Heavens" (*Hideous Strength* 289). They are of the very highest order of angelic beings, and their descent to earth to empower mere mortals is the most divinely terrifying thing that Lewis created in any work of fiction. The mighty visitants appear in the room where Ransom and Merlin are waiting, but they are not *in* the room in the sense of being "at rest" in it. Instead, occupants of Deep Space as they are, they are intentionally "keeping their beams" focused on this particular spot on the Earth's surface, while they continue to wheel "through the packed reality of Heaven" (320).

First the angel Mercury, the lord of language, enters, and agitation seizes the people in the house, "a kind of boiling and bubbling in mind and heart which shook their bodies" and rose to such a peak that "they feared their sanity must be shaken into a thousand fragments." The mighty Mercury, "the lord of Meaning himself," has come down to them (*Hideous Strength* 321–22). Next Venus appears, bringing warmth and intoxicating fragrance: "The room was rocking. They were afloat. . . . As the whole of her virtue seized, focused, and held, that spot of the rolling Earth in her long beam, something harder, shriller, more perilously ecstatic, came out of the centre of all the softness. . . . It was fiery, sharp, bright and ruthless, ready to kill, ready to die, outspeeding light: it was Charity, . . . unmitigated. They were blinded, scorched, deafened. . . . They could not bear that it should continue. They could not bear that it should cease" (323).

The next three angelic visitants are equally terrifying, according to their unique defining essence. With the arrival of the archangel of Mars comes a sense of "the ordered rhythm of the universe, side by side with punctual seasons and patterned atoms and the obeying Seraphim," and the humans are overwhelmed by "the clear, taut splendour of that celestial spirit which now flashed between them" (*Hideous Strength* 325). Saturn's spirit next lies on the house, bearing down with "the lead-like burden of his antiquity" and "with a cold pressure such as might flatten the very orb of Tellus to a wafer" (326). Then, finally, comes the heroic, dancing energy of the mighty Jove, sending out mighty flashes of "Kingship and power and festal pomp and courtesy" (326).

This shattering visitation is the culmination of Lewis's imaginative depiction of angels, a depiction that has its roots in his knowledge of scripture and in his belief in their actual existence. In his discursive interpretation and fictional depiction of angelic beings, Lewis provides a serious view of them that replaces his readers' sentimental notions about their nature with a holy awe of them as mighty beings who accomplish God's redemptive purposes. His work reshapes our understanding and allows us to vicariously encounter the terrifying splendor of beings whom Lewis suggests are often so hidden that they are mistaken "for a sunbeam or even a moving of the leaves" (*Silent Planet* 76).

Angelic Beings in Eliot's Family Reunion

Popular books on angels, personal testimonials telling of encounters with angels, and movies and television programs featuring angels as characters all seem to have one thing in common: the angels are benevolently helpful. Clarence Oddbody in the movie *It's a Wonderful Life* (1946) and Michael Landon in the television series *Highway to Heaven* (1984–89) portrayed angels as kind and loveable. Even when they assume more brittle personalities, popular angel characters are usually committed to helping people get on better. The movie *Angels in the Outfield* (1994) has them helping players make incredible catches and run with otherworldly speed. In the British movie *Angel in the House,*[13] compassionate angels take the form of a precocious foster child and a mysteriously well-informed hobo. Even the TV series *Touched by an Angel* (1994–2003), though admirably representing the love of God and people's need for him, fleshed out angels as friendly, comforting individuals doling out advice and encouragement. Since the 1990s, a plethora of angel shows and movies have been released, ranging from silly, crude, and satiric to hellish.

Like Sayers and Lewis, T. S. Eliot followed scripture in depicting both the fearsomeness of angels and their ultimately redemptive purposes as ministering spirits seeking to draw people toward salvation (Heb. 1.14). The nonhuman characters in two of Eliot's plays, *The Family Reunion* and *The Cocktail Party,* are such "ministering spirits" facilitating redemption, but they are as ruthless and free of sentiment as those of Sayers and Lewis.

E. Martin Browne, who was intimately associated with the production of Eliot's plays, regards *The Family Reunion* (first performed in 1939) as "the most difficult to apprehend" of all of them (Browne 90). It is loosely based on the plot of the *Oresteia,* a trilogy by the ancient Greek dramatist Aeschylus. In Eliot's play, the central character, Harry, a distraught individual haunted by guilt, returns home to his family's manor house in the north of England, to a cold, demanding mother and a cluster of visiting relatives ranging from the astute to the stupid. The play's action is, as Browne points out, based on "the family relationships, and the interruption into them of the force represented by the Furies" (93).

The avenging Furies of Greek mythology were female deities connected with justice; they were also called the Erinyes, or angry ones. They pursued the guilty (usually people who had murdered family members), driving them mad. In the third play of the *Oresteia* trilogy, the goddess Athena succeeds in calming the anger of the Furies, and they are transformed into a benevolent form, becoming the Eumenides (or "kindly ones"). In this gracious form, they are no longer fearsome, but exude good will and behave with honor, helping to protect the city of Athens from harm.

In Eliot's *Family Reunion,* the Furies appear as malignant spirits pursuing the guilt-ridden Harry. They are not initially connected with biblical concepts. Near the end of the play, however, they are transformed, as in the myth, and become the Eumenides. When Harry identifies them as "bright angels" (281), we begin to see the mythic and biblical layers of their significance. Just as Lewis blended Greek mythology with the biblical portrayal of angels, Eliot takes the mythic figures of avenging deities and merges them with the concept of avenging angels—holy administrators of the judgment of God—and then seamlessly shifts their function to one of mercy. At the end, they are agents of redemption.

Russell Kirk, in his literary biography *Eliot and His Age,* explains that Eliot's intention, in *The Family Reunion* was to convey the Christian message to a post-Christian world: "Eliot knew that his audiences would refuse assent—in an era so soon to be called 'post-Christian'—to a drama openly drawn from what they would call the Christian Myth. A classical myth, nevertheless, they might tolerate as remote, harmless, and undemanding. Let Christ or Saint Paul never be mentioned, and those audiences might listen. Eliot will be all things to all men" (222). Kirk observes that the thrust of the play is that Harry, by accepting the past and the fact of sin (his own and that of his parents), comes to understand the causes of his misery, and is "redeemed" (222). Kirk considers the play "Christian teaching in the riddle of a mirror—though the words of theology and faith are not uttered explicitly" (222). D. E. Jones, in *The Plays of T. S. Eliot,* agrees that in this play Eliot was trying to reach an audience not only ignorant of Christianity but also prejudiced against it (87). Jones points out that in giving the Eumenides a Christian dimension, Eliot was essentially "showing the way in which Christianity completes the intuitions of the Greek poet" (87). In doing so, Eliot makes use of the same bridge that Lewis had used, the bridge that connects the ancient belief in celestial intelligences with the Christian idea of angels as agents of the divine.

Accordingly, in *The Family Reunion,* the Furies are celestial agents assigned to pursue the erring soul and drive it toward redemption. Yet how to represent the Furies on stage proved to be a more difficult challenge than any other performance issue in Eliot's plays. This problem was rooted in a larger issue Lewis mentioned in *The Discarded Image* and in his letters: whether or not angels should be thought of as having a material form. The Furies, destined to be recognized as benevolent Eumenides or "bright angels" by the end of *Family Reunion* (281), are a key part of the play's visual spectacle as Eliot first conceived it, but the problem of how to manage their appearance was virtually unsolvable. In part 1, scene 1, they are seen by Harry, through a window, but are not seen by the audience. This

is indicated in the stage directions only by the fact that Harry stops
suddenly and stares at the window (231). He cries out," Look there,
look there; do you see them?" But the other characters do not (232).
E. Martin Browne explains that in the first production, Harry was
looking out through the window and the audience saw "nothing
but a change of lighting" (Browne 137). Harry shows fear, naturally,
but his fear at actually seeing them is less traumatic than the earlier
horror, throughout his travels, of knowing they were always there,
though invisible. A little later, in scene 2 of part 1, Harry, sensing
their presence, describes them as "sleepless hunters" who insist that
he is always aware of them, who will not let him sleep, and who pre-
empt the moment of falling asleep by showing their distended claws
(253). Harry cries, "Come out!" and there is the stage direction: "The
curtains part, revealing the Eumenides in the window embrasure"
(253). Following Eliot's suggestion in his initial stage directions, the
first production of the play had these apparitions of the Furies appear
as "a man and two women in evening dress" (Browne 117). Nonetheless, they are intended to be recognized as supernatural beings. They
never speak or move. In some later productions, in an attempt to
add a surreal quality, the actors playing the Eumenides wore masks,
sometimes the sort of masks worn in Greek theater.

The physical manifestations of angels posed greater difficulties
for Eliot than for Lewis, since suggesting unpredictability, fluid
form, and elusiveness was more problematic on stage than in fantasy fiction. Eliot worked many conflicting elements into his presentation of these demanding spiritual beings, relying on Harry's
words to convey their otherworldliness, but there was unavoid-
able incongruity. Harry recalls the apparitions as having distended
claws; yet they stand silently in evening dress. They are relentless
pursuers, always "flickering at the corner of [Harry's] eye" (*Family
Reunion* 250), yet Harry's valet tells the curious relatives that he has
seen them and soon "got used to them," adding that he could "see
them cheerful-like" because he was sure that there was "no harm in
them" (289). The implication in that last point, with the word *them*

italicized, was that there *was* real harm in Harry's situation, and the business of the Furies (or "ghosts," as the valet calls them) was to protect Harry from it.

The use of ominous mythic personas in a modern play was an innovative move, but the actual onstage presentation remained a challenge that neither Browne as producer nor Eliot as writer ever felt had been properly met. In an article written some thirteen years later, Eliot called the Furies "ill-fated figures" and said he should have either stuck closer to Aeschylus (whose plotline provided the model for his own) or else "taken a great deal more liberty with his myth" ("Poetry and Drama" 90). He spoke, with wry amusement, of the various failed attempts to present the Furies in a way that was impressive and appropriate. In future, he says, they must "be omitted from the cast, and be understood to be visible only to certain of my characters" (90). There was, however, a much later production that managed to achieve the appropriate level of terror—an achievement never seen in Eliot's lifetime. Lyndall Gordon, in *Eliot's New Life,* speaks of the importance of the Furies' presence, and describes one production in which their appearance reached the necessary peak of power:

> The crucial trial is the Furies, who are real in the terms of a play in which the real and unreal change places. . . . The insubstantiality of reported phantoms should be confounded by a dramatic shock when they enter. The spectacle should be overwhelming as in Michael Elliott's Royal Exchange production in 1979, when they appeared suddenly at every entrance of the Roundhouse theatre at about twice the human size, hooded in white like the Ku Klux Klan, to a grinding noise almost unendurable to the ear. They loomed over the audience on every side in the sudden darkness, blocking all exits. Such terror was never achieved in Eliot's lifetime. (87)

The terror evoked by the nonhuman presences in this production, forty years after the play was first staged, was appropriate to Eliot's original intention of communicating the terror of the gospel to a post-Christian world by using angelic beings as fearsome agents of redemption.

The original intention was to create discomfort and awe. Writing to Browne during the early stages of planning, Eliot indicated the spiritual purpose behind these supernatural figures:

> This attraction[14] glimmers for a moment in [Harry's] mind, half-consciously as a possible "way of escape"; and the Furies (for the Furies are *divine* instruments, not simply hell-hounds) come in the nick of time to warn him away from this evasion—though at that moment he misunderstands their function. . . . [T]he second appearance of the Furies, more patently in their role of divine messengers, . . . [lets] him know clearly that the only way out is the way of purgation and holiness. They become exactly "hounds of heaven." . . . Only after the second visit of the Furies does he begin to understand what the Way of Liberation is: and he follows the Furies as immediately and as intelligibly as the Disciples dropping their nets. (qtd. in Browne 107–8)

Eliot's italicization of the word *divine* adds emphasis to the Christian purpose and redemptive theme that he had in mind. This letter also explains the nature of the surprising change in Harry near the end of the play. Agatha, Harry's aunt, reveals to Harry dark secrets of his own family and the shadow they have cast over both Harry and herself. She tells him, however, that it is not a story of "crime and punishment," but one of "sin and expiation" (*Family Reunion* 275). Harry is cleansed and freed; he has "come into a quiet place" (278). The Furies appear again in the window embrasure, and Harry speaks to them calmly and gladly, saying he is no longer surprised or afraid to see them. This time he recognizes them as "real" and he is ready to follow them (278). He tries to explain to his mother that he has lived all his life in flight, and in "ignorance of invisible pursuers" (280). He says that what he is doing is "at once the hardest thing, and the only thing possible." He knows that these divine beings will now lead him, and that he will be safe with them (281). The scene concludes with Harry saying that he does not understand why he has "this election." He feels that something has always been preparing him for it, and that it was, in some sense, "what [he] always wanted." Now the strength he needed has been given to him and he declares, "I must follow the bright angels" (281). Following them completes the process of redemption for Harry.

The "bright angels" are the most unusual feature of this remarkable play. In spite of the production challenges that the supernatural beings posed, D. E. Jones, in *The Plays of T. S. Eliot,* recognizes in this play a "richness and complexity" that sets it next to the greatest of Eliot's works (122). Admitting that it may not have been a "complete success as drama," Jones suggests that *The Family Reunion* may be "an important extension of drama that we have not yet understood" and that it is unique as "an attempt to communicate with the audience on the level of spiritual experience" (122). Russell Kirk agrees, observing that in this play Eliot "unbarred a gate to the realm of the spirit" (224).

Angelic Beings in The Cocktail Party

In Eliot's next play, *The Cocktail Party,* the gate into the realm of the spirit stands wide open, and the "bright angels," who are agents of redemption, are no longer aloof and inscrutable. Appearing in human form, they are efficient "Guardians" moving and functioning with ease in the world of upper-class Londoners, incognito. They manipulate and prod; they protect the foolish, salvage a broken marriage, and facilitate a tragic and glorious martyrdom.

The most astonishing thing about the public response to this powerful play is that—with very few exceptions[15]—the scholars and critics who have discussed it and praised it have been unwilling to say directly that the Guardians are angelic beings. Their reticence reflects the embarrassment felt by educated people in modern times at the mention of angels. Admittedly, the real identity of the Guardians in *The Cocktail Party* is not revealed initially, and the other characters in the play are never able to perceive it. Nevertheless, their identity is abundantly apparent to anyone who takes the play seriously and is not afraid to speak the word *angels.*

This work is integral to Eliot's understanding of the intersection of the eternal world with the temporal. It is also fascinating in what it suggests about the role of angels in the redemptive process. Both fantastical and solemn, it deserves to be examined closely.

Eliot, in harmony with scriptural precedents and the thinking of Lewis on the forms angels may assume, created in *The Cocktail Party* three characters who are divine agents that have taken on human form. The play presented angels in disguise many decades before such characters became a fashion. In scripture, the functioning of angels is often subversive, and they are mistaken for human beings because they look like ordinary people.[16] The angel sitting by Jesus's empty tomb is described as simply "a young man . . . clothed in a long white garment" (Mark 16.5). Wings and ghostliness are *not* usual features, even when angelic appearances in biblical narrative are recognized as supernatural. As Lewis says in *The Discarded Image,* the physical forms in which angels appear are assumed forms, not forms that are natural to them.

Neville Coghill's "An Essay on the Structure and Meaning of the Play," which provides a close examination of Eliot's intention in *The Cocktail Party,*[17] begins by recognizing that Eliot's treatment of the problems of holiness—first raised in *Murder in the Cathedral*—reappears in this play. This time, however, Eliot has taken such spiritual issues "out of the Church in order to show them to us in our comparatively godless daily lives" (237). Coghill summarizes the matter of the play thus:

> It gives an amusingly satirical picture of the fashionable West End world of London between the two wars, and yet is charged with a sense of the mystical destiny of a soul chosen for something greater. . . . This is the greatness of the play, that it not only convincingly presents a spiritual calling of this kind, but also the antics of our secular, modern world of troubled sexual relationships, in what

seems a maladjusted marriage, for the cure of which a brilliant psy-
choanalysis is amusingly presented. . . . No other English comedy
has linked these two kinds of spiritual quest—the quest for love in
marriage and the quest for the love of God. (237)

The play begins with a cocktail party from which the hostess is
unaccountably absent, and at which the host, Edward, is confused
and bumbling. His distress is caused partly by his wife's absence
(and his suspicion that she may have left him) and partly by the
presence of an Unidentified Guest, whom he has never seen before,
but whom he assumes his wife has invited. This Guest appears to
be equally unknown to the other guests—Celia, Peter, Julia, and
Alex—but later we learn that two of them, Julia and Alex, not only
know this man well but are working covertly with him to promote
the self-knowledge and spiritual health of the other characters. In
the humorous opening scene, Eliot has depicted literally the scriptural admonition: "Do not neglect to show hospitality to strangers,
for by this some have entertained angels without knowing it" (Heb.
13.2 *NIV*). *Strangers* is a key word. The Unidentified Guest (who in
later scenes is revealed to be a psychotherapist named Reilly), flam-
boyant Julia, and pushy Alex are strangers in the sense that they are
strange in seemingly random ways; but their strangeness congeals
and declares itself as the play progresses. They are referred to in the
stage directions as "Guardians."

Russell Kirk is one of the few critics to directly acknowledge their
unearthly nature. He observes that the three "troublesome" guests
are not what they appear. They don't seem to be "guests" in the
ordinary sense of the word; they are in reality in a much more dominating position. They are Guardians, and "their intervention in the
lives of the other four people produces recovery in the soul" (Kirk
288). Kirk advises that to understand the meaning of the play, we
should understand what the Guardians are: "Superficially, the three
Guardians may be taken for sensible people whose understanding of
human nature is far deeper than one might surmise from a meeting
at a cocktail party. . . . But Eliot makes it sufficiently clear that also

the Guardians have greater power than any ordinary well intentioned friend might possess. . . . Eliot offers strong hints that these three Guardians, though operating with human powers—more by suggestion than direction—upon human wills, in essence are other than human, . . . possibly a different sort of angel" (289–90).

Kirk recognizes that the subject of angels is a very sensitive one, and one that is both "neglected" and important: "The doctrine of angels—Jewish, Stoic, Mithraic, and Christian in its origins—is no less credible than many other dogmas which Eliot had learned to accept. . . . It is a mark of democratic ages, Alexis de Tocqueville mentions, that the common man denies or ignores any invisible hierarchy separating him from direct relationship with God. . . . [For Eliot] there was nothing repugnant or incredible in conceiving of tutelary beings of another order than human" (290–91).

Russell Kirk's recognition that the Guardians may be "a different sort of angel" differs from the cautious reluctance of other critics. Even the critics who provide the most insightful analysis of this play are reluctant to admit the otherworldliness of these beings: they hover on the edge of acknowledging the supernatural but cannot bring themselves to do so. The possibility of the interference of angels is intensely embarrassing to modern educated people, especially literary critics. A close reading of the play, however, supports the view that these unusual characters are indeed "a different sort of angel."

Gradually, through successive scenes, Eliot uncovers the layered personalities of the three *strangers* and slowly reveals their true purposes. Initially they are more comic than threatening, and even their most worryingly inscrutable utterances are clearly rooted in goodness and kindness. Julia's cover persona is a talkative old lady with a disorganized mind, a talent for recounting humorous incidents (made even more hilarious by her erratic style of narrative), an impulse for taking control of the movements of others, and a tendency to lose her glasses. The fact that there is more to her than appears on the surface is leaked early in the play by Alex's remark: "She never misses anything unless she wants to" (*Cocktail Party* 298). Words flow from her with a haphazard wit and babbling energy that amuses and bemuses. In his notes to the play, Coghill describes Julia's speech patterns as "irresponsible rotations of tongue" (204). She controls the scene by her torrent of words—words that appear to come from a disordered consciousness. But even before we learn more of who she really is, we wonder how anyone can be so clever and so foolish at the same time.

Alex's cover is less showy. During the cocktail party he functions occasionally to set Julia up, but his personality seems unremarkable. When, near the end of the first scene, he comes back to Edward's apartment, and insists (despite all protests and obstacles) on cooking dinner for him, his oddness become apparent. But it is a very comic oddness. He tells them that his special talent is the ability to produce something tasty out of any mere scraps he can find in the kitchen; when he lived in the East, he says, he learned how to concoct a variety of dishes out of "a handful of rice and a little dried fish." He silences protests with, "Don't say a word. / I shall begin at once" (313). As a caricature of a would-be gourmet, oblivious to the attempts of his friends to protect others from him, Alex has an amusing aggressiveness that parallels that of Julia. Both are pushy interferers, but not in the least offensive.

The third interferer, the Unidentified Guest, is silent and aloof throughout the cocktail party in the opening scene, replying in noncommital monosyllables when he is prodded by the other guests, who are curious to find out who he is. When the other guests leave, and the host, Edward, initiates a conversation about his personal situation, the Unidentified Guest quickly reverses his earlier aloofness. Showing concern for Edward in his dismay over his wife's departure, he pushes Edward, with well-directed questions, to see some truths about himself (like his cowardice and his unfaithfulness to his wife) that he has never before faced. The Unidentified Guest is benevolently belittling (as the *edila* were to Random in *Perelandra*). When Edward begins to take offense at his prying questions and comments, the Unidentified Guest reveals his mysterious authority and his access to privileged information. He tells Edward that he knows him as well as he knows Lavinia, his wife, and that he is

aware that Edward initiated the conversation simply for the pleasure of sharing a personal matter with "a stranger" with whom he
shares no past or future connection. The Guest unnerves Edward,
announcing that, though he will "remain a stranger," Edward has
opened a door that he will not be able to shut. By so approaching
a stranger, the Unidentified Guest tells Edward, he has "invited the
unexpected," released "a new force into the situation," and begun
a sequence of events beyond his control. He has "let the genie out
of the bottle" (*Cocktail Party* 306). The Guest, so silent earlier in
the scene, now talks on and on, pressuring Edward to try to think
clearly and honestly about his marital situation and to find out who
he really is and what he really feels (307). When Edward admits
(to his own surprise) that he truly does want his wife to return, the
Guest's knowledge and control of the larger circumstances are more
openly revealed. This "stranger" not only knows where Lavinia is
but will bring her back to Edward. She will return in twenty-four
hours, provided Edward agrees to the terms the Unidentified Guest
lays down. Edward has indeed shown hospitality to a "stranger" —
an uncontrollable "stranger" who is *no* stranger to the intimate details of his psyche.

In the second scene of act 1, Edward and Celia (the young woman
with whom he has been having an affair) are bombarded by inter-
ruptions from Julia, while they try to struggle through an honest ap-
praisal of their relationship. They realize that what they had wanted
from each other was based on a hopeless dream. The spiritual issues
at the core of the play begin to surface, and Celia realizes that in
pursuing the affair with Edward she has been looking for happiness
in the wrong place (*Cocktail Party* 304) and contributing to her own
"humiliation" (324). For his part, Edward realizes that he is feeling
"old" (325), that his life is characterized by dullness and "medioc-
rity" (326), and that he probably deserves Celia's description of him
as "a beetle the size of a man" (327). The scene concludes with Celia
and Edward asking forgiveness of one another and drinking a toast
to the "Guardians." The word *Guardians* is a jolt; it seems to have
come to them out of nowhere. Yet it was slightly foreshadowed by

Edward's earlier comment that the inner unspeaking "self" may for some men "be the guardian" that prevents spiritual disaster (326). Edward and Celia seem at this point to know intuitively that they are being watched over and directed, and they are beginning to accept that it must be so. Celia speculates that "it may be that even Julia is a guardian"—perhaps even Celia's own "guardian" (328).

In the next scene, which takes place the following day, the Unidentified Guest returns to hold Edward to his decision to try to rebuild his marriage. The Guest stresses the importance of decisions. Paralleling the view of time Eliot expresses in "Burnt Norton,"[18] the Guest suggests that the past and the future are less real than the present moment, and says that when Edward and Lavinia meet again (by his arrangement), they must not "strangle each other with knotted memories" (*Cocktail Party* 330). We are reminded of Scrooge's terrified conversation with the ghost of Marley, when the Guest tells the alarmed Edward that he must await "visitors"—"strangers" (330). To Edward's distressed question, "Who are you?" he will only answer mysteriously, "I also am a stranger" (330).

In subsequent scenes, Alex and Julia continue to maneuver the spiritually needy characters in subtle ways, and the Unidentified Guest—having revealed himself as Reilly, a psychiatrist—manipulates them in direct ways. The characters, although under the Guardians' spiritual compulsion (*Cocktail Party* 339), are never permitted to consciously recognize the three as supernatural agents. Yet they have their suspicions. Lavinia complains, "If it's a machine, someone else is running it. / But who? Somebody is always interfering" (336). There is, however, less resentment as it becomes increasingly apparent that the interference is redemptive.

When, in act 2, the three Guardians converse in Reilly's office with none of the other characters present, the demeanor of Julia and Alex is starkly different. It becomes apparent that they are divinely appointed beings who are compassionate but unsentimental. They divest themselves of the bumbling aspects of their cover personalities and speak of the needs of the patients in a businesslike way. They recognize that Celia is the one who perceives most intensely the issues of sin and failure and expresses deep longings for love, healing, and even "ecstasy" (*Cocktail Party* 363). With the help of the Guardians, she chooses the second of the two possible spiritual paths offered to her—a particularly fearsome redemption. It is the higher way, the one that, in Reilly's words, requires a "terrifying journey" (365). She is sent off to "work out [her] salvation with diligence" (366), and the Guardians turn their attention to the other patients.

Julia reflects that their work as Guardians requires that they "always take risks" (*Cocktail Party* 367). The risks, which are part of their angelic "destiny" (367), are not personal risks to themselves, but uncertainties as to what outcomes their interfering will produce. Because they operate within time, they cannot always foresee what mortals will choose to do when they have been "stripped naked to their souls" as the Guardians ruthlessly urge them toward salvation (367). Julia, speaking to Reilly of the painful journey lying ahead for Celia, muses, "But what do we know of the terrors of the journey?" (367). In saying this, she reveals that Reilly, Alex, and herself have a mode of spiritual existence that is quite different from that of the other characters, and admits that they have never traveled, and can never travel, the road that Celia is taking.

Eliot's depiction of the limited understanding of the Guardians highlights both the uncanny otherness of these divinely commissioned beings and the glorious mystery of redemption. Julia continues, emphasizing the difference between their mode of being and that of the humans: "You and I don't know the process by which the human is / Transhumanised" (*Cocktail Party* 367). The Guardians, though they frequently seem all-knowing, have limited knowledge of the inner changes that occur during the process of redemption.[19] Julia reiterates this ignorance, asking the rhetorical question, "What do we know / Of the kind of suffering they must undergo / On the way of illumination?" (367). And Reilly admits that when he says to one like Celia, "Work out your salvation with diligence," he does not really understand what he is saying (368). Julia is speaking for all three of them when she tells Reilly that he must "accept [his] limitations" (368).

The third and final act, set two years later, reveals that *The Cocktail Party* is not a "comedy" in the popular sense of the term. The tone has changed. There are no moments of humor or lightheartedness; instead, tragedy is introduced. The same people, except for Celia, are gathered for a cocktail party, but they receive shocking news: Celia has died violently by crucifixion in a savage land. Edward, Lavinia, and Peter are stunned, horrified, and grief-stricken, while the Guardians (Reilly, Julia, and Alex) seem to take the news calmly. Lavinia rebukes Reilly for expressing no "surprise or horror" but instead something that seems almost like "satisfaction" (*Cocktail Party* 383). In response to this accusation Reilly recounts his own prophetic vision when he first met Celia. Looking into the future, he saw the astonished ecstasy on her face in "the first five minutes after a violent death" as she encounters the sublimity of the "other" world—the glorious reality beyond this world (383–84). Reilly rejects the view that Celia's life was wasted, declaring, "It was a triumph" (385).

The play is not the light social comedy it appeared to be at the beginning, but it *is* a comedy in the highest sense of the term, the sense in which Dante's great work is a "comedy." It recounts journeying and struggle and pain but ends with the resolution of problems and joyous union. Reilly's announcement of the redemptive triumph with which Celia's life ended makes this play a kind of "divine comedy."

On a much more ordinary level, the resolution of another thread of the plot makes the play a "comedy" in another sense—the sense in which *comedy* is used when applied to the comedies of Shakespeare, where separated lovers come together at the end. Thanks to the interference of the Guardians, a broken love relationship has been mended. Through self-knowledge, repentance, and forgiveness, the marriage of Edward and Lavinia has been rebuilt. They have allowed divine grace to operate, and they have learned how to appreciate, enjoy, and love one another. This is another redemptive triumph. The three Guardians, making no further attempt to deny their complicity, leave together, observing that they "have another engagement" (*Cocktail Party* 387). The Christian message of redemption makes happy endings possible because all is of grace.

In Eliot's choruses to the pageant play *The Rock*, there is a cryptic warning: "Oh my soul, be prepared for the coming of the Stranger. / Be prepared for him who knows how to ask questions." (103) Like the "Stranger" mentioned in *The Rock*, the Guardians in *The Cocktail Party* "know how to ask questions." Although they blend in with the social scene and provide a good deal of the initial entertainment in what starts out as a humorous play, they soon become disconcerting because the other characters are not prepared for the questions they raise. The intrusive questions arouse fear, but it is a good fear, leading to honesty, repentance, and spiritual health. Eliot intended his play to disturb, and it did.[20] He wanted to startle the audience with the realization that divinely appointed strangers may intrude in many lives, even their own. One critic commented, "Perhaps the Guardian Angels, whom [Reilly, Julia, and Alex] symbolize, are more familiar than we guess" (qtd. in Browne 237).

Images of the Unseen

Lewis, Sayers, and Eliot do not suggest that we should seek greater awareness of the presence and intervention of angels. Such awareness is not a component of godliness. Even the unfallen Green Lady of *Perelandra* was for a long period unaware of the presence of the archangel who ruled her planet. Their depictions of supernatural interference suggest that it is right that we remain largely oblivious to the angels who watch over us, and refrain from trying to identify those who come into our lives incognito, perhaps even as strangers at a party (as suggested in Heb. 13.2). Nonetheless, dismissiveness toward angels may be a bad thing if it means we refuse to see our lives as overshadowed by divine providence, and we assume that we have no need of protection and guidance. Perhaps we do not want to see our lives as hedged in by benevolent provision and overshadowed by redemptive forces.

In their accounts of the supernatural agents of God's mercy and grace, Sayers, Lewis, and Eliot draw attention to things that are normally unseen. All three writers suggest that unexpected and uncontrollable presences may influence and direct us in ways that we perceive only dimly, if at all. Such a possibility is terrifying, but despite the initial fearsomeness of such intrusion, the biblical greeting "Fear not" assures us of the ultimate goodness these presences represent.

Similar thoughts about the elusiveness and redemptive role of angelic presence have been poignantly expressed by two poets who seem remote from Lewis, Sayers, and Eliot, but whose awareness of angels beautifully complements theirs.

In his poem "The Kingdom of God," the nineteenth-century poet Francis Thompson describes human blindness to angelic presences while asserting that the Kingdom of God is not distant from us in a strange, faraway realm, but is as close as our breathing.

O world invisible, we view thee,
O world intangible, we touch thee,
O world unknowable, we know thee,
Inapprehensible, we clutch thee!

. . . .

Not where the wheeling systems darken,
And our benumbed conceiving soars!—
The drift of pinions, would we hearken,
Beats at our own clay-shuttered doors.

The angels keep their ancient places;—
Turn but a stone, and start a wing!
'Tis ye, 'tis your estrangèd faces,
That miss the many-splendoured thing. (226–27)

Here Thompson, like Eliot, Lewis, and Sayers, challenges our tendency to think of the divine as residing far away, out in space, "Where the wheeling systems darken, /And our benumbed conceiving soars!" Instead, the movement of angels' wings, "the drift of pinions" (representing the proof of God's presence and care that we so long for) is right beside us, but we cannot hear the sound because we have our "clay-shuttered doors" closed so tightly against the supernatural.

Thompson asserts that the guardian angels have not forsaken us: they keep their ancient, divinely appointed places. Psalm 91 speaks of angels protecting us from striking our foot against a stone (91:12), and, working off that image, Thompson affirms, "The angels keep their ancient places— / Turn but a stone, and start a wing." He envisions a walker stumbling a little and turning over a stone in the path, causing a watchful angel to lurch forward with wings protectively outspread. He goes on, "Tis ye, 'tis your estrangèd faces, / That miss the many-splendored thing." Like Lewis, Sayers, and Eliot, he believes the fault lies with us; it is our estrangement from the holy that causes us, time and time again, to "miss the many-splendored thing."

The twentieth-century poet Sylvia Plath[21] likewise expresses the deep-rooted human craving for the kind of angelic presence that Eliot, Lewis, and Sayers describe. In a poem called "Black Rook in Rainy Weather," Plath—though she does not "expect a miracle" (41)—admits that she occasionally desires "backtalk / From the mute sky" (41) and cautiously yearns for "whatever angel may choose to flare / Suddenly at [her] elbow" (42). Plath is one of the most celebrated and controversial poets of the twentieth century—one who never embraced religious faith and never stooped to sentiment. Yet in this poem she describes a "celestial burning" that seems to take possession "of the most obtuse objects now and then" (41)—a burning that bestows holiness on inconsequential moments. Plath fears the idea of "total neutrality" in the universe. She describes herself as journeying, "Trekking stubborn through this season / Of fatigue," and patching together "a content / Of sorts." Though she has absorbed the worldview of a secular age, part of her believes that "Miracles occur, / If you care to call those spasmodic / Tricks of radiance miracles" (42). The poem ends wistfully:

> The wait's begun again,
> The long wait for the angel,
> For that rare, random descent. (42)

The longing Plath expresses here is the same longing that Eliot, Lewis, and Sayers sensed and responded to, the longing to connect with the unseen world and with God, "the long wait" for the descent of the angel and the miracle of redemption.

6

Fiery Trials

World War II and Redemptive Suffering

✣ ✣ ✣

Pondering the futile plotting of kings and rulers, Psalm 2 asks, "Why do the nations rage?" The answer sets the question in the larger context of the rebellion of men against God, and against Christ, his Anointed One (Psalm 2.1–2 *ESV*). According to scripture, the terrible suffering caused by war has its roots in the general fallen state of mankind and in the specific sinfulness of individual men. War takes a heavy toll, but in the midst of its greatest horrors, God's grace and mercy can operate.

The suffering caused by World War II was the crucible in which the prophetic function of Lewis, Eliot, and Sayers was refined and focused. In this time of national and international crisis, those on the front lines were not the only ones to experience intense suffering; physical deprivation and anguish engulfed Europe's civilian population. People who had lived through the enormity of World War I a few decades earlier were horrified to find devastation and death on their very doorsteps again.

Anguished Questions and Hard Answers

The evening of Wednesday, November 14, 1940, was clear and moonlit in the English Midlands—a perfect night for Operation Moonlight Sonata, the horrific German raid on the ancient city of Coventry. That night German planes dropped 450 tons of high explosives and 36,000 incendiary bombs, destroying or damaging tens of thousands of buildings (including many factories and the fourteenth-century cathedral), killing about 600 civilians, and injuring about 1000 others. The term *Coventrate* was coined by the Germans for their brilliant new strategy for leveling British towns and cities; it was used to mean "annihilate or reduce to rubble."

Six days later, the first of several mass burials took place. The Bishop of Coventry commended the dead to "the mercy and care of God," and reminded the stricken people that though the Germans could kill their loved ones, they themselves could choose whether or not their own spirits would be broken. He called on those who believed in the life to come, to live on in the strength of their faith. "Let us go out to try and live unbroken and unembittered," he urged, "asking the help of God's Holy Spirit to support us and to strengthen us that these dead may be prouder of us when we meet again" ("Coventry Buries Her Dead" 6).

The attack on Coventry was one of the worst events of the period of intense bombing carried out by the Germans from September 1940 to May 1941, a period that came to be known as the Blitz. The destruction was greatly aggravated by the raging fires that the bombing caused: it was a veritable *firestorm*. Yet some good emerged from the devastation. The tragedy at Coventry cemented the intense resolve of the British people to resist despair and to press on toward what Prime Minister Churchill called "victory in spite of all terror" (169).

Sayers hailed Churchill as a fellow prophet: one who did not seek to lull people's fears by "the rumble of abstractions" and who knew that only intense words like "blood and toil; tears and sweat" would make sense in these desperate conditions. She saw that Churchill, unlike other leaders, was not attempting to soothe people "with assertions of confidence—recapitulations of our vast resources." The attempts by other leaders to soothe had had the opposite of their intended effect, producing "a heart-shaking lack of confidence" (Sayers, "Notes on the Way" 633). But now, suddenly, Winston Churchill was courageously addressing the hard questions, telling people that suffering is what it will take, and that their strength lay in the endurance of blood, toil, tears, and sweat. Churchill's blunt honesty set the tone for others who would turn away from pat answers to the problem of pain.

It was through the radio broadcasts of the British Broadcasting Corporation that Churchill's words went out to the nation. The BBC was a key factor in the determination of the British to resist despair, and it provided the most important means by which public morale was maintained. BBC broadcasts that brought courage and hope to people battling despair featured Christian spokespersons, including Dorothy L. Sayers, T. S. Eliot, and C. S. Lewis.

As Justin Philips recounts in *C. S. Lewis in a Time of War,* the BBC directors, particularly the Rev. James Welch, director of religious broadcasting, knew that radio programs providing music, comedy, and other diversions were not what people really needed at a time like this. Radio broadcasts would be inexcusably irrelevant if they did not respond directly to the terror and dismay caused by the relentless bombing. People needed programs that addressed the agonizing questions: "'Why has it happened? Whose fault is it? How can we prevent its happening again? What kind of world are we fighting for?'" (Phillips 78). Welch determined that "the best formats to deal with these four fundamental questions were discussion programmes and the scripted single-person broadcast talk" (78). Welch also wanted to "find some new names to reach the ordinary [person and] to do something original" (79). He found the right people. In Lewis, Eliot, and Sayers, he had radio speakers who would put these questions in the context of the larger questions that "the Church has perpetually to answer."—the questions: "To what purpose were we born? What is the end of Man?" (Eliot, *The Idea of a Christian Society* 77). As Lewis, Eliot, and Sayers addressed these questions through their broadcast talks and their writing during the war years, the goal that the Rev. Welch had hoped for was achieved, and also the unforeseen.

The Blitz Becomes a Crucible

More prophetically than he could have foreseen when he wrote "East Coker" a few years before the war, Eliot's image "old timbers to new fires" described the fate that awaited London during the intense period of bombing. It was a trial by fire both literally and figuratively, but while the fire destroyed much that was old, it brought new zeal, and purged and strengthened the witness of the church.

To better understand what was happening during the Blitz in the lives of Sayers, Eliot, and Lewis, I would like to turn back the calendar and reconstruct a scene from the life of each of them.

A crucial wartime experience for Dorothy L. Sayers occurs on the morning of November 22, 1940. In her home in Witham, just east of London, Sayers is taking in her mail, and finds a letter from a Miss Jenkin, an assistant producer at the BBC. The letter is in response to Sayers's submission of the first play of a series of twelve radio plays on the life of Christ that she has been commissioned to write for the radio slot called *The Children's Hour*. Sayers's face tightens in annoyance as she reads. This intolerable woman has the gall to suggest that, though the play Sayers submitted is "profound and beautiful" it needs extensive editing to simplify the language so that it will be understood by young listeners (qtd. in Sayers, *Letters of DLS* 2: 195). As a professional writer, Sayers is greatly offended. Further correspondence on this subject with the BBC editors only adds fuel to the fire, transforming Sayers's annoyance into one of the worse attacks of righteous indignation she has ever had, and a huge battle ensues—by mail.[1] Sayers comes very close to abandoning the whole project.

It was an inauspicious beginning for a religious writing project, but—thanks to the skillful arbitration of James Welch—the project was not abandoned. *The Man Born to Be King* came to be one of the most loved series aired during the war, and one of the most acclaimed biblically based works of drama written in the twentieth century.

The re-creation of a significant wartime experience for Eliot brings us to the evening of April 16th, 1941. In South Kensington, a region of London, Eliot puts on Wellington boots, a black metal helmet with a large white *W* painted on it, and an air raid warden armband. His shift starts late and lasts till dawn. Before starting his patrol, he stops at the Air Raid Precautions Depot and picks up other equipment he will need while making his rounds of the blacked-out streets. The most cumbersome things to carry are the first aid kit, the bucket and hand-pump for putting out fires, and the two-sided sign saying "Alert" and "All Clear." Less likely to be needed are the gas mask and the hook for removing damaged ceilings, but he takes them too. He also takes the hooter used to sound the alarm if a raid occurs, and the siren to announce the all clear. With the streets in deep darkness in accordance with blackout regulations, the spirit lamp is one of the most important things he has to carry.

Enforcing the blackout regulations is part of Eliot's duty as an air raid warden. Because it is essential that no house lights be visible, the wardens are required to knock on the doors of people whose blackout curtains are leaking light and tell them to do something about it. That sort of intrusion is probably the part of the job Eliot likes least—that and taking a tally of the number of people sleeping in each house so that all can be accounted for if a house is demolished in a raid. The most taxing part of the air raid warden's work occurs during the actual raids, when he must help old and physically disabled people leave their houses and reach a bomb shelter. Eliot feels most weary at the end of the shift when he has to record a detailed account of the events of the night, and then head home to prepare for the day's work at Faber and Faber, the publishing house where he is a senior editor. He is exhausted before the regular workday starts.

Many nights are relatively uneventful, but others are horrific. On this particular evening, of April 16, 1941, the Germans drop thousands of high explosives and incendiary bombs on London, starting more than 2,000 fires and killing more than 1,000 people. Many of London's old churches are destroyed or severely damaged— churches that had defined the texture of the city for centuries.

Twenty years earlier, Eliot had depicted such London churches in *The Waste Land,* churches whose clocks steadily kept "the hours" (39), and whose structures had "inexplicable splendour" (45).

Ten years earlier, in the choruses he wrote for the pageant play *The Rock,* he had depicted the old churches of London in offering a response to the question, "What is the meaning of this city?" ("Choruses from *The Rock*" 103). Many of these historic churches are now reduced to rubble: their keeping of the hours ended, their splendor ruined, and their answers silenced. During the raid of April 16, St. Paul's Cathedral is struck and severely damaged; the fact that it is not destroyed is nothing short of a miracle. The firestorm of the Blitz is one of the blackest periods of London's history, and it is one of the blackest periods of Eliot's life. Yet out of the disorientation and horror of those dark nights patrolling the London streets comes his greatest work of poetry, the last of the four poems composing *Four Quartets,* the poem called "Little Gidding."

The re-creation of a significant wartime experience for Lewis brings us to 6:45 P.M. on August 6, 1941. At the BBC's London studios in Great Portland Street, C. S. Lewis is rehearsing for his first radio broadcast. It will go on the air, live, in exactly one hour. This broadcast is an audacious undertaking for an Oxford lecturer in English literature, who has, up to this point, never addressed the general public on any subject: furthermore, this talk will be on religion, a subject in which he does not have academic qualifications. It is, perhaps, even more risky for the BBC. They are not sure how this experiment will be received. As Justin Philips records, the radio programming for this particular day in war-ravaged England has been a mixed bag: a few religious items early in the day, then alternating music, news, and humor. From 7:00 to 7:30, shortly before Lewis's talk, a show called *Under Your Hat* is scheduled, with content ranging from the Hillbilly Swingers to a speech giving recognition to those in the Civil Defense Force who have won medals for bravery. During this program, Lewis is already in the studio, but he is oblivious to what is on the air; he is practicing his timing (which must be very precise). At 7:30, fifteen minutes before Lewis's talk, there is a news broadcast—in Norwegian.[2] Clearly, Lewis has not been given the best slot of the day for his fifteen-minute talk, called "Right and Wrong: A Clue to the Meaning of the Universe." Many English-speaking people will probably turn off the radio during the Norwegian news, and may not bother to turn it back on at 7:45, to hear this unknown speaker, billed in the BBC's schedule publication as "C. S. Lewis, Fellow of Magdalen College, Oxford."

This was an inauspicious start for a radio series. As Lewis made his way through the blackened streets of bombed-out London to catch the train back to Oxford, his hope of providing light in a dark time may have seemed like an idle dream. But those radio talks continued through several more series, reached hundreds of thousands of listeners, and became the basis of one of Lewis's most acclaimed books: *Mere Christianity*.

As a defense of the faith, the apologetic work *Mere Christianity* is the best of its kind. Similarly Eliot's "Little Gidding" is the greatest Christian poem of the modern age, and Sayers's *Man Born to Be King* is the most comprehensive and impressive biblically based work of drama in English literature. All three were written during this black period of England's history, and came into being not despite the war, but because of it.

Visible Witness

The war was fought at home as well as on the battle fronts: the people of England toiled and sacrificed and suffered as never before. In the midst of the destruction, many good things emerged—things like fortitude, hope, and faith. And it was through the medium of radio, as much as through the written word, that Lewis, Eliot, and Sayers played a major part in that strengthening, as historian Adrian Hastings observes:

> [Throughout the millions of recorded] personal responses to the hard facts of war, . . . one senses not only the seemingly unlimited human ability to adjust to the unusual and the tortuous, not only a

simple almost crusade-like heroism, . . . but also a widespread . . .
re-appropriation of Christian faith as the key to the meaning of life.
. . . Thus, on the literary front, the war was the golden age of that
Anglican lay literary and theological foursome—Charles Williams,
C. S. Lewis, T. S. Eliot, Dorothy L. Sayers. . . . The most critical
phase of the Second World War was a time of very considerable
Christian literary creativity, but of a non-sectarian sort. The BBC
was its natural medium. (388)

Lewis, Sayers, and Eliot worked tirelessly on scripts, spoke live on the
radio, and endured the hardships of wartime travel to give lectures.
Through it all, they maintained clarity of focus and the ability to see
the war in the context of larger issues. The immediate challenges of
wartime conditions were constantly in their minds as they produced
works in a range of literary modes on many diverse subjects.

It was during the war years that Lewis produced the two philosophical works, *The Problem of Pain* and *The Abolition of Man;*
a work of literary criticism called *Preface to Paradise Lost;* and the
three imaginative works, *The Screwtape Letters, Perelandra,* and
That Hideous Strength. During World War II, Eliot also reached
his peak both as a poet and as a critic of culture, producing the last
three parts of his four-part magnum opus, *Four Quartets,* between
1940 and 1942, and numerous essays and lectures. Sayers's output
was likewise at its peak during the war years. It was during this
period that she produced the cathedral play *The Just Vengeance,*
her masterpiece of critical theory *The Mind of the Maker,* and a
massive number of hard-hitting newspaper articles, radio talks, and
public lectures. Sayers's journalism during 1939 and 1940 focused
primarily on coping mentally with the war and the daily deprivations and problems it created. In one article about how to endure—
even enjoy—the gloomy evenings of the blackout, Sayers looked for
the positive side of the dearth of usual entertainments like theater
and concerts. Devoid of trivial amusements, she observed, one is
forced to endure one's own company, to think, to become more self-
aware, and to learn to enjoy *oneself.* The blackout and the absence

of social diversions, she believed, granted people the opportunity to live less superficially and to think about things of real consequence ("How to Enjoy the Dark Nights" 2).

Though Lewis, Eliot, and Sayers made no claim to speak for the church in any official capacity, their words rang with authority. The essays and lectures they produced in response to the war were not precisely "theological" in nature, yet they were shoring up and rebuilding something that had been crumbling into ruin—Christian witness in the midst of a secular culture. Eliot's choruses for the pageant play *The Rock* (1934) emphasize that the Church must be continually rebuilding because it is always "decaying within" and being "attacked from without." There is much that has to be knocked down, and much that has to be rebuilt ("Choruses from *The Rock*" 101). The Church has to be visible, like a "light set on a hill / In a world confused and dark and disturbed by portents of fear" (112). The confused, dark, and fearful world of the 1940s needed the light of faith and hope; people needed a more visible and more audible Church.

In 1940, reviewing a book called *The Art of Preaching,* Sayers spoke of the urgency of the situation: "To the interesting and valuable matter of [this] book the layman would like to add one word. 'Remember,' he would say to his parson, 'we no longer live in a Christian atmosphere. We are bombarded, six days of the week, with definitely anti-Christian teaching, much of it very skillfully worded. If you are to counteract the effects of this in fifteen minutes on Sunday, you will have to be very convincing indeed.' The task of the preacher has never been harder than it is at this moment; and never, perhaps, in the history of the world has it been more urgent" ("The Technique of the Sermon" 150). Lewis, Eliot, and Sayers took up the challenge as lay preachers, as they reaffirmed Christian truths to a non-Christian culture and thus provided a basis for hope. The light they offered in the darkness of war reflected Jesus's description of his disciples as a light set on a hill (Matt. 5.14–16).

Through the light imagery in *The Rock,* Eliot stresses the need for continual renewal of the Church's witness to the world. This pageant-like work combines the images of rebuilding and relighting, and, as it concludes, praises God for moving his people to the work of reconstructing crumbling structures and building "an altar to the Invisible Light" so that we may set on it our own "little lights." We endure the darkness because it "reminds us of light," and in that darkness, the Church must be visible like a "light set on a hill ("Choruses from *The Rock*" 112).

The idea that the light is "set on a hill" has several possible implications. There is a sense in which speaking from a point of elevation is a bad thing, as when a writer seeks isolation and protection by positioning himself above the turmoil, and contemplating conflicts from a safe distance. This potential negative implication of "on a hill" does not apply to the light that Eliot, Lewis, and Sayers brought to war-torn Britain. Their efforts demonstrated quite the reverse: the horrors of the Blitz allowed no retreat to an ivory tower but instead impelled these writers to light a beacon visible to their beleaguered readers. In an article on the wartime responsibilities of a writer, Eliot expressed the personal accountability they all felt when he observed that a writer "should be no less devoted to his country than other men" and should undertake the same duties as other citizens.[3] Eliot also affirmed that the writer's duty is to write as well as he can about the war, even though his experience may seem trivial compared to that of people on the front lines. Sometimes he can only convey a very specific situation, "some limited experience, such as cold, discomfort, or the boredom of waiting at an isolated post" ("Poetry in Wartime" 351). But the position that Eliot, Lewis, and Sayers occupied as writers was not an "isolated post." They were "set on a hill," in the sense that Jesus meant, in that their message was highly visible. Their written and spoken words were so widely received that, as Hastings observed, they led to the "widespread . . . re-appropriation of Christian faith" during the years of war. Hastings actually saw this dark period as a "golden age" because of the "Christian literary creativity" of Eliot, Lewis, and Sayers (388). They all continued to affirm what Eliot called "the first principles which it is the business of the Church to repeat in and out of season" ("The Idea of a Christian Society" 76), and they wrote out of both the immediacy of their war-ridden personal situations and the larger perspective on suffering afforded by the good news of the gospel.

The Tangled Issues of Guilt, Injustice, Pacifism, and Patriotism

Eliot, writing in the spring of 1939, anticipated the doom that was to come. He observed that "a great deal of the machinery of modern life is merely a sanction for un-Christian aims"—aims that are "hostile" to "virtue and well-being in community" ("The Idea of a Christian Society" 27). He foresaw the result of a mechanistic, aggressive, mercenary culture; he said, "a wrong attitude toward nature" leads to "a wrong attitude toward God," and "the consequence is an inevitable doom" (49).

Christ said, "I have not come to bring peace, but a sword" (Matt. 10.34). The Christian life is pictured as a spiritual warfare, and it is partly for this reason that most Christians have accepted physical war as inevitable. War is certainly dreadful, but to dread it too much, and to try to avoid it at all costs, is to ensure that when it does come it will be all the more horrible. That is precisely the mistake that the leaders of Europe made in the 1930s. In November 1939, shortly after the start of the war, Sayers described the errors that led to it: "If one looks back at the last twenty years, one sees at how many points we might have prevented this war, if it hadn't been for our inflexible will to peace. We said 'Never again'—as though 'never' wasn't the rashest word in the language. ' . . . We will never go to war again, . . . we will never interfere in other people's wars, we will always keep the peace.' We wooed peace as [a sickly person] woos health, by brooding over it till we became really ill" ("Wimsey Papers—II" 736).

Lewis's and Eliot's thoughts on the attempt to avoid war were similar to those of Sayers. The Church had for centuries supported the Aristotelian and Augustinian concept of "just war," but in their repulsion at the thought of another war some church leaders turned to a pacifist position. Lewis observed, however, "If war is ever lawful, then peace is sometimes sinful" ("The Conditions for a Just

War" 374). In his *Criterion* editorial of July 1936, Eliot took issue
with a recent statement by the Bishop of Durham that no war could
be just. He exposed the simplistic thinking behind common arguments for the injustice or justice of war:

> If we refuse to consider the causes, and consider a war only at the mo-
> ment when it breaks out, there is likely to be a good deal of justice on
> both sides: and if we do consider its causes we are likely to find a good
> deal of injustice on both sides. The believer in just war is in danger
> of inferring, at the moment when war is seen to be inevitable, that
> the war is necessarily just: on the other hand the person who sees the
> injustice behind war may be equally in error in assuming that because
> war is unjust he is justified in refusing to take part in it. And it is almost
> impossible to say anything about the subject without being misunder-
> stood by one or both parties of *simplifiers*. (qtd. in Kirk 209–10)

Recognizing the complexities that led to World War II, Eliot saw
the injustice of Britain's desertion of Austria and Hungary in February 1938. Speaking of it in a conversation two decades later he said,
"I felt a deep personal guilt and shame for my country. . . . If our
culture led to an act of betrayal of that kind, then such a culture
was worthless, worthless because it was bankrupt. It had no morality because it did not finally believe in anything. We were concerned
with safety, with our possessions, with money, not with right and
wrong" (qtd. in Kirk 214).

Sayers had a similar view of the situation that led to World War
II, and saw that there was guilt on both sides. The BBC asked her to
be one of seven speakers in a series of talks broadcast in the spring
of 1941 under the title *The Church Looks Ahead*. In the lecture she
delivered for this series, she identified the increasing de-Christianization of European culture as a root cause of the war. Incisively cut-
ting to the core of the spiritual crises that had brought on the war,
she also, at the same time, issued an even bolder challenge, saying,
"What we have been trying to do for some time is to keep the Christian ethic without the connecting thread of Christian theology—the

beads without the string" ("The Religions Behind the Nation" 46).
She pointed out that the leaders of Germany had thrown out Christian theology, and then, realizing that "Christian ethics will not
work without it, . . . jettisoned the ethics as well" (48). It is illogi-
cal, Sayers argued, for the British to be "shocked" and "surprised"
by this sequence of events, because "if Christ is the only guaran-
tee that reason is rational and goodness is good, then, the logical
result of repudiating Christianity is the repudiation of reason and
virtue" (46–47). Sayers believed the people of her own country to
be caught between the two extremes: "neither vigorously Christian
nor boldly anti-Christian; unwilling to give up Christian ethics, but
unable to assert them positively because we can no longer give any
good grounds to justify our faith in them, . . . [and we are] 'living
on our Christian capital'" (48). Sayers saw the position of England
as extremely vulnerable, in a spiritual sense: "We are at present on
the defensive—fighting a desperate and bewildered rearguard action, cut off from our spiritual reinforcements. We cannot do that
forever. We must know what we are fighting about and what we are
fighting for. And it would be well that we should begin by grasping
this plain fact: that we can make no intelligent and wholehearted
fight for our 'European culture' unless we are also ready to fight
for the Christendom upon which (whether we realize it or not) it is
founded" ("The Religions Behind the Nation" 48). Sayers is insisting that people *think*—that they understand the basic underlying
issues, and that they recognize what is at stake on a spiritual level.
Knowing what they were fighting about and what they were fighting
for was essential, she asserted, if the people of Britain were to cope
intelligently and courageously with the devastation of war.

Despite the convoluted issues of justice and injustice, pacifism was
not an option for these three writers. In an essay called "Why I Am
Not a Pacifist," Lewis carefully works through some of the moral
issues that caused him to support the war. He points out that all our
moral judgments involve "facts, intuition, and reasoning, and . . .
some regard for authority" (71–72). The first fact he deals with is the
agreed consensus that war is a very bad thing, but he disagrees that

this justifies the pacifist assertion that wars "always do more harm than good" (73). Both that opinion and its opposite—that war is generally beneficial—are extremes that Lewis cannot embrace. He says that the view that "wars do no good is then so far from being a fact that it hardly ranks as a historical opinion" (73). He dismisses the pacifist conclusion that wars are always useless. "It seems to me," he says, "that history is full of useful wars as well as useless wars" (74).

Lewis's rebuttal of pacifism then turns to the issue of "intuition," and exposes the limitation of the popular intuition that "love is good and hatred is bad, or that helping is good and harming is bad" (75). Such an intuition cannot, however, produce significant action until it is qualified in some way. "You cannot," Lewis argues, "do *simply* good to *simply* Man; you must do this or that good to this or that man" (75). He builds his point carefully, explaining how this applies in specific instances:

> If you do *this* good, you can't at the same time do that; and if you do it to *these* men, you can't also do it to *those.* . . . And this in fact most often means helping A at the expense of B, who drowns while you pull A on board. And sooner or later it involves helping A by actually doing some degree of violence to B. When B is up to mischief against A, you must either do nothing (which disobeys the intuition) or you must help one against the other. . . . [Violence against B should be] equally efficient in restraining him, and equally good for everyone concerned, including B, whose claim is inferior to all the other claims involved but not nonexistent. But I do not therefore conclude that to kill B is always wrong. ("Why I Am Not a Pacifist" 71–76)

Having used reason to demonstrate that violence is sometimes necessary if justice is to be done, Lewis goes on to show that neither the authority of the historical church nor the Christian's ultimate authority—scripture—support the pacifist position ("Why I Am Not a Pacifist" 80–88).

Lewis's attitude toward the war was not naïvely patriotic. The war was to push him into unfamiliar spheres, but Lewis's first direct and public discussion of the war occurred in the context of his life as an Oxford academic. He was asked to preach the University Sermon at Oxford in the autumn of 1939, just after the outbreak of World War II. The sermon was delivered in the University Church of St. Mary the Virgin, an even more venerable institution than the University Sermon itself.[4] Lewis's sermon title was "Learning in War-Time," and students crowded in to hear him. Lewis clarified his support of the war on the basis of his Christian worldview, saying, "I believe our cause to be, as human causes go, very righteous, and I therefore believe it to be a duty to participate in this war. And every duty is a religious duty, and our obligation to perform every duty is therefore absolute" ("Learning in War-Time" 30). Yet Lewis also saw the danger of confusing patriotism with godliness. He went on (as we saw when we considered this passage in chapter 2) to make it clear that the claims of God must take precedence over all other loyalties: "A man may have to die for our country: but no man must, in any exclusive sense, live for his country. He who surrenders himself without reservation to the temporal claims of a nation, or a party, or a class is rendering to Caesar that which, of all things, most emphatically belongs to God: himself." This is why, he said, our religion cannot exclude "all our natural activities," even though it must, in a higher sense, "occupy the whole of life." There is, Lewis affirmed, no compromise possible between "the claims of God and the claims of culture, or politics, or anything else." God's claim on our lives is uncompromisingly "infinite and inexorable" (30–31).

In *The Screwtape Letters,* written a few years later, Lewis illustrates the spiritual confusion and entrapment that results when commitment to a nationalistic or patriotic cause is considered to be synonymous with commitment to Christ himself. The senior demonic tempter, Screwtape, advises that the new Christian (whom the tempters view as their "patient") be encouraged to make this very error of substituting patriotism for godliness. Screwtape counsels the less experienced tempter to make the most of the opportunity that war affords. Whichever side the patient adopts, patriotic or pacifist, the temper's main task will be the same. "Let him," advises Screwtape,

"begin by treating the Patriotism or the Pacifism as a part of his religion. Then let him, under the influence of the partisan spirit, come to
regard it as the most important part." The technique is very subtle.
The patient is gently led by his tempter to "the stage at which religion
becomes merely part of the 'cause' and his [faith] is valued chiefly
for the excellent arguments it can produce in favour of the British
war effort or of Pacifism." The tempter must ensure that "meetings,
pamphlets, policies, movements, causes, and crusades mean more
to him than prayer and sacraments and charity." The more "religious" he becomes, in this sense, the more "securely" he is damned
(*Screwtape Letters* 42–43). Through Screwtape's reverse perspective,
Lewis shows what one's personal devotion to the war effort should
be, and what it should not be. Patriotism must not be substituted for
godliness, but honorable loyalty to one's country will be stronger and
wiser when one's highest accountability is to eternal things.

In a poem called "Defense of the Islands,"[5] Eliot similarly recognizes the right sort of patriotism. He urges people to honor and me-
morialize those who heroically defend "these British islands"—men
who are assigned to the grey battleships, and the merchant vessels,
and the trawlers, who take responsibility for the nation's welfare and
are willing to contribute theirs to the bones of past Englishmen that
now pave the floor of the sea. Such seamen take part in "man's new-
est form of gamble / with death" and undertake to wage warfare
with the "powers of darkness in air and fire." They follow in the
footsteps of their ancestors, fighting in Flanders and in France. Eliot
praises their resilient spirit, calling them "undefeated in defeat" and
"unalterable in triumph." Continuing the heroic patterns of their
ancestors, they have changed nothing—nothing except the kind of
weapons they use. Redeeming the dark gloominess of Thomas Gray's
line "the paths of glory lead but to the grave,"[6] Eliot describes these
men as those "for whom the paths of glory are / the lanes and the
streets of Britain." Unlike Gray, Eliot does not depict the heroes as
simply descending to "graves." Death does not extinguish the glory
achieved in battle; the glory lives on in peaceful "lanes and streets"
trodden by the next generation ("Defense of the Islands" 227–28).

Like Lewis and Eliot, Sayers distrusted naïve nationalism, but valued the love of country, the ideals of camaraderie, and the call to sacrifice inspired by the challenges of the war. These ennobling aspects of the war experience are reflected in the poems that she wrote during the war years. The first of these poems, "The English War," was published in *The Times Literary Supplement* in September 1940, and was reprinted at least three more times in poetry collections between 1941 and 1966.[7] It was the most popular of her war poems because it inspired hope. It reminded readers that Britain's honor and strength had always come through most victoriously when the odds were worst, when allies had deserted, and when there was no political game left to be played. The poem begins with an epigraph taken from a radio broadcast, a surprisingly optimistic comment on the fact that Britain was now standing alone: "*What other race on earth, well aware of its danger, isolated to fight, would utter a great sigh of relief that all had abandoned it, and say to itself: 'Well, thank goodness for that; now we know where we are'?*"

Sayers's first stanza thanks God himself for the extremity in which England now finds itself: "Praise God, now, for an English war— / The grey tide and the sullen coast, / The menace of the urgent hour, / The single island, like a tower, / Ringed with an angry host" (*Poetry of DLS* 120). The poem goes on to recognize the familiarity of the situation: "This is the war that England knows, . . . When no allies are left, no help / To count upon from alien hands, / No waverers remain to woo, / No more advice to listen to, / And only England stands" (120). The isolation, the necessity of relying solely on its own resources, was a situation well known from past wars. The absence of allies also meant the absence of wavering support and dubious advice. It is reassuring to recognize that "This is the war that we have known / And fought in every hundred years" (121). The last four stanzas become a prayer in which Sayers petitions the Almighty for the "will and power / To do as we have done before" and for the kind of national peace that is accompanied by the virtues of common sense, decency, justice, and the absence of treacherous neighbors. The request to be separated from the "dangerous dreams of wishful men /

Whose homes are safe" could be a reference to the unwelcome political influence of America, with its detached position from the realities of the war.[8] In the last stanza, the prayer is for practical realism: "No dreams . . . but vigilance." What is needed most is a valid perspective on actualities and a spirit of tireless dedication and watchfulness. What England is fighting for, the final lines affirm, is not merely her own safety, but the "inviolate seas" and "skies" of a world in which tyranny will not be tolerated (122). The old-school patriotism expressed here had a wide appeal, but it is not a blind, unthinking loyalty to country. The optimism is not naïve; it recognizes that victory will come at a price and is dependent on God's mercies.

The Deprivations of Life in Wartime

With blunt realism, Sayers's poem "The English War" recognizes that war is a time of stripping away, a time of dispossession. Living is reduced to the mere basics, the most elemental things: the simple requirements of eating, sleeping, and finding shelter. Another of Sayers's war poems, "Lord, I Thank Thee," deals more directly, but more lightly, with this stripping away of nonessentials. Its tone is jovial as it catalogs the inconveniences caused by wartime restrictions and rationing. The speaker claims that the war suits her preferred lifestyle, since she does not particularly like most of the things that the war precludes—things like traveling for pleasure, consuming bananas and sugar, buying new clothes, and wearing silk stockings. She is relieved by the thinner newspapers, because of the "ruthless restrictions of twaddle" and the minimizing of the "blare of advertisements / Imploring . . . An apathetic public / Into buying what it neither needs nor desires." Before the war, people had "too much of everything," she declares. Indeed, the war affords new and interesting challenges, such as the delight of finding in the stores something that is in short supply (like a tin of mustard or packet of hairpins) and "bearing it home in triumph." The poem ends as it began, declaring ironically, "If it were not for the war, / This war / Would suit me down to the ground" (*Poetry of DLS* 123–26). Even

though the poem depicts trivialities of daily life during wartime, it is
not a trivial poem. The humor is uplifting, because it is encouraging
people to *grin* and bear it. Sayers knew well that wartime suffering
meant enduring much more serious deprivations than the absence
of bananas and silk stockings.

The war stripped away usual points of reference, leaving people
baffled and disoriented. The complexities of all that the war machine
involved boggled the mind. In Sayers's poem "Aerial Reconnais-
sance," written in 1943, two people are looking at aerial reconnais-
sance photographs in the newspaper and trying to make sense of
them. Their bewilderment, mixed with humble confidence in those in
charge, comes through in remarks like "doubtless the bomb exploded
and damaged something important," and "these things, / naturally . . .
don't mean much to a layman." The feeling of confidence is shaky,
however, and there is pathetic misgiving apparent in the foundering
lines "but of course, I am quite convinced / that the destruction was
enormous— / absolutely convinced— / absolutely." The disoriented
speaker then looks at the next set of newspaper aerial photos and sees
something she *can* connect with—a landscape she can identify because she knew it as a child. Suddenly the effects of the bombing
touch her in a way that is not hypothetical, but real. She pours over
the pictures taken from the air, recognizing every landmark, and realizing that a bridge *she knew* has been bombed, and a village *she knew*
flooded. Yet her reaction is stoically calm. Though the bombs will
not (as she ironically understates it) have done "much good" to machines and power plants, they also will not have permanently damaged the land. The confidence of the speaker returns, subtly modified,
in the last section of the poem:

> Well, I must say,
> those are wonderful pictures,
> I am delighted to have seen them—
> let me have the paper when you are finished with it.
> I want to look again, and go on looking
> because I recognize this,

because I know what it means and understand it,
because I can see exactly what we have done —[9]
we have blown up the dams,
burst the sluices,
unshackled the waters. (*Poetry of DLS* 142–45)

In those final lines, the poem is no longer mimicking the voice of a bemused reader of newspaper war reports. The tone has changed: the staggering magnitude of what is going on is solemnly and subtly acknowledged. Though the land will be renewed in time, there is an irrevocability in the destruction.

Eliot also writes of the damage done by war. In the second Quartet, "East Coker," written during the first year of the war,[10] Eliot anticipates the disorientation and destruction the war will bring, as he depicts old buildings crumbling. In movement 2, the disordered seasons anticipate the way "the knowledge derived from experience" will be proved false, and how, in the coming onslaught, "every moment [will become] a new and shocking / Valuation of all we have been" (*Four Quartets* 125). The Dante-like experience of being found, in middle life, lost "in a dark wood" is intensified in this movement; we find ourselves caught in brambles and tottering on the brink of disaster—"On the edge of a grimpen [a treacherous marsh], where is no secure foothold, / And menaced by monsters" (125).

The absence of a "secure foothold" and of familiar reference points is connected, both literally and figuratively, with darkness. In the third movement of *East Coker* Eliot speaks of darkness as a great leveler—darkness like the darkness of blacked-out London during the Blitz: "O dark dark dark. They all go into the dark. . . . / Distinguished civil servants, chairmen of many committees, / Industrial lords and petty contractors, all go into the dark." The blackout was intended to make it difficult for the German bombers to find populous areas to target. But, nonetheless, the bombs fell relentlessly on public buildings and homes. They did not select their targets according to class or income bracket. As Eliot said, *all* went "into the dark"—from the "distinguished" to the "petty." The structure of life, indeed the very fabric of existence as it had been before the war, was being steadily stripped away (*Four Quartets* 126).

This ordeal had much in common with the Way of Negation spoken of by Christian mystics. Eliot, also in movement 3 of *East Coker,* describes this journey into the darkness of the unknown as, paradoxically, a way to beatitude or blessedness. Passing through the most difficult of trials and deprivations is essential if we are to come to the end of ourselves—if we are to come to God. He tells us that we must go by a way that affords "no ecstasy." If we want to gain real knowledge we must "go by a way which is the way of ignorance." If we want to possess something we do not yet own, we must let go of the notion of ownership altogether, and "go by the way of dispossession." As everything is taken away, ignorance becomes the gateway to real knowledge, and loss of material possessions, the road to true wealth (*Four Quartets* 127).

Even with the promise of obtaining things of real spiritual value, the kind of utter dispossession Eliot describes would hardly be anyone's choice. But in war there is little choice, as layer after layer of what is familiar and comfortable is peeled away.

In the most personal and poignant of her war poems, Sayers portrays the pathos and spiritual devastation of war in terms of individual lives and personal culpability. "Target Area," published in *The Fortnightly* in March 1944, was written in response to the bombing of Frankfurt by British bombers, and out of Sayers's compassion for a German woman she had known years before, who now lived in Frankfurt. Fraulein Fehmer had been Dorothy Sayers's piano teacher when she was at boarding school in Salisbury. The Fräulein had been a stern woman, but a good teacher and a great musician. Sayers's poem begins with a report on British air raids: "*Our bombers were out over Germany last night, in very great strength; their main target was Frankfurt.*" The bombs are dropped by "The grim young men in the blue uniforms, / professionally laconic, charting, over the intercom, / the soundings of the channel of death." These laconic young men "have carried / another basket of eggs to Fräulein Fehmer." The understatement created by the image of delivering a needed food item, like eggs, makes the destructive intention of the bombing raid all the more horrific. Sayers is uncertain whether her teacher was hit: "I do not know, of course, whether she got them" (*Poetry of DLS* 140).[11] The poem becomes very human and tender as Sayers recalls the recent correspondence she had, some years before the war, with Fräulein Fehmer. The ageing pianist told her that she "remembered England with much affection" and that she had heard Sayers was a writer, and would like to read something she had written:

>   –would I send her a copy
> for old sake's sake? It cost more than she could afford
> to order a book from England; times were hard,
> it was very hard indeed for musicians to live
> in Germany nowadays; "of course," she added,
> I am an ardent Nazi."
>   She used to wear
> a shawl, as I have said, when the weather was pinching.
>   Memory
> tells me it was grey. Hitler rose to power
> on the despair of the middle classes. I sent her books,
>   and she thanked me;
> for a long time we exchanged polite greetings at Christmas. (Sayers,
>   *Poetry of DLS* 142–43)

Having provided us with the background, Sayers returns us to the present: "*Last night our bombers / were out in very great strength over Germany; / Fräulein Fehmer was in the target area*" (143). Sayers ponders with compassion the physical and emotional vulnerability of such women: "There are so many things that one does not know— / what, for example, becomes of ageing women / whose skill is rooted in the wrong memories." She wonders about the fondness her teacher had for Chopin, thinking, "it may be / that ardent Nazis are not encouraged to play / Polish music." Sayers rhetorically questions her former teacher asking, "Tell me, Fräulein Fehmer, / were you playing Chopin when the bombs went down?"

and probing the irony of a woman who so loved the music of a Polish composer being supportive of Poland's destruction: "Did the old, heart breaking melody cry to you / Poland's agony through the crashing anger of England?" (*Poetry of DLS* 143).

The questions turn in a different direction as Sayers tries to imagine what it felt like for the old woman when the British air strike began:

> Did we strike you, perhaps, quickly,
> tossing the soul out through the rent ribs or merciful
> splitting of the skull? Or did you
> find yourself suddenly awake at midnight,
> peering from the blankets, fumbling for your glasses to see,
> by flare-light and fire-light,
> the unexpected precipice by the bedside,
> the piano shattered aslant, with all its music
> coiling out of it in a tangle of metallic entrails,
> dust, books, ashes, splintered wood, old photographs,
> the sordid indecency of bathroom furniture
> laid open to the sky? . . . (*Poetry of DLS* 144)

This hypothetical scene of destruction in Frankfurt intentionally parallels the destruction in London after German air raids, when the victims of the Blitz waited "in a passion of nightly expectation." And so "the death sent out" in 1941 returns to Germany in 1944 (*Poetry of DLS* 144).

Sayers muses on the way her life and that of her old piano teacher diverged and then reconnected, first through letters, and then through the tragedy of war. Her teacher had declared herself a Nazi. Instead of judging Fräulein Fehmer for this, Sayers sees herself as similarly accountable, one of those who, figuratively, "filled bombs" and "loaded" the planes (*Poetry of DLS* 144). She wonders whether her life choices and those of her former teacher had contributed to the war, whether individuals like themselves could have made any difference in the big scheme of things. She wonders to what extent each person is accountable for the evil in the world:

for this you learned to play Chopin and I to write
that we might exchange these messages and these replies.
Neither of us can stop what is happening now,
nor would we if we could; the discord of private harmonies
must be resolved in the deafening cataract of calamity;
the first to cry "Halt!" utters a cry of defeat,
and makes a breach in the dam through which the water
floods over the house-tops.
      This I write
with the same hand that wrote the books I sent you,
knowing that we are responsible for what we do,
knowing that all men stand convicted of blood
in the High Court, the judge with the accused.
The solidarity of mankind is solidarity in guilt,
and all out virtues stand in need of forgiveness,
being deadly. (*Poetry of DLS* 144)

In any war, Sayers points out, there is guilt on both sides, and—without the redemption and forgiveness provided by Christ—all of us "stand convicted" in the "High Court" of heaven. The solidarity of humanity is, indeed, "solidarity in guilt" and even the most virtuous "stand in need of forgiveness" (*Poetry of DLS* 144). Sayers's humble and compassionate poem affords a Christian perspective on the war. Experiencing the ravages of war and seeking to understand it from such a perspective means being dispossessed of more than material comforts; it strips away self-centered detachment and moral complacency.

The Annihilation of Complacency

The war forced people to think about many things they preferred to ignore; one of them was their own mortality. The demonic tempter Lewis created in *The Screwtape Letters* spoke of the way war interferes with the satanic goal of human complacency, observing that the "continual remembrance of death which war enforces" is disastrous to the agenda of hell, because it encourages people to consider

what may lie beyond this life. One of hell's best weapons, the demon says, is "contented worldliness," but such naïve contentment
cannot exist in wartime. In war, no one can pretend to himself that
he is going to live forever (Lewis, *Screwtape Letters* 39).

In the sermon "Learning in War-Time," Lewis addresses the
complex questions that the war would press home, challenging
people to "see the present calamity in a true perspective." He argues
that war does not create a new situation, but "simply aggravates
the permanent human situation so that we can no longer ignore it."
What he says next is perhaps the most pertinent point Lewis makes
in all his wartime speaking and writing: "Human life has always
been lived on the edge of a precipice" ("Learning in War-Time"
27). Accepting that fact is the key to spiritual health, in both time
of war and time of peace. Lewis clarifies what he means by *precipice,* observing: "Human culture has always had to exist under the
shadow of something infinitely more important than itself. If men
had postponed the search for knowledge and beauty until they were
secure, the search would never have begun. We are mistaken when
we compare war with 'normal life'. Life has never been normal"
(27–28). The image Lewis uses of living "on the edge of a precipice" is strikingly similar to Eliot's image (in *East Coker*) of living
"on the edge of a grimpen." Both men saw the precariousness of
life in wartime as simply an intensification of conditions that always exist—while recognizing that during war it is a precariousness
that we cannot ignore.

In a poem called "A Note on War Poetry," Eliot probes the impact of war on the individual spirit and soul.[12] He describes the
generalized public response to wartime destruction as a "collective
emotion / Imperfectly reflected in the daily papers," and observes
that what the papers record is very different from the personal response—the "individual / Explosion" or internal trauma—which
must be contained, as each devastated citizen doggedly pursues "the
path of . . . [daily] action." Yet out of the seeming insignificance of
"merely individual" suffering (and he uses the word "merely" twice
within three lines to underscore the *apparent* unimportance of what

occurs on the individual level), something emerges that is of great significance—something he calls "universal." What emerges out of "the impact" of the war on individual lives is far from trivial. Living on the edge, during the extremities of war, brings inner changes of great importance. Spiritual forces of "Nature and the Spirit" that are beyond our puny control operate on us in times of suffering. In such intense moments, individual experiences cannot be processed; they appear "too large, or too small" for analysis. While we are enduring the extremities of suffering, we have to manage our emotions, keeping them at the level of mere "incidents" in our dogged efforts to "keep day and night together," and just keep on going, putting one foot ahead of the other. We are in "a situation . . . which may neither be ignored nor accepted." We simply have to cope with it, without accepting it, sometimes by using "ambush," or direct methods of confronting the horror, and sometimes by using "stratagem," or indirect methods. War will pass, it is transient; but the moments of "private experience" within it may be truly significant and thus connect us with things that are "enduring" and "universal"—what Eliot calls, in another context, "permanent things" ("A Note on War Poetry" 229–30).

The poem is called "A Note on War Poetry" because Eliot is trying to express what happened inside himself during the war, in order to show how poetry of significance may eventually arise out of personal traumatic experiences. Most people will not write poems, but what Eliot is saying here pertains not only to the process within a poet but also to what happens within any individual when the force of "the Spirit," operating beyond human control, moves him beyond his "private experience" of suffering into something "universal."

The last section of "East Coker" similarly depicts the movement toward something larger than "private experience." It describes the world becoming "stranger," and the pattern of life and death becoming "more complicated" and requiring much more of the individual. There is an intense "burning in every moment" that will not allow one to live in isolation from the pain of others, or in isolation from the past and future. The strongest image near the end of this second poem of *Four Quartets* is a combination of stillness and movement: "We must be still and still moving / Into another intensity / For a further union, a deeper communion." The intensity of the war forced people out of their comfort zones, forced them to live on the edge, and encouraged them to move toward that ultimate "union" and "communion" with the divine (*Four Quartets* 129).

Eliot himself moved into "another intensity" and "deeper communion" during the war. His experience as an air raid warden, patrolling the streets at night, is recreated in the second movement of "Little Gidding." The scene opens on an almost unearthly setting, in the "uncertain hour" just before dawn, when a seemingly endless night of bombing and flames is about to end. The last bomber, "the dark dove with the flickering tongue" has just disappeared over the faint horizon, and dry leaves rustle on the silent and deserted streets. Though the rising "smoke" comes from fires caused by the bombing, Eliot, on night patrol, discerns a figure. He says, "I met one walking." It is a vision, almost a nightmare, full of images that are deliberately reminiscent of the opening scene of Dante's *Inferno*. As in *Inferno*, an encounter takes place between a living human being and a specter who appears to be a "dead master." The conversation that ensues between Eliot and the ghost reminds him, in the midst of the harsh realities of war, of other harsh realities that he would rather not face. Eliot is forced to recognize that what is wrong in the world at large—the folly that brought the world into this terrible war—is paralleled by the wrong in his own life. Seemingly, he has nowhere to turn, nothing on which to construct meaning and peace. Like so many others in wartime, he is a broken man, an "exasperated spirit." But the ghost suddenly utters a word of hope—"unless." For just a moment, the ghost of the dead master points to another sort of fire, as intense as the fires caused by the bombs—but restorative, rather than destructive: "From wrong to wrong the exasperated spirit / Proceeds, unless restored by that refining fire / Where you must move in measure like a dancer." That is the last thing the ghost says (*Four Quartets* 140–42).

Movement 4 of "Little Gidding" resumes the imagery of fire and depicts the nature of the "refining fire" referred to in movement 2. The passage opens, "The dove descending breaks the air / With flame of incandescent terror" (*Four Quartets* 143). The terrifying dove that bursts over the head of the speaker is both a death-bringing enemy bomber and the life-bringing Holy Spirit. It is the "Spirit" who, in Milton's terms, presided over the creation of the world "with mighty wings outspread" and brooded over "the vast abyss" to engender life (*Paradise Lost* 1.17–21). The message that comes with the descent of the dove is that the only way to escape from "sin and error" and the "despair" that they bring is to make "the choice of pyre or pyre— / To be redeemed from fire by fire" (*Four Quartets* 144). The searing, purifying fire of the Holy Spirit is the means of escape from the burning of sin—the "burning, burning" described in "The Fire Sermon" in *The Waste Land*. We may despair and reject it, or we may hope and receive it. We must choose one fire or the other.

The "terror" caused by the Blitz may, in the purposes of God, also be the terror of redemption; the flames of the burning buildings may, in the purposes of God, also be the cleansing flames of the Holy Spirit. The second stanza of Eliot's two-stanza "dove-descending" passage asserts that it is the severe "Love" of God that has "devised the torment" and has woven the "intolerable shirt of flame" (*Four Quartets* 144). The fire of war brings destruction and despair, but fire also represents divine intervention. Redemption is provided, but it will be by fire. A "choice" must be made about which fire will consume us, and we must be prepared, as the ghost said at the conclusion of movement 2, to "move in measure like a dancer"—that is, to take our place and perform our steps in the great plan, choreographed by God himself (142).

The Mystery of Suffering

Dorothy L. Sayers believed that we must expect to be saved, "not *from* danger and suffering, but *in* danger and suffering" ("What Do We Believe?" 20).[13] Like Lewis and Eliot, Sayers believed in the

potential redemptive value of wartime suffering; she too knew that
we can be "redeemed from fire" only by fire. Although such ideas
may seem to offer poor consolation, and little hope, people truly
did draw strength and purpose from the Christian view of suffering that Sayers expounded, and she was flooded with invitations to
speak and write about the Christian faith (Bray 2).

In "Creed or Chaos?" a talk delivered at a church festival in Derby
in May 1940,[14] Sayers, responding to the agonized question "Why?,"
explained the connection between evil and suffering. She described
the current war as "a war of religion [and] a war of dogma [or]
ideology" (25–26). She said, "The rulers of Germany have seen quite
clearly that [Christian] dogma and ethics are inextricably bound together. Having renounced the dogma they have renounced the ethics
as well—and from their point of view they are perfectly right. They
have adopted an entirely different dogma, whose ethical scheme has
no value for peace or truth, mercy or justice, faith or freedom; and
they see no reason why they should practice a set of virtues incom-
patible with their dogma" (26).

Sayers pointed out that this is something the people of England
had been very slow to understand, and they therefore continued to
expect Germany to behave according to traditional Christian values, "as though that standard was something which [Germany] still
acknowledged." She said that people needed to "grasp that there
is no failure in Germany to live up to her own standards of right
conduct," and to accept the terrifying fact that "what we believe to
be evil, Germany believes to be good, [in] direct repudiation of the
basic Christian dogma on which our Mediterranean civilization,
such as it is, is grounded" ("Creed or Chaos?" 26).

By pinpointing the immorality of Nazism, Sayers was not locat-
ing the problem of evil in Germany. She was identifying it as something rooted in all of us, and something that is especially apparent in the godlessness of modernity. It is pointless, she declared, to
place value on Christian morality unless we are prepared to defend
"the fundamentals of Christian theology" ("Creed or Chaos?" 28).
In this talk, she went on to summarize the Christian view of God,

man, sin, judgment, work, and society. It is impossible, she said, to abolish wars and wickedness by moral law, because of the basic fact of human sinfulness (44). The only solution is grace.

A month later, in a column called "Notes on the Way," Sayers again spoke about the connection between the Christian understanding of sin, grace, and redemption and the suffering caused by war. She pointed out that "the dislocation in human nature [the evil that causes war] cannot be eliminated; it can only be redeemed," and that the "redemption is always, and necessarily, accompanied by . . . sacrifice" ("Notes on the Way" 657). Enduring these sacrifices and the harsh conditions required hardening: the people of England had to become stronger and tougher, but, Sayers admonished, "we can only win the fight by ensuring that the necessary hardening takes place only in our conditions of living, and not in our hearts" (657).

In another 1940 article, "Devil, Who Made Thee?" Sayers worked through the Christian view of good and evil and showed how a great evil like Nazism can occur in a world presided over by an all-loving, all-wise, and all-powerful God. She explained that evil is permitted "in the divine scheme of things" because God intends that we have choice, and because we cannot have good without the possibility of evil. We have the choice of good or evil and we also have the choice of allowing God to "transmute evil into good by the way of grace. . . . [and] use the destruction-tending evil for the creation of new forms of good." Sayers reasoned that when good is redeemed out of evil it is a higher sort of good than "the good that has had no encounter with evil." She argued that "the consequences of evil [can never] . . . be annulled; they can *only* be redeemed." Thus, she affirmed, "the Christian religion is essentially an active and heroic religion [because its] saints are all soldier-saints, engaged in the struggle to wrest victory out of defeat ("Devil, Who Made Thee?" 38–39).

In Sayers's view, the fact that good that *could* emerge—and, for many, *did* emerge—from the horrors of war was much more than a fortunate coincidence. The resilience, courage, and hope that rose from the ashes of bombed London was part of a miraculous, redemptive process—the work of God himself. There was, as Sayers observed, a necessary hardening of the will to endure and the will to go on, but there was also a softening of the heart and an embracing of fearsome redemption.

Redemptive Suffering

Sayers believed, as did many, that the pain of war was given meaning by the eternal value of what was being fought for, but she went even further. What was unusual in her view of suffering was the idea that the individual's suffering could become part of the redemptive process. In several letters to the Rev. John Welch,[15] Sayers argued with passionate conviction for the spiritual significance of suffering, and applied this idea to the suffering of the ordinary individual in wartime. She insisted that, in order to deal rightly with their own suffering, people had to stop viewing themselves as completely innocent "victims of undeserved misfortunes" and to recognize that they share the sinful nature common to all men and the human tendency "to fight against the right order of things" (qtd. in Bray 92). People must understand, Sayers said, that in enduring suffering (including the suffering of war) they are actually bearing, or "carrying," the consequences of both their own sinfulness and the sinfulness of the world in general. In speaking of "carrying" the consequences of sin, Sayers does not mean sheer teeth-gritting endurance; this is something quite different. It involves acknowledging "the relevancy of the Cross" and the fact that "the Power which made and sustains the Universe, with its iron laws, is the Power that makes evil good" (qtd. in Bray 94). There is a choice involved—a spiritual choice of attitude—in which people cease to regard themselves as innocent victims. Suffering the effects of the war, with an awareness of their own fallen state and the "relevancy of the Cross" (94), meant participating in the process of redemption.

By the humble acceptance of that "little daily crucifixion," Sayers believed, people were facilitating the work of God in dealing with evil, but if they refused to take the right attitude in enduring the rationing restrictions and deprivations, "armies are destroyed and battles are lost for lack of coal [and] the evil continues to propagate itself" (qtd. in Bray 87). In the same letter, Sayers explains how the right sort of acceptance of suffering facilitated the atoning work of God in the world:

> If we violently resent the sacrifice, we start a fresh cycle of anger and hatred and trouble. As a matter of fact, *in an emergency,* when we are strongly conscious of our solidarity with ministers and miners, however sinful, because they and we are one in blood, we do feel that the act of atonement is not only expedient, but *right*—for a brief moment we really see the pattern of the Cross as the pattern of life. God, being Incarnate, therefore *solid in blood and nature* with man can "carry the guilt" of mankind because He is at once perfect Innocence and perfect Charity (which we can never be); it is the Incarnation which at one and the same time confirms the validity of the pattern and *gives the power to live the pattern.* (qtd. in Bray 87–88)

Sayers's message to pain-ravaged people, then and now, is that we can, in our personal suffering, identify with Christ in his suffering.

Although these ideas may seem more extreme than the usual Christian teaching on suffering, they do recall the words of St. Paul, indicating that bodily suffering connects us with Christ:

> I bear in my body the marks of the Lord Jesus. (Gal. 6.17)
> Always bearing about in the body the dying of the Lord Jesus, that the life also of Jesus might be made manifest in our body. (2 Cor. 4.10)
> That I may know him, and the power of his resurrection, and the fellowship of his sufferings, being made conformable unto his death. (Phil. 3.10)

Sayers applied such scriptures more literally than most people. She believed that Christ's suffering undergirds and makes possible the vast process of redemption that operates throughout all time and space, and that our little sufferings may become part of the pattern of redemption—the operation by which Christ ultimately subdues all things to himself (Phil. 3.21).

Lewis similarly connected the suffering of the war with the redemptive work of God in individual lives, and with the suffering of Christ himself. In May 1939, he wrote to a friend, "I do not doubt that whatever misery He permits will be for our ultimate good unless, by rebellious will, we convert it to evil. But I get no further than Gethsemane" (*Collected Letters of CSL* 2: 258). Returning to this idea in a later letter, he said he had met "so many innocent sufferers who seem to be gladly offering their pain to God in Christ as part of the Atonement . . . that we can hardly doubt they are being, as St. Paul says, 'made perfect by suffering'" (3: 257).

What Sayers and Lewis believed about the redemptive function of suffering has some resemblance to the Christian virtue of fortitude, in the sense of patient endurance, but it is of a much different and higher order. What it means is most fully explored in Sayers's cathedral play *The Just Vengeance*.[16] First performed in 1946, it was a timely subject, and, as Barbara Reynolds records in her notes to the letters, the play was an enormous success: "The play was scheduled to run for eleven days but the demand for seats was so great that the period was extended for another three. It was attended by Queen Elizabeth [the wife of George VI, known as the Queen Mother during the reign of Elizabeth II] . . . and was seen by an audience of over 10,000 people" (*Letters of DLS* 3: 243).

As noted earlier in the discussion of conversion, the central character is an Airman shot down during World War II. His spirit returns—at the moment of his death—to his home community and to the church he had known from boyhood, Lichfield Cathedral. The Airman is confused and unable to reconcile himself to the immense suffering he has seen in the war; he is bitter and angry about the injustice of war. He is a representative young man, preoccupied with the gross unfairness of it all and regarding himself as one of the many innocent victims of an evil with which they have no innate connection. The Airman realizes that he himself has died, and that—according to traditional religion—some sort of "judgment" must await him. He challenges the very idea of judgment, and protests angrily against the false assumption that people like him have had a clear choice between doing right and doing wrong, and can therefore be held accountable for their choices. Even when we try to do right, he says, someone may get hurt, and "very likely the wrong person" (*The Just Vengeance* 288). And if we choose to do wrong, or do nothing, he exclaims, the outcome is the same in the end. Any action in wartime ends in horrific results: "We drop a bomb / And condemn a thousand people to sudden death, / The guiltless along with the guilty. Or we refuse / To drop a bomb, and condemn a thousand people / To a lingering death in a concentration camp / As surely as if we had set our hands to the warrant" (288). It is no good, he argues, to say we should have waited, and not acted till we had means of making a wiser judgment. "We did wait, / And innocent people died" (288). The alternatives contain no good outcomes. The Airman sums up the mesmerizing dilemma of wartime:

> We have no choice between killing and not killing;
> We can only choose which set of people to kill—
> And even at that, the choice is made for us;
> I did not choose; perhaps I ought to have chosen?
> I was told to go and I went. I killed; I was killed.
> Did any of us deserve it? I don't know.
> You can stand there and say your hands are clean;
> I cannot. But you were lucky. You could be meek
> And go to prison, and not take others with you.
> We who are tied in this damnable cat's cradle
> Where there is no choice except between bloody alternatives
> Have a fraternity which you know nothing about. (*The Just Vengeance* 288)

"Fraternity" becomes a key idea in the drama—an idea that operates on several different levels. The Airman is aware that he is intrinsically connected to others who have suffered, but he is thinking only of the present, of those caught in *this* damnable mess, with only bloody choices. But the idea of the *fraternity of blood* calls up voices from the past—people of Lichfield's past from a wide variety of periods, but all from situations involving suffering. Some were the victims; others, the victimizers. These people form a Chorus who interact with and challenge the Airman.

When the Airman is asked what he believes and attempts to state his own personal creed, beginning with the words "I believe," the voices of the Chorus take over, reciting the Apostles' Creed. At the creedal words "suffered under Pontius Pilate" (*The Just Vengeance* 295), the Airman seizes on the issue that has been his main stumbling block: suffering. He interrupts, telling them to stop. He announces that "suffering" is exactly what he does *not* believe in, and that he sees no sense in the idea of "a suffering God," asking, "Why should anyone suffer?" (295). When he exclaims, "We have seen too many people crucified. . . ." (296), the Chorus interrupts, picking up on the word *crucified* and going on with the recitation of the creed:

> . . . . crucified, dead, and buried; He descended into Hell.
> The third day He rose again from the dead; He ascended
> into Heaven; from thence He shall come to judge the quick
> and the dead. . . . (*The Just Vengeance* 296)

At the word "judge" the Airman recognizes something deeper down that is at the root of his anger: the incompatibility between the harsh reality of suffering on the one hand and the traditional idea of a just and loving God on the other. He shouts,

> Judgment! wait—there is something I want to believe—
> They say there is no such thing as Heaven or Hell,
> Or anything after death; I do not know;
> It seems I am dead, and therefore there must be something.
> Somehow. That being so, I have this to say:
> That if there is going to be judgment, I want justice. (296)

The Airman's angry demands are received with respect and love, and the main action of the play begins to unfold as he is shown scenes from the biblical narrative: the fall of man, the first murder, and the healing ministry of Christ. Throughout this panorama, he is essentially an onlooker, but as the scenes leading up to the crucifixion are shown, the Airman is drawn into the action, and is horrified to find himself joining with the crowd who cried, "Crucify, crucify" (*The Just Vengeance* 337). The shock of his own identification with the murderous crowd forces him to accept his complicity with the sinfulness of mankind. He submits to Christ, saying, "Sir, I understand now what I ought to do. / Am I too late to bring to the wood of your Cross / Whatever in me is guilty and ought to be crucified? / Whatever, being innocent, is privileged to die in Your Death?" (345). Though he has been the victim of the sins of others, he himself is also a sinner, but now a repentant one. Christ invites him to become a disciple: "Take up the Cross and come and follow Me, / For you shall carry the burden of bewilderment: / We shall find one another in the darkest hour of all (345).

The Just Vengeance was a deeply moving experience for the participants and for the audience. One actor affirmed the play's immense relevance, observing, "It was exactly right for the time . . . we had come through the war, but many of our friends had not. Like the Airman, we were bewildered." A reviewer praised its powerful impact, observing that it "shocked the audience into silence, . . . [and was] a feast of dramatic intensity . . . [pointing to] the spiritual and moral power behind the mystery of the universe." Still another comment, this time from an audience member remembering it forty-one years later, affirmed the play's power in conveying the theme of redemption for those "fresh from the war, and only dimly comprehending the world into which one was 'launched back.'" It had, he said, a lasting effect on his "personal pilgrimage" (qtd. in Reynolds, *Passionate Intellect* 92, 94–95, 95).

To the secular mind, in 1945, there seemed to be no way out of the maze of bitterness and disorientation. The way out was dramatized in *The Just Vengeance,* conceived during the intensity of the conflict and staged soon after the war concluded. Dorothy L. Sayers brought the pattern of the times into juxtaposition with the pattern of the cross.

Eliot, in movement 4 of "East Coker," makes the same connection between suffering and redemption, pointing similarly to the "only" way out.[17] Christ is the "wounded surgeon" who alone can bring about our healing. The image of the Cross comes into focus in the last stanza, when the broken body and shed blood of Christ are declared to be our "only" food and drink. The "sickness" that must "grow worse" before it can be cured is our awareness of our own sinfulness and our own complicity in the rudimentary sinfulness of humanity, the sinfulness that caused the suffering of war (*Four Quartets* 127–28).

During the war, many people, even those not particularly religious, clung to the idea that suffering was a sort of spiritual investment—something from which some sort of good would come, in some way, ultimately. This may have been for many a kind of naïve optimism that allowed them to get through horror and devastation, believing there is a purpose in all things and believing in a better future. The Christian view of suffering depicted by Lewis, Eliot, and Sayers is different. It is a wise optimism that hopes for little from this world, but is confident in the goodness of the redemptive purposes of God.

A similar line of thought from centuries earlier shows how firmly rooted these ideas are in the traditional wisdom of the Church. A striking and succinct explanation of the theology of suffering occurs in John Donne's *Meditation 17*—the meditation so famous for the "no man is an island" image. What Donne says about affliction and tribulation in this context is, however, far more profound:

> Affliction is a treasure, and scarce any man hath enough of it. No man hath affliction enough that is not matured and ripened by it, and made fit for God by that affliction. If a man carry treasure in bullion, or in a wedge of gold, and have none coined into current money, his treasure will not [cover his expenses] as he travels. Tribulation is treasure in the

nature of it, but it is not current money in the use of it, except we get nearer and nearer our home, heaven, by it. (440–41)

Lewis, Eliot, and Sayers believed in the redemptive potential of suffering and believed, like Donne, that affliction and tribulation are potential treasures. Whether the purchase was worth the high cost depended on what the sufferer did with the suffering, on whether he—through it—came into contact with the "pattern of the Cross."

The Cost of the War for Eliot, Lewis, and Sayers

World War II was costly in every sense. No one could avoid paying a high price, not even those who had the stability of a deep Christian faith. The war cost Eliot his comfortable pattern of life, forcing him into an exhausting routine of working as a publisher by day and as an air raid warden by night. It cost Sayers the relative ease of the comfortable point she had reached in her writing career before the war, writing only in literary genres in which she was experienced and accomplished.

The war meant loss of comfort and security for Lewis as well. It cost him his privacy, as he opened his home to accommodate children evacuated from London. More painfully, his deep commitment to supporting the war effort through public speaking required that he travel almost constantly. He journeyed back and forth to London for the live BBC broadcasts and undertook even more arduous traveling to speak to soldiers in military camps. Jill Freud, one of the young evacuees staying at Lewis's house during the war, recalled what she knew of his wartime travel:

He did lectures in RAF and Army bases all over the country with terrible train journeys to get to them. And he suffered dreadfully from sinus . . . and he was always going off on these long journeys in tremendous pain. The trains were cold and then they'd stop for half an hour and then start again. All the lights were blue'd [to fulfill] the blackout regulations. (qtd. in Phillips 133)

Lewis's wartime writing also meant the loss of the approval of his Oxford colleagues. As we noted in chapter 2, the academic community of Oxford strongly disapproved of his Christian writing. Though Lewis was very aware of the rejection such speaking and writing would produce, he felt compelled to do it, particularly because of the gravity of the wartime situation (Phillips 222). He saw the "claims of God" to be, as he said in his University Sermon of September 1939, "inexorable" ("Learning in War-Time" 31). The result of his choice was that, although his scholarly publications and his prestige as a lecturer surpassed that of his colleagues at Oxford, he was never given the promotion to full professorship.

Although war was costly for Lewis, it also brought good things into his life—changes that were crucial in positive ways. It brought him, as George Sayer (his friend and biographer) pointed out, the close association with children without which the Narnia books may never have been written (Sayer 269), and it modified his perception of himself as, primarily, an academic whose religious writing had to remain on the fringe of his life. The war jolted Lewis out of his comfortable pattern of life as an Oxford don. He said, in a letter to a friend, "For me, personally, [the war] has come in the nick of time: I was just beginning to get too well settled in my profession, too successful, and probably self-complacent" (Sayer 266–67).

Some of the costliness of wartime was not a matter of choice—not the choosing one action over another, not the performing of courageous and noble deeds. Instead it was the toll taken simply by the trauma of the war. That is what was so difficult for people. When there is seemingly no choice to be made, nothing that one can do except suffer and endure, it seems there is no opportunity for choosing the virtuous path over the sinful one. But the idea that one has no choice is false. Free will is always in operation, even in the seemingly passive and trapped position of being a victim of German bombs.

Eliot deals with this dilemma in *Murder in the Cathedral,* when the main character, Thomas Becket, is contemplating the martyr's death that almost certainly awaits him. He recognizes that suffering in the right way, accepting what comes with a patient spirit, is itself a choice. Such godly *in*action becomes, paradoxically, action—and sometimes action of great magnitude. Like Thomas Becket, many of those who suffered through the war would come to know "that action is suffering / And suffering is action," and that the *active* role of being the doer of an action and the *passive* role of being the receiver of an action are both fixed within the sovereignty of God—fixed "In an eternal action, an eternal patience /To which all must consent" (*Murder in the Cathedral* 182). Such consent to God's purposes, though it seems passive, is—in truth—a costly *action*.

In the last movement of "Little Gidding" (movement 5), Eliot observes that "any action" is potentially a drastic and crucial one—"a step to the block, to the fire, down the sea's throat." Such actions are a kind of death, a coming to the end of oneself. But they may also be a beginning, a point from which "we start." From such a point of decision and consent we can move onward and upward. "We shall not cease from exploration," Eliot says. The goal to be reached is, he affirms, "A condition of complete simplicity / (Costing not less than everything)." Here, in the closing lines of this last movement of "Little Gidding," the flames of wartime bombing are modulated into the redemptive fire that heals and restores, and makes sense of all we have endured. "Little Gidding" concludes with consoling words quoted from Juliana of Norwich, "And all shall be well and / All manner of thing shall be well." Finally, the torturous "fire" of all our sufferings and the rose-like beauty of all the joy and love we have ever known or longed for are harmonized: "When the tongues of flames are in-folded / Into the crowned knot of fire / And the fire and the rose are one" (*Four Quartets* 145).

7

The Journey to Joy

Life as a Pilgrimage to Heaven

✝ ✝ ✝

The movement of the soul through time and toward God is often seen as a physical journey across a treacherous landscape. This traveling motif is the dominating feature in works of widely different sorts, ranging from Bunyan's simple narrative in *Pilgrim's Progress* to Robert Browning's complex and disorienting poem "Childe Roland to the Dark Tower Came." The image of the Christian life as a pilgrimage, so prevalent in medieval and Renaissance literature, developed in the early centuries of Church history, but the roots of the idea go back even farther. The New Testament depicts the follower of Christ as a citizen of heaven, a stranger and foreigner traveling through this present world en route to a better one. Augustine's concept of the journey to heaven, in his great work *City of God,* is based in part on the Old Testament account of the pilgrimage of the Israelites to the Promised Land, and on the reference to Abraham in Hebrews 11 as an alien in this world looking forward to a heavenly city (Heb. 11.8–10).

Traveling Homeward

The most impressive use of the journey motif in Christian literature occurred in the fourteenth century, when Dante used it in *The Divine Comedy* to depict what Sayers called "the drama of the soul's choice" (Introduction to *The Comedy of Dante Aligieri: Hell (L'Inferno)* 11). Dante, who is both author and traveler, is taken on a three-part journey: first (in *Inferno*), downward through the lostness of Hell, and out from the bottom of the pit; second (in *Pugatorio*), upward through the gate of conversion, and up a mountain representing the levels of sanctification to reach the Earthly Paradise, the recovered Eden; and third (in *Paradiso*), into the celestial realm peopled with the hosts of the redeemed and, finally, to a brief, glorious glimpse of God himself.

Dante's use of the allegory of a journey resonated with Lewis, Sayers, and Eliot. Lewis described the last part of *The Divine Comedy* as suggesting "spacious gliding movement," recognizing its rare achievement of depicting, simultaneously, "the freedom and liquidity of empty space and the triumphant certainty of movement" (*Collected Letters of CSL* 1: 857).[1] In her introduction to her translation of the first canto of Dante's work, *Inferno,* Sayers elucidates Dante's use of travel as an allegory and the biblical inspiration for it. She quotes from a letter written by Dante to his patron, explaining that "the exodus of the Children of Israel from Egypt in the days of Moses" may be seen as an allegory of "our redemption wrought by Christ" (Introduction to *The Comedy of Dante Aligieri: Hell (L'Inferno)* 15). *The Divine Comedy,* she observed, is "an allegory of the Way to God" that has a universal quality, in that it uses the situation of a particular man in a particular time and place to represent "all Heaven and Earth and Hell" (19). Dante set himself, Sayers said, "to write the great Comedy of Redemption and of the return of all things by the Way of Self-Knowledge and Purification, to the beatitude of the Presence of God" (49).

Eliot, similarly intimate with *The Divine Comedy,* advises the reader of Dante to "clear his mind" of any prejudice against allegory and to accept the fact that it was a "mental habit" of an earlier era, that, "when raised to the point of genius [could] make a great poet as well as a great mystic or saint" ("Dante" 243). Eliot understood that the allegorical mode of describing a journey is what makes Dante appealing, because it allows the reader to travel along with him, and see through his eyes (243).

Eliot's comments on *The Divine Comedy* recognize that, although modern readers have difficulty with some forms of allegory, the idea of a journey is easily assimilated as a representation of an individual life span, or a portion of it, because journeying represents the linear nature of time as most of us perceive it. The ideas of pilgrimage and quest overlap with the idea of journeying, but the image of journeying—traveling across a physical space—is the simplest, broadest, and most open-ended. Pilgrimage and quest have more specific connotations: both suggest that the journey is directed toward a goal. In the case of pilgrimage, the journey is associated with spiritual aspiration and the expectation of arriving at a destination that is sacred, even heavenly. A quest is a search for something not necessarily religious or spiritual, although many of the best-known accounts of quests have been spiritual in nature.

The Grail Quest—a scenario associated with, but predating, the Arthurian legend—is the underlying image of Eliot's most celebrated work, *The Waste Land*. The phrase "the Waste Land" was used in Thomas Malory's fifteenth-century retelling of Arthurian legend, *Morte d'Arthur,* to describe the terrain traversed by those seeking the Holy Grail. The term was taken up by others writing of the Grail quest. Lyndall Gordon tells us that from the earliest stages of his work on *The Waste Land,* "Eliot had in mind the traditional form of the spiritual journey through deathly ordeals" (*Imperfect Life* 148).

C. S. Lewis's depiction of journeys through "deadly ordeals" in his Narnia books reflects his lifelong fondness for Arthurian legend. George Sayer records that, in adolescence, Lewis's imagination was so captivated by the legends of the knights of the Round Table that he addressed his friend Arthur Greeves as "Galahad" and believed that "life without a copy of Malory's *Morte d'Arthur* . . . would be quite unbearable" (Sayer 103–4). Lewis delighted in the kind of chivalric adventures found in Malory and other reworkings of Arthurian material, particularly Edmund Spenser's *Fairie Queene*. Although Lewis's seven Narnia books do not attempt to recast incidents or characters from the canon of Arthurian legend, elements of the Grail quest tales hover in the background of the challenging and dangerous journeys the books depict. In writing the Narnia books, Lewis had in mind the same archetype that Eliot used—the journey of the Christian through the Waste Land of this world in obedience to a spiritual calling. The quest is rooted in passionate longings, is painfully long, and is beset by struggle, ignorance, and discouragement. Yet the ordeal is worth it because of the joy that awaits the traveler when redemption is complete and the destination is reached.[2]

The Call of Beauty

Movement across a geographical expanse is the dominant image in Lewis's first work of prose fiction, the allegorical *Pilgrim's Regress*. As in Bunyan's *Pilgrim's Progress,* the hero turns from his own house, and falteringly makes his way across a bewildering and dangerous terrain. But unlike Bunyan's hero, Lewis's protagonist John sets out, not in fear of damnation and a desire to "flee from the wrath to come," but in longing for something almost indescribable but painfully beautiful. John has had a vision, catching a glimpse of something his heart yearns for. The image is fleeting and insubstantial, but it appears to resemble a peaceful and beautiful island. What is most unmistakable is the intensity of the desire it inspires; it is "a sweetness and a pang so piercing that instantly he forgot his father's house" (Lewis, *Pilgrim's Regress* 34). Glimpsing it for the first time, John believes that he knows now what he wants. He leaves home, and sets out in search of it (35).

This loosely autobiographical work, written when Lewis was a new convert, anticipates his later, more literal, account of his personal spiritual journey. In *Surprised by Joy,* published in 1955, he speaks literally, rather than allegorically, of specific episodes in early life which initiated a spiritual longing that never left him. He said that he "desired with almost sickening intensity" something that he could not describe, but that defined the "central story" of his life. Paradoxically, Lewis viewed this "unsatisfied desire" as "more desirable than any other satisfaction," adding, "I call it Joy, which is here a technical term and must be sharply distinguished both from

Happiness and from Pleasure. . . . I doubt whether anyone who has tasted it would ever . . . exchange it for all the pleasures in the world" (*Surprised by Joy* 17–18). As he grew older, he became more aware of what the longing meant for him, and for others who experience it, explaining, "Joy was not a deception. Its visitations were rather the moments of clearest consciousness we had, when we became aware of our fragmentary and phantasmal nature and ached for that impossible reunion. . . . It matters more that Heaven should exist than that we should ever get there" (222).

Lewis's longing, recounted in *The Pilgrim's Regress* and *Surprised by Joy*, is connected with intense moments of heightened conscious-ness: moments containing an almost physical apprehension of things of supreme beauty and significance, moments when one's own frailty touches stupendous power. What is experienced in such moments is essentially a longing for heaven, the place that is our true home—the supremely desirable and supremely desired destination.

In *Four Quartets* Eliot depicts such moments of intense aware-ness and of unexplainable ecstasy that begin in early life, and that recur as moments of heightened spiritual consciousness. In "Burnt Norton" (the first of the four poems composing *Four Quartets*), the scene is a garden visited by an unidentified "we." The garden contains echoes of the past, and is inhabited by presences that are described in the first movement of the poem as "dignified" and "in-visible" and also by the presences of children. The cry of a bird— "Quick, . . . find them, find them"—seems a summons to follow the bird, and to try to find something or someone that is just around the corner, just outside the normal range of vision and consciousness. The bird urges the listeners to follow quickly, as though playing a game of tag, or hide-and-seek: "Quick, said the bird, find them, find them, / Round the corner. Through the first gate, / Into our first world, shall we follow / The deception of the thrush?" The phrase "our first world" implies the world of childhood (*Four Quartets* 117–18).

The bird's invitation in this passage suggests the desire to roll back the calendar and return to innocence. But the idea that it is possible to do so may be a mere "deception"—an invitation that it would be foolish to accept. The leaves of the trees and shrubbery are "full of children," children who are hidden, and laughing with excitement. The bird urges, "Go, go, go," but then momentum ends, and the tone of the poem is clouded by the limiting observation: "human kind / Cannot bear very much reality." Although there is joy and exuberance in the scene, there is also solemnity and sadness, because the glimpse of perfect joy and innocence is a glimpse of the lost Eden—a "reality" that we cannot bear very much of (*Four Quartets* 118).

Glimpses of Heaven

Such "timeless moments" (as Eliot calls them later in "Little Gidding," the final poem of *Four Quartets*) occur when one is connected to something outside of time. They occur near the axis of all things, that Eliot calls, in movement 2 of "Burnt Norton," "the still point of the turning world." As we approach this "still point," we experience something that is not a bodily sensation, even though we have not been removed from our bodily existence. Eliot says it is "neither flesh" (that is, not a literal bodily experience) "nor fleshless" (that is, not totally separated from what we perceive through the senses). It is a point that likewise is neither absence of movement nor movement: "Neither from nor towards; at the still point, there the dance is, /But neither arrest nor movement. And do not call it fixity." Similarly, in temporal terms, such a moment is neither progression nor regression, ascent nor descent. It is a point outside our normal temporal existence—"where past and future are gathered." These rare moments of connectedness to the divine are, Eliot believes, essential to the spiritual life: "Except for the point, the still point, / There would be no dance, and there is only the dance" (*Four Quartets* 119).

The image of the dance is difficult, but quite important. Eliot's use of *dance* in this context is reminiscent of Yeats's haunting question at the end of the poem "Among School Children": "How can we know the dancer from the dance?" (Yeats 185). Yeats's question is

asking, "How can we distinguish between 'the dancer'—the movements of the person dancing (or the actions of an individual life)—
and the larger pattern—the divinely choreographed 'dance'?" Eliot
uses the dance image similarly in movement 2 of "Burnt Norton," in
the statement "Except for the point, the still point, / There would be
no dance, and there is only the dance." This alludes to the supremely
ordered plan of God (the eternal dance) as the ultimate reference
point for every gesture and movement within our temporal existence
(*Four Quartets* 119). The word *dance* also suggests a rotating movement that can, in turn, connect with the "still point" that is the axis
on which all of reality turns.[3]

Movement 2 of "Burnt Norton" presents these divine moments
as essentially mysterious occurrences, defying analysis: "I can only
say, *there* we have been: but I cannot say where. / And I cannot say,
how long, for that is to place it in time." This connectedness to the
divine affords brief periods of release from the bondage of our selfhood, when we have "inner freedom" from our usual motivations
and compulsions, and when we feel encompassed and borne up by
grace. Eliot describes it as being surrounded by "a grace of sense, a
white light still and moving." He describes the moment as "*Erhe-
bung,*" a German term suggesting sublime elevation or exaltation
of the spirit because of contact with the divine. Eliot connects these
intensely charged points in time with changed perception: the ability to perceive "a new world / And the old made explicit, understood." Through these elevated moments, we are able to perceive
new things, and we are able to perceive the old more clearly and
wisely (*Four Quartets* 119).

Like Lewis, Eliot connects such experiences with ecstasy, but it is
"partial ecstasy" compared to what will come at the end of the journey. Both men felt the mysterious and exhilarating pull Eliot describes
in the closing passage of "Burnt Norton" (movement 5): "Sudden in
a shaft of sunlight . . . / There rises the hidden laughter /. . . . Of children in the foliage / Quick now, here, now, always." These moments
of sudden joy and clarity are perhaps the most significant of all human experiences; they stir up precious memories, recalling the merri-

ment and laughter of childhood. "Burnt Norton" ends by setting up a contrast between these timeless moments and the mundane moments that make up most of our days: "Ridiculous the waste sad time / Stretching before and after." These closing lines suggest that the glimpse of transcendence that we receive in such moments of ecstasy makes us feel the absurdity of much of the sad and futile time spent trudging through the Waste Land (*Four Quartets* 122).

Homesick for Eden

It is the initial longing that gives impetus to the journey. Paradoxically, it is both a journey forward to something never yet experienced and a return journey, back to our place of origin, the place which is truly "home." It is a journey onward and upward to a heavenly destination beyond anything we could ever have experienced or even imagined we experienced in the past, but it is also a return journey, a recovery of the lost Eden-home of all humanity. We have all lost Eden. We are all homesick for the perfect beauty of that lost garden.

Lewis's poem "The Ecstasy" offers us a foretaste of heaven. It depicts the entering of a garden, a place of perfect beauty, and moving forward, toward "the centre of / The garden, hand in hand, finger on lip." There are fountains on both sides of us, and "the air grows warmer." It is very silent. The forward movement continues: "So on we fared and forded / A brook with lilies bordered" and eventually arrive at the "quiet centre." We have passed beyond the burdensome sphere of time, and come to the place where "True stillness dwells and will not change, / Never has changed, never begins or ends." But it has just been a vision or a foretaste, and in the last lines of the poem we are jolted back to present reality; suddenly we are back outside the garden, "back in the wavering world" (*Poems* 36–37).

Lewis describes another unusual experience of joy is described in "The Day with a White Mark," but the joy is briefer and less visionary. The poem begins, "All day I have been tossed and whirled in a preposterous happiness." The speaker speculates that the cause of this unexpected delight (on a very ordinary day) might even be the movement of an angel somewhere in his vicinity. He asks if his unexplained happiness is caused by "the cloudily crested, fifty-league-long wave / Of a journeying angel's transit roaring over and through my heart?" There is no logical connection between his circumstances and the feeling of "preposterous happiness." The poem reviews the dismal facts of his present situation: his garden is ruined, his holidays are canceled, and other "miseries" abound. Reason tells him that his joy is out of line with reality, but nonetheless he continues to feel "ripplings and dewy sprinklings of delight," that are partly connected to "memory." He recalls the "inaccessible longings and ice-sharp joys that shook [his] body" in early life. The whole experience is a kind of "sudden heaven" —a foretaste of the heavenly garden at the end of the journey (*Poems* 28–29).

Eliot uses similar garden imagery to express the longings of the heart, longings for something precious and elusive. In the first movement of *The Waste Land,* "The Burial of the Dead," there is a passage that suggests desire for and failure to grasp the beauty of romantic love. The German passage, *"Frisch weht der Wind / Der Heimat zu, / Mein Irisch Kind, / Wo weilest du?"* means "Wind fresh from my homeland, my Irish girl, where are you?" After this cry of heartache for the lost beauty of home and sweetheart, there is a conversation between a woman and a man. A young woman says, "You gave me hyacinths first a year ago." The man's response expresses his inability to seize this opportunity to embrace beauty and love: "Yet when we came back, late, from the hyacinth garden / . . . I could not / Speak, and my eyes failed, I was neither / Living nor dead, and I knew nothing." The intensity of the experience offered overwhelms him: he feels he is "looking into the heart of light," into ultimate "silence" (*The Waste Land* 30).

In contrast, in Eliot's poem "Marina," written years later, the beauty and happiness represented by a young girl *is* embraced by the speaker. Using characters from Shakespeare's play *Pericles,* the poem depicts the reunion of Pericles with his daughter Marina, whose form and face bring intense joy and take him beyond himself into a rich and deep silence ("Marina" 72–73). Similarly, the "lucid stillness" encountered in the third movement of "Burnt Norton" is capable of "Turning shadow into transient beauty / With slow rotation suggesting permanence." The beauty that is "transient" because it is of this world points to that which has "permanence" because it is not of this world. Movement 4 of "Burnt Norton" ends with an image of natural beauty, that of light reflecting off the colors of a "kingfisher's wing," leading to an intense experience of silence and stillness: "After the kingfisher's wing / Has answered light to light, and is silent, the light is still / At the still point of the turning world." Finally, movement 5 of "Burnt Norton" shows how such transcendent stillness can arise from a different source of earthly beauty—the beauty of art, like that of Chinese vases and violin music. The experience of such things can sometimes reach the "stillness" where we become aware of the "co-existence" of the temporal and the eternal (*Four Quartets* 121).

Characters in Eliot's plays long for such experiences. Sometimes what they desire is the unspoiled loveliness of the unfallen world, the perfection of a supremely beautiful garden. In *The Family Reunion,* Harry feels trapped in the Waste Land, trapped by "shrieking forms in a circular desert" (277), and wants to go "through the little door . . . [into] the rose-garden" (277). In doing so he will be free for the first time, and will have "come into a quiet place" (278). In Act 2 of *The Cocktail Party,* Celia describes herself as "lost" and longing for "ecstasy" (363). In *The Confidential Clerk,* the protagonist, Colby, believes that people need a secret garden somewhere in which to find themselves and be themselves (49–50). But the Edenic garden that Colby alludes to is not just a place of self-discovery; it is a place of relationship with God. Colby's cravings are spiritual; he does not want to use his garden merely as a place of escape. He says, "If I were religious, God would walk in my garden / And that would make the world outside real / And acceptable, I think" (51). In such scenes, Eliot uses the longing for a garden to represent the inner sterility and isolation of modern secular man, alienated from all that would truly satisfy his deepest self.

Traversing the Waste Land

Eliot's concern with sterility and isolation in the plays he wrote in later life was the same concern he expressed earlier in his depiction of the bleakness of the modern world in *The Waste Land*. A garden suggests the spiritual perfection of the unfallen world. The antithesis of a garden is a bleak, infertile terrain suggesting spiritual sterility and destitution. Jewell Spears Brooker identifies the barren landscape of *The Waste Land* as the dominant and most important thread running through the barrage of images that make up the poem:

> The single and most important group of images in Eliot's poem are those having to do with literal wastelands, for these refer to the ancient myth that provides Eliot with his title and his major symbol. The myth describes a land cursed with sterility, a land in which crops will not grow, woman cannot bear children, cattle cannot reproduce. The sterility in the land and its occupants is connected in some mysterious way to impotence in the ruler of the land. The ruler, who is both a god and a king has been wounded in his genitals (by such causes as war, sickness, old age), and this sexual incapacity affects his entire kingdom by depriving it of regenerative power. Just as the curse on the divine ruler has blighted his people and land, so would his healing lead to their health. (Brooker 240–41)

Eliot identified the work of James Frazer and Jessie Weston[4] as the scholarly sources influencing his understanding of the Grail myth and the role of the wounded king, often called the Fisher King. However, Brooker points out that Eliot's interest, unlike that of Frazer and Weston, lies not in the myth itself but in "the myth's power to suggest truths about contemporary life and in its claim to support an underlying unity for modern society" (242). She proposes that Eliot's use of the myth "suggests a mysterious but particular relationship between the wounding of God and the existence of a wasteland" (243).

The Waste Land is dense with imagery of loneliness, futility, and disappointment; but it is the fifth and last movement, "What the

Thunder Said," that alludes to figures traversing a death-ridden land-scape. The most important of the poem's faintly drawn characters, or presences, are the questing knights of the Grail legend. The Holy Grail (if it could be found) would be restorative and nurturing, like a garden, but the journey in search of it takes the knights through regions of utter desolation. The knights toil through "mountains of rock," past "mud-cracked houses," "empty cisterns," and "tumbled graves," only to find the Grail chapel[5] standing "empty" and to realize that "there is no water" (*The Waste Land* 48).

For the knights of *The Waste Land* there does not seem to be a clear or satisfying conclusion to the quest. Yet, near the end of the poem, there are suggestions of the hope implicit in the Grail myth: hope that healing *may* come to the king and to the land. As Brooker explains, "This healing [as the myth depicts it] could be accomplished by undergoing certain trials and by asking certain questions about the meaning of life. The healing, interestingly, happens because the questor asks the right questions rather than because he receives the right answers" (243). Near the end of "What the Thunder Said," Eliot alludes to a different myth, a Hindu myth, containing a scene of questions and answers. The asking of questions allows for hope, and hope is implicit in the fact that the rain finally does come and the Thunder that accompanies the rain speaks words that offer some spiritual wisdom.

Imagery of traveling through a figurative Waste Land recurs in Eliot's later works, but with firmer hopefulness. In *The Cocktail Party*, Celia describes herself as being like "a child / Lost in a forest, wanting to go home," but there is also with her "the inconsolable memory / Of the treasure [she] went into the forest to find" (363). She connects that treasure with "moments" of "ecstasy"—moments of "intensity" full of a "vibration of delight" (363). She is craving the home that she has never known, but for which she was made and which she finally finds. Though it culminated in painful death, Celia's dark journey brings her to the home she had long craved. It is a journey to joy.

Lewis, similarly, depicts travelers seeking that which is ultimately beautiful, and journeying through a vast, desolate landscape. In *The*

Pilgrim's Regress, the protagonist, John, traverses a cold, rocky, and barren land. He encounters a few individuals who wistfully believe they have a garden, but the climate is so severe and the soil so poor that all they can grow are radishes. It is a travesty of a true garden. A deep gorge separates John from a region that appears far richer and warmer. Hoping to find a way to cross the gorge, he and his two companions travel northward, to still more miserable regions (122–23). This is the wrong way to go; frustrated, they must turn south again. There is no clear set of directions, no reliable map.

Traveling without Directions

In many tales of quest, the pilgrim is given little direction and minimal information on the nature of the road ahead. This was true even of Jesus's disciples. When Jesus told them, "You know the way to where I am going," Thomas, in frustration, protested, "Lord, we do not know where you are going. How can we know the way?" (John 14.4 *ESV*). Although Jesus had told them earlier, "I am the Way," Thomas's dismay is understandable. Lacking specific directions, and being unable to anticipate what the future would hold, the disciples were forced to rely solely on Christ. He promised never to leave them, but to continue to teach them and be with them (John 14.18 *ESV*), but it was still unsettling to be told so little about the direction the journey would take.

In *The Pilgrim's Regress,* the problems John faces because of the initial lack of clear directions are compounded by the fact that he is misdirected by many of the people he encounters. He frequently misunderstands the truths he is shown, and begins to doubt the reliability of his deepest desire—the desire that was the initial impetus for the journey. He sets out from his home, in the land of Puritania, to journey west because he wishes to escape the tyranny of the Landlord, whose castle is in the mountains to the east. Stories of the cruelty of this Landlord and the harsh arbitrariness of his rules haunted John's childhood. The young man's dual motivation for

the journey is to escape the tyrant in the east and to find the beautiful Island in the west, which he had glimpsed in a vision in early life,
and for which he passionately longs. Since he hates the Landlord
and loves the Island, it is clear that he must travel westward. But,
like our world, the world of *The Pilgrim's Regress* is round. Paradoxically, in traveling west, John has been heading away from the
Landlord and toward the Landlord simultaneously.

For much of John's difficult journey, he is helped by a friend
called Vertue, who has no definite destination but is firmly committed to the journey for its own sake. With Vertue as his companion,
John often avoids dangers, but eventually Vertue weakens, sickens,
and abandons him. When John encounters an old woman called
Mother Kirk (representing the Church) and learns that he must
cross a dangerous chasm, he ceases to be directionless, and begins
to understand the way that he must go. Yet now, even with definite
direction, he finds the going harder than ever, as he moves along
a narrow ledge with an abyss on one side and a towering cliff on
the other. His way is soon barred by a spur of rock, and to mount
it, he must climb up unstable boulders. He is overwhelmed with
confusion, shame, sorrow, and (above all) fear. It seems his journey
is at an end; he can advance no further. He thinks, "I will sit here
and rest, till I get my wind, and then I will go back." But suddenly
a Man calls to him from above and urges him onward.

"I cannot get up the rocks," said John.

"I will give you a hand," said the Man. And he came down till he
was within reach of John, and held out his hand. And John grew pale
as paper and nausea came upon him.

"It's now or never," said the Man.

Then John set his teeth and took the hand that was offered him.
. . . What with pushing and pulling the Man got him right up to the
top and there he fell down on his belly in the grass to pant and to
groan at the pains in his chest. When he sat up the Man was gone.
(*The Pilgrim's Regress* 179–80)

John's journey is still far from over; but he realizes he can advance no further on his own. In bitterness of soul, he cries, "Help. Help. I want Help." He realizes with horror that he has been praying, and that it is only the Landlord who can send help (181). The Man returns, and gives him bread and guidance for his next movements. From this point on, the journey is easier and the right direction clearer, but in spite of this, John feels trapped and resentful. He believes that the "return of the Landlord" means he must give up his hope of reaching the Island. He thinks that there still may be such a place of beauty and joy, but knows that he is "no longer free to spend his soul in seeking it, but must follow whatever designs the Landlord had for him." He is now thinking that the ultimate that one can experience—what he calls the "last of things"—does not seem to be much like a place (such as an island), but seems to be more like "a person."

John is wrong in thinking that his desire for the Island has been completely invalidated, but right in realizing that, for now, he cannot focus on reaching it. Talking with the hermit called History helps him understand the things he encountered on his journey, and the rightness and wrongness of the various philosophies he has been exposed to. History makes it clear that those who never travel "never learn anything" (190); that the Landlord is the source of the beautiful pictures—like that of the Island—that create profound desires (193); and that such a desire "is a starting point from which one road leads home and a thousand roads lead into the wilderness" (196). John's journey finally leads him out of the Waste Land; he takes the road that leads "home."

The journeys in Lewis's Narnia books are similarly fraught with difficulties because of the absence of detailed maps and clear directions. Disorientation and discouragement frequently overwhelm the children who are brought into Narnia to undertake missions they cannot fully understand. They are frequently lost, confused, exhausted, and upset. It may seem surprising that Lewis chose to present his young readers with such worrying, and often inglorious, scenarios, and even more surprising that these children—who are seeking to do good and be obedient to the will of Aslan—have not been provided in advance with ample information and clear guidance. Yet the children's uncertainty about where they are going and how to get there does not detract from the appeal of the stories. Although the settings and events are those of fantasy, the plotlines ring true because they frankly represent the confusion and misunderstanding that so often occur during life's most important ventures.

The struggle of weary and uncertain travelers is also depicted memorably in Eliot's poem "Journey of the Magi." The poem is a dramatic monologue, and the speaker is one of the Wise Men, who is recalling, many years later, the journey to Bethlehem. Oddly, the poem's emphasis is not on the Magi's arrival, worship, and presentation of gifts to the Christ child, but instead on the struggle of the journey. The Magus recounts the difficulties of their travels, speaking of the cold and sharpness of the weather at that time of year—"the dead of winter"—the length of the journey, and the exhaustion of the camels. In the midst of deprivation and frustration, they recall the comforts of home, and almost regret having left their luxuries to embark on such an unpromising expedition. It gets harder toward the end, and voices in their ears whisper that the journey is "all folly." Although the physical conditions of their travel get a little better as they near their destination, they really have "no information." They believe that initially they were being "led," yet it often seems that they are traveling blindly, with directions that are maddeningly insufficient ("Journey of the Magi" 68–69). But they travel on.

What they find when they finally reach "the place" is, astonishingly, described as merely "satisfactory" ("Journey of the Magi" 69). The Christian reader—expecting the familiar Magi storyline with the emphasis on the gifts they present and the worship they offer—is shocked that, after this detailed account of the struggle, Eliot does not even mention the joy that (as Matthew records) the Magi felt as the star led them to the place where the child was.

In this poem, Eliot's purpose is not to recreate the traditional image of the Wise Men as mythic figures, who come mysteriously and picturesquely, and then disappear completely. They were, Eliot is insisting, historical characters, real men inhabiting the real world of the biblical Middle East. The poem traces the probable line of thought of these divinely led questers, and the probable result of their experience. The traveling was hard enough, and fraught with uncertainties. Harder still, in Eliot's re-creation of the experience, was their encounter with the newborn Christ child. The Magus recalls and ponders, "All this was a long time ago, I remember, / And I would do it again" ("Journey of the Magi" 69).

Yet, having said that, he abruptly changes the tone of his utterance, not once, but twice. The musing tone of "long time ago . . . would do it again" is abandoned, and he shifts to the imperative voice, suggesting that he is about to say something firm that needs to be recorded. He speaks in a *command*, "but set down / This," and repeats the phrase a second time for emphasis. We are expecting a *statement*—and one of some clarity and importance. Instead, we get another change, as he poses a *question:* "were we led all that way for / Birth or Death?" The question affirms that the Wise Men had understood the journey as something they were "led" to undertake, but it surprises us that they associate it so closely with death. "There was a Birth, certainly, / . . . I had seen birth and death, / But had thought they were different; this Birth was / Hard and bitter agony for us, like Death, our death" ("Journey of the Magi" 69).

The speaker seems to grasp, intuitively, that Christ's death would be even more important than his birth. However, the death spoken of is also their own death; the agony involved is their agony. He says, "We returned to our places, these Kingdoms, / But no longer at ease here." They can no longer feel at home in these old Eastern cultures that are part of the "Before Christ" world, what the speaker calls "the old dispensation." The Wise Men, as Eliot envisions them, are standing on the crack between the two dispensations. They have died to what they used to be, but—because they have not been granted a full revelation of Christ's Kingdom—they are unclear about what it is they have been reborn into. Having returned to their former kingdoms, they now know that they do not belong there, among what they now see as "alien people, clutching their gods" ("Journey of the Magi" 69). The journey brought them into the presence of the true God.

Theirs was a life-changing journey, but a tortuous one, with little clarity to it. For the Magus, who is looking back on the experience years later, there are still more questions than answers. The poem ends disconcertingly, with the Magus reaching no firm conclusion, and just waiting for death. Yet the last lines make two important points. First, the Magus says emphatically that he would "do it again." The journey was worth it: the pain and uncertainty they endured count for nothing compared to what was gained. Second, the final object of the quest has not yet been attained. The poem ends with the Magus saying he will be "glad of another death," because then he will have arrived at the true end of the journey and achieved full understanding and lasting joy ("Journey of the Magi" 69).

Eliot and Lewis both depict life as a spiritual journey fraught with uncertainties. We resemble John in *The Pilgrim's Regress,* the children in the Narnia books, and the Magi: we have minimal understanding of the road we travel. We cannot see very far ahead and cannot comprehend the full import of what we encounter. While we do not travel haphazardly, we err most when we envision ourselves as being in control. Lewis, in his poem "A Pageant Played in Vain," describes such futile posturing, and the assumption of being in control:

> Holding what seems the helm,
> I make a show to steer,
> But winds, for worse or better, overwhelm
> My purpose, and I veer. (*Poems* 96)

Eliot uses similar imagery of steering a boat to illustrate our need to have a higher power control the direction of our lives. The concluding section of *The Waste Land* expands on the cryptic message spoken by "the Thunder." In the elaboration on the word *Damyata* — loosely translated as "control" — Eliot uses the image of traveling in a boat to suggest, *not* that we should each take control of our own lives,[6] but to illustrate our dependency on "expert" hands to rightly direct the journey of our lives:

> The boat responded
> Gaily, to the hand expert with sail and oar
> The sea was calm, your heart would have responded
> Gaily, when invited, beating obedient
> To controlling hands. (*The Waste Land* 49–50)

Just eleven lines after this point, *The Waste Land* concludes with the Hindu word s*hantih* uttered three times.[7] The poem ends without any firm resolution of the prevailing disorder and fragmentation. Yet here in this boat-steering image, so close to the end, joy intrudes briefly: the sea is "calm" and the word "gaily" is used twice. These words are the first sign of real hope the poem affords: they indicate that peace and happiness may be found in submissiveness to "controlling hands." The use of the conditional tense "would have" is significant. Eliot's later poetry builds on this wistful suggestion of the gaiety and security that "would"—hypothetically—come with obedience. The traveler need feel no anxiety about his direction in the voyage of life if he is in the "controlling hands" of a captain who is "expert with sail and oar" (*The Waste Land* 49).

Nearing the Destination

Although they depict moments of joy and reassurance along the way, Eliot and Lewis depict the Godward journey of the soul as long and wearisome. As we grow old, we feel like travelers worn down by the cycle of time, the weary rotation of the seasons, and weight of the passing years. So often it seems that no progress is occurring and that we are nowhere close to our anticipated destination. Long ago we set out on the journey with the sense that we could measure our progress by the accomplishment of certain goals, but we come to realize—as Eliot says in the third movement

of "Little Gidding"—that our "attachment to our own field of action" has been largely ineffectual, and that a particular "action," or
activity, that we formerly valued is ultimately "of little importance"
(*Four Quartets* 142). Time itself is draining us, and many of the
wounds we have received are still open, for, as Eliot says in the
third movement of "The Dry Salvages," time "is no healer" (*Four
Quartets* 134). The journey is far longer and more arduous that we
expected; we thought we would have been able to rest by now, or
at least have passed the difficult part.

In Lewis's poem "Pilgrim's Problem," the speaker is a traveler
who had estimated that he was nearing the end of his journey and
about to reach the pleasant, reassuring part of the landscape, an easy
walk in the "late afternoon" with the anxieties and heat of the day
behind him. Soon he should see "the majestic / Rivers of foamless
charity that glide beneath / Forests of contemplation." He should
be at the stage when, if storms did arise, he would have ready access
to places of refuge and secure rest. Yet, disappointingly, he "can see
nothing at all like this." He wonders whether his map was wrong,
but then realizes, as an experienced walker, that "the other explanation is more often true." The "other explanation" is that the traveler
still has a long way to go. The journey is longer than he thought,
and it is not always easy to stay on the right road. The process of
redemption has not yet been completed in him; much ground must
still be covered before he enters that "supreme stage" and glorious
landscape (*Poems* 119–20).

Eliot's similar themes of travel, change, and the passage of time
are worked and re-worked through dismal imagery that, like the
imagery of Lewis, confounds any naïve expectations readers may
have of easy, cheerful outcomes. Hopefulness has traditionally been
associated with springtime, and yet, as Eliot points out at the start of
The Waste Land, April can be the cruelest month because it awakens
hopes that will only be dashed. Nothing is more discouraging than
hope deferred again and again; it is (as scripture says) something
that "makes the heart sick" (Prov. 13.12 *ESV*). In the second movement of "East Coker," Eliot expresses a disappointment similar to

that of Lewis in "Pilgrim's Problem." It is a dark picture of old age, but it is accurate in many respects. "Autumnal serenity" and true "wisdom" do not come simply from the accumulation of years, even though some "quiet-voiced elders" of earlier generations have encouraged us to think so. Long years of experience may produce a kind of knowledge, of "limited value," but do not produce wisdom. Eliot exclaims, "Do not let me hear / Of the wisdom of old men, but rather of their folly." He views old people as characterized more by folly than by wisdom—especially the folly of fearing the wrong things: "Their fear of fear and frenzy, their fear of possession, / Of belonging to another, or to others, or to God." The fear of aging, with the inevitable loss of physical strength, is accompanied by fear of the inevitable dependency that comes with old age. Eliot recognizes that many are terrified by the thought of no longer "belonging" to themselves, and of being in the control of other people. But most of all they fear "belonging . . . to God." It is pride that leads to such fear, and Eliot follows this passage by proclaiming that humility is the only solution to the foolish and prideful fears of old age: "The only wisdom we can hope to acquire / Is the wisdom of humility" (*Four Quartets* 125–26).

Old age is depicted even more bleakly, and with more detail in the second movement of "Little Gidding" than in the passage from "East Coker." In "Little Gidding," the regret and frustration of old age are especially intense because Eliot is speaking more personally. As we saw earlier,[8] the scene is set during the bombing of London, when Eliot is walking the streets on night patrol. In the nightmarish darkness, he has a visionary encounter with an unexpected, ill-defined figure. He says, "I met one walking." He feels initially that the person is a "stranger"; then he senses something that reminds him of "some dead master"—a wise man, perhaps a writer, whose legacy he has received. It is not, however, the ghost of one particular person, but a "compound ghost" with whom he feels connected, although he cannot identify him specifically (*Four Quartets* 140).

The ghost talks to Eliot of the need to let go of the past, and speaks of the seemingly futile struggle of poets to communicate truth and wisdom. He speaks, almost brutally, of what can be expected in one's declining years, and calls the changes of aging, ironically, the "gifts reserved for age." First there is physical deterioration—the "cold friction of expiring sense . . . / As body and soul begin to fall asunder." Then there is anger at the foolishness of so many people—the "conscious impotence of rage / At human folly" (*Four Quartets* 141–42). And finally, anguished remorse over our own mistakes, wrong things that we did when we thought we were doing good. The ghost observes that the memory of all that we have done and been brings shame, rather than self-satisfaction. We look back on our motives and realize that they were not pure, and that many things we did, believing we were acting virtuously, were actually harmful to others. What a misery of regret awaits us in old age! The ghost describes an aging person as an "exasperated spirit" with a deteriorating body, who is angered by human folly and deeply ashamed of his own misguided actions. The aging person proceeds "from wrong to wrong," caught between the wrongness of the world and the wrongness inside himself (*Four Quartets* 142). What can relieve this picture of frustration and despair in old age?

In the next lines, Eliot begins to open the door to the solution. The ghost observes that there is nowhere to go to escape this entrapment, "unless restored by that refining fire / Where you must move in measure, like a dancer" (*Four Quartets* 142). The word *unless,* as Eliot uses it here, is a word of hope. There *is* a way out of the misery of failure and regret. There exists "that refining fire"—a very specific sort of fire—that can free us from frailty, anger, and guilt, and restore to us, as the prophet says, "the years that the . . . locust has eaten" (Joel 2.25 *ESV*). This miraculous restoration frees us from the bondage of the past to take our place within the rhythm—the dancelike pattern—of God's supreme purposes.[9]

The account of conversion in *Ash Wednesday,* which we looked at in chapter 4, depicts such miraculous restoration, and shows how time can be redeemed. The pleasant springtime imagery of this poem contrasts with the cruelty of April depicted in the opening lines of *The Waste Land.* In the second movement, the speaker talks of coming to the end of what had seemed an "endless journey," and arriving at "the garden / Where all love ends" (*Ash Wednesday*

62). The fourth movement expresses hope for "restoring . . . the years," and a fountain springs up and birds sing. (*Ash Wednesday* 64). The images of hope continue in the final two movements: a garden has sprung up in "the desert / Of drouth" (movement 5); while in movement 6, "the lost heart . . . rejoices . . . [and] the weak spirit quickens" (*Ash Wednesday* 66). In contrast to the foolishness and fear of the old men depicted in "East Coker," this poem asserts that old age can be a time of restoration, quickening, and rejoicing.

In Eliot's poem "A Song for Simeon," the speaker is Simeon, the aged man of God who appears in the second chapter of Luke's gospel. He has, according to God's promise, lived long enough to hold in his arms the infant Christ—"the still unspeaking and un-spoken Word." Eliot's poem depicts the old man as one who has "kept faith and fast, [and] provided for the poor," but for whom old age has not been particularly pleasant. Simeon describes himself as "waiting for the death wind"—a chill wind—reflecting, "I am tired with my own life." But now, holding the infant Christ, he is given, at the very end of life, a glimpse of God's glory, and is able to pray, serenely, "Grant me thy peace. / . . . Let thy servant depart, / Having seen thy salvation." Old age is, for such a man of faith, a time of joy and fulfillment. ("A Song for Simeon" 69–70).

In the poem "The Cultivation of Christmas Trees," Eliot con-trasts the impact of passing time on two contrasting sorts of people. The title teasingly suggests that the poem will be about the farming of Christmas trees. It is not; it is about the "cultivation" of the right sort of attitude toward all that Christmas can and should mean. Eliot begins the poem by observing that there are a variety of re-sponses to the Christmas season, but he quickly dismisses some of the most common: "the social, the torpid, the patently commercial" and "the rowdy." Another wrong attitude is the sentimental or "childish," but Eliot quickly distinguishes *childishness* from *child-likeness*. The right attitude toward Christmas is "that of the child," who is able to connect with the meaning behind Christmas tree decorations like candles and plastic angels. The glow of the candle reflects the light of the Star of Bethlehem, and the "gilded angel / Spreading its wings at the summit of the tree" is much more to the child than a tree ornament: it *is* an angel. The child's response to the Christmas tree represents the right attitude not only to Christmas but to life itself. It is a spirit of credulity, awe, and joy: "The child wonders at the Christmas Tree," Eliot says, adding, "Let him continue in the spirit of wonder." This spirit of wonder is worshipful and festive, and reflects the true meaning of Christmas. Eliot points out that Christmas is one of the great "Feast" days of the Church calendar, a glorious "event" that is an end in itself, not just an excuse or "pretext" to legitimize foolish activities—the social, commercial, and childish forms of celebration. To the young child, the Christmas tree embodies the essence of Christmas itself—the "star," the "angel," all that generates "wonder" ("The Cultivation of Christmas Trees" 117–18).

The poem proclaims that we, as adults, even as aging adults, must cultivate the spirit of wonder that we first knew as children. As we recall the amazement and rapture we felt when, as children, we first beheld a Christmas tree, and as we recall the delight we had in the gifts and the "expectation of the goose or turkey," we return in our spirits to that childlike combination of "reverence" and "gaiety." These are the things that can be lost in "the bored habituation, the fatigue, the tedium, / The awareness of death, the consciousness of failure" that we experience in later life. Yet for the person of faith, Eliot believes, the process should operate in reverse: Christmas joy should accumulate, not diminish, with the passage of time. The combined emotion of all the Christmases of all the years of our lives is the basis for even greater awe, reverence, and gaiety than those we experienced as children. This joy cannot be stifled by the world-weariness and fear that so often accompanies later life—fatigue, thoughts of death, memories of failure. For the Christian, life is not winding down in the later years; it is intensifying. By the end of our lives, our last Christmas, "the accumulated memories of annual emotion / May be concentrated into a great joy." Christmases should keep getting better and better, because we increasingly perceive our lives as being within the larger expanse of God's mercy and love. Contemplating, at Christmas time, the beginning of the gospel story with the first coming of Christ, we are reminded of the big picture of God's purposes, "Because the beginning shall remind us of the end / And the first coming of the second coming" ("The Cultivation of Christmas Trees" 117–18). In these last two lines of the poem, Eliot echoes one of the themes of the Church's Advent season: the divine triumph that will culminate in Christ's Second Coming. This is the basis for joy in old age.

Sayers's essay "Strong Meat" (originally published as "The Food of the Full Grown") paints a similar picture of the way time and aging impact a person who—in the sense Christ meant it—becomes "a little child":

> Paradoxical as it may seem, to believe in youth is to look backward; to look forward, we must believe in age. "Except," said Christ, "ye become as little children"—and the words are sometimes quoted to justify the flight into infantilism. Now, children differ in many ways, but they have one thing in common. . . . All normal children (however much we discourage them) look forward to growing up. "Except ye become as little children," except you can wake on your fiftieth birthday with the same forward-looking excitement and interest in life that you enjoyed when you were five, "ye cannot see the Kingdom of God." One must not only die daily, but every day one must be born again. ("Strong Meat" 18–19)

The experience of later life is radically different for the person who has been, as "Little Gidding" puts it, "restored by that refining fire," and who, in spite of the weariness and disintegration caused by age, experiences "the garden blossoming in the desert," the rejoicing of the "lost heart," and the quickening of the "weak spirit" (*Ash Wednesday* 66).

Joyous Arrival

In the poem "As One Oldster to Another," Lewis describes the later stages of life as a train ride that is nearing its end. We are on a "night train [that] rushes on with us," screaming through the stations. We wonder how many more stations there will be, and if it will soon be time "to think of taking down one's / Case from the rack." We ask "Are we nearly there now?" The speaker in this poem is Lewis himself, but he uses "we" because he believes that his state of mind as he approaches the end of life's journey will be shared by many of his readers. Lewis's mood is one of anticipation, not gloom or dread. Even though many things in later life have been disappointing for him—"loss of friends," "an emptying future," and the shattering of "long-builded hopes"—there is still a dancing within his spirit. His "obstinate heart" has never been so subdued by life's trials as to adopt a solemn and "sedate deportment." The longing for ultimate joy and beauty that he felt so strongly as a child is still with him: "Still beauty calls as once in the mazes of / Boyhood. The bird-like soul quivers. Into her[10] / Flash darts of unfulfill'd desire and / Pierce with a bright, unabated anguish." His soul quivers, like a bird, in its excitement, and intense longing pierces through him. The pangs of this desire are a kind of "anguish"—an anguish of longing he had known in youth and never forgotten: "Armed thus with anguish, joy met us even in / Youth—who forgets?" It is anguish mingled with joy. He is just on the brink of its fulfillment, having not quite arrived at the "terminus" that is heaven, where—finally—the "doors of delight [will be] set open" (*Poems* 41–42).

Here we see various elements of the journey motif coming together: the sense of our movement being under compulsion from another force, the longing for the end, the memory of disappointed hopes. Most important, though, is the buildup of excited expectation, as the call of that incredibly beautiful reality is renewed, and remains as strong as ever. It is a piecing sweetness, resembling anguish, but it is also joy—the same joy that called to us in youth, and that has given impetus to the whole journey, a joy that will be finally complete as the gates open, and we pass through—home at last.

The opening of gates into a place of perfect joy is depicted at the end of another of Lewis's poems, "What the Bird Said Early in the Year." On a fine spring day, a bird is singing in Addison's Walk—a lovely woodland path on the grounds of Magdalen College where

Lewis loved to walk.[11] The bird encourages us to believe that the future will be wonderful. The poem begins, "I heard in Addison's Walk a bird sing clear / 'This year the summer will come true. This year. This year. / Winds will not strip the blossoms from the apple trees / This year, nor want of rain destroy the peas'" (Lewis, *Poems* 71). The promises are so optimistic that they seem much too good to be true. Spring's seductive beauty encourages us to believe that the world is a more kindly place than it really is. Can we really count on consistently good weather?

The promise of good weather is broadened out into something even more improbable, as the bird announces, "This year time's nature will no more defeat you, / Nor all the moments in their passing cheat you. / This time they will not lead you round and back / To Autumn, one year older, by the well-worn track." Again, the reader is skeptical. How can we expect to triumph over "time's nature" and avoid the process of aging? The bird's impossibly optimistic message continues, telling us that "this year" will be different, and we will "escape the circle and undo the spell." The "circle" and "spell," that the bird suggests we can break free, of represent the bondage of time and mortality (Lewis, *Poems* 71).

Up to this point, the poem seems to be promoting, in the reader, not optimism but pessimism. We are reminded of the cynicism toward spring's promises suggested by the opening of Eliot's poem, *The Waste Land:* "April is the cruelest month" (37). Perhaps the cry heard in Addison's Walk represents the same sort of "deception" by a bird that we encounter in the first movement of Eliot's "Burnt Norton" ("shall we follow / The deception of the thrush?"), when we are invited to follow quickly and enter a world of innocence, perfection, and hopefulness (*Four Quartets* 118). The reader of Lewis's poem questions whether the promises made by the bird's song "Early in the Year" can be trusted. Lewis is prompting the reader to respond with cynicism: "We weren't born yesterday! Why should we for one moment think that *this* year the seasons will be kindly, that *this* year all our hopes and dreams will be fulfilled?" Many timeworn people would feel that the wise response to what the bird said, the response born of experience, would be at best a guarded one. Those who have been often disappointed find it hard to be this hopeful of the goodness of the future. And Lewis recognizes that, being "often deceived," our reaction will be to close our hearts to hope. Yet, the poem's closing lines dismiss the idea that pessimism, reserve, and caution are the best responses to the promise of a good outcome. We are urged to open our hearts to the hope of ultimate joy: "Often deceived, yet open once again your heart, / Quick, quick, quick, quick!—the gates are drawn apart" (Lewis, *Poems* 71).

The bird's words, "Quick, quick, quick, quick!" correspond to the urging of the bird in Eliot's "Burnt Norton": "'Quick,' said the bird" (*Four Quartets* 117). The gates referred to in Lewis's poem are not gates in Addison's Walk, not gates in any earthy location. They are reminiscent of the entrance to bliss Eliot mentions in "Burnt Norton," as "the door we never opened / Into the rose-garden" (*Four Quartets* 117). They have even more similarity to "the unknown, remembered gate" we pass through at the end of "Little Gidding" (*Four Quartets* 145). They are all, in essence, the same gate—the threshold of the garden that is our true home. In movements 1 and 5 of "East Coker," Eliot says, "In my beginning is my end" and "Home is where one starts from" However, since in movement 5 of the same poem, he also says "in my end is my beginning" (*Four Quartets* 123–29), home is also where one ends.

Until the end is reached, the steady plodding onward must continue. Old age is not a time for spiritual inertia. Near the end of "East Coker," Eliot stresses, not the dismal nature of old age, but its challenges: "Old men ought to be explorers / Here and there does not matter / We must be still and still moving" (*Four Quartets* 129). There are always new things to be discovered and experienced, and though the line "Here or there does not matter" suggests a kind of recklessness, it is recklessness rooted in faith, not foolhardiness. The paradox of being "still" and yet "moving" in the third line of this "East Coker" passage is very important. The stillness reflects our recognition that we are not in charge of the journey and that all our momentum comes from God; the continuing movement is our faithful obedience—pressing onward.

In "The Dry Salvages" (the third poem of *Four Quartets*) Eliot stresses the transforming nature of the journey, comparing it to both train travel and an ocean voyage. The imagery of the third movement indicates that our destination is a home that may be reached only by a long, difficult, and traumatic journey. It is traumatic because we are not in control, and because we are being changed from what we have been, but are not yet in our final form: "You are not the same people who left the station / Or who will arrive at any terminus. / . . . You are not those who saw the harbor / Receding, or those who will disembark" (*Four Quartets* 134).

As "Little Gidding" moves toward a conclusion, the imagery of exploration and travel rises to a crescendo and resolves. We are told that we will not "cease from exploration" as we continue on our journey, but that the purpose and culmination of it all will be to arrive at the place we started from, and "know the place for the first time." In our temporal existence we are pilgrims, called to ceaselessly move into new territory. Yet all that fearful venturing into the unknown, brings us finally—like John in Lewis's *Pilgrim's Regress*—back to where we started, to God, who is our source, and to the place where we will finally know, "even as we are known" (1 Cor. 13.12). In the last movement of "Little Gidding, Eliot depicts us passing, at the end, through an "unknown, remembered gate" (*Four Quartets* 145)—a gate that is "unknown" because we are passing through into eternal life and we have never passed through death before. The journey ends in great joy as we pass through the gate into the lost garden, the garden where, in the words of *Ash Wednesday,* "all loves end." The journey of life, the journey toward heaven, forces us across a Waste Land dense with frustrations and regrets. But we are drawn steadily forward by the relentless love that calls us, the love that redeems us.

8

Ask for the Old Paths

Redeeming the Time

✠ ✠ ✠

C. S. Lewis, Dorothy L. Sayers, and T. S. Eliot affirmed the validity of old views and values. Their treatment of the subjects we have discussed—the nature of Christ, experience of conversion, the ministry of angels, the meaning of suffering, and the hope of heaven—reveals, not an esoteric perspective, but the traditional Christian one. Their challenge to a secular, modernist age is reflected in the words of the prophet: "Thus saith the LORD, Stand ye in the ways, and see, and ask for the old paths, where is the good way, and walk therein, and ye shall find rest for your souls. But they said, We will not walk therein" (Jer. 6:16). The phrase "Thus saith the Lord" points to the divine impetus under which each of them spoke. Standing "in the ways" points to the high visibility that their message had in their own day. Asking for "the old paths" and walking in "the good way" as a means to "find rest for [their] souls" points to the strong appeal they made for a return to Christian orthodoxy and for acceptance of the redemption offered by the gospel. Jeremiah's following sentence, "But they said, We will not walk therein," points to the resistant secularism of the modern world and the godlessness that these three writers diligently opposed.

The Value of Permanent Things

The "good old way" was the ideal of Nicholas Ferrar, who founded a godly conclave in a tiny Cambridgeshire village in the early seventeenth century. It was this devout community, called Little Gidding, that inspired Eliot's last and greatest poem. To modern ears the "good old way" sounds unpleasantly like the cliché of the "good old days," with its simplistic idealization of bygone eras. Many modern people dislike the sentimentality associated with a nostalgia for the past, even though they may secretly long to recover moments of joy from their own earlier lives and reclaim things of beauty from earlier periods of history. For Lewis, Eliot, and Sayers, however, asking for "the old paths" was not based on sentiment and nostalgia. Their dismay over contemporary trends and their high esteem for the past was rooted in their commitment to what Eliot called "permanent things" (*Christianity and Culture* 76).

Lewis, Sayers, and Eliot played a key role in strengthening the Church in the first half of the twentieth century because they stood at the meeting point of ways—at a crossroads—warning people against the wrong-mindedness of the modern world and directing them toward the old and good paths. Lewis set out the choice of ways clearly near the beginning of his book *Miracles,* observing that the first choice to be made in our thinking is the choice between "Naturalism and Supernaturalism" (11). In her 1940 lecture "Creed or Chaos?" Sayers stated, "Something is happening today which has not happened for a very long time. We are waging a war of religion. Not a civil war between adherents of the same religion, but a life-and-death struggle between Christian and pagan" ("Creed or Chaos?" 25). Eliot made a similar point about the alternative presented by the two ways, observing, "Our choice now is not between one abstract form and another, but between a pagan, and necessarily stunted culture, and a religious, and necessarily imperfect culture" ("The Idea of a Christian Society" 14). He argued that it is "the Church's business to interfere with the world" and further asserted that "to accept two ways of life in the same society, one for the Christian and another for the rest, would be for the Church to abandon its task of evangelizing the world" ("The Idea of a Christian Society" 71).

Like many who love old literature, these writers regarded themselves as belonging to an earlier time, spiritually and intellectually.

Eliot, writing to a friend in 1928, confessed that he felt like a dis-
placed person in the modern world, but felt an affinity for America
as it had been a hundred years earlier (Reade 15). Ezra Pound's
nickname for Eliot was "Old Possum"[1]—a name probably intended
to poke fun at Eliot's caution and reserve. But the nickname also
reflects Eliot's affinity for an earlier, simpler time. The name sat so
comfortably with Eliot that he used it of himself in the title of his
collection of cat poems, *Old Possum's Book of Practical Cats*.[2]

Lewis clearly had a similar feeling of displacement. In his poem
"Re-Adjustment" (*Poems* 102), he refers to himself as being the last
of his kind, and in "*De Descriptione Temporum*," his 1954 Inaugural Lecture at Cambridge, he describes himself as a rare relic of the
past—a species that had survived from prehistoric times. "I read as a
native texts that you must read as foreigners," he said. " . . . Where
I fail as a critic, I may yet be useful as a specimen. I would even
dare to go further. Speaking not only for myself but for all other Old
Western men whom you may meet, I would say, use your specimens
while you can. There are not going to be many more dinosaurs" ("*De
Descriptione Temporum*" 24–25).

Disintegration and Loss

In "The Idea of a Christian Society" Eliot argued that modern society, influenced by what was called liberalism, was moving "away
from, rather than towards, something definite" (12). He observed
the trends leading to disintegration: the destruction of "traditional
social habits . . . by licensing the opinions of the most foolish, by
substituting instruction for education, by encouraging cleverness
rather than wisdom, the upstart rather than the qualified, by fos-
tering a notion of *getting on* to which the alternative is a hopeless
apathy" (12). He believed that the traditional rhythms and patterns
of life were fading. In the pageant play *The Rock*, Eliot pointed to
the loss of traditional bonds between family members and to the
disconnectedness of people from one another, living in neighbor-
hoods where they don't know who their neighbors are and don't

really care—unless they happen to be disruptive. *The Rock* depicts modern families no longer spending most of their waking hours together but rushing here and there in cars and seldom coming together as a family. The teenage boys have their motorcycles, and the girls are picked up by their boyfriends. They are all "familiar with the roads and settled nowhere" (101–2).

All three saw loss of respect for education as a particularly alarming aspect of society's deterioration. Sayers's 1940 essay "The Contempt of Learning in Twentieth-Century England" described the increasing dominance of a "prosperous middle class" whose members see no value in real education and whose entire lives are "based on the notion that everything has its price."[3] Such people resent the kind of mental integrity "that cannot be bought or sold," she asserted, because a value system not based on monetary rewards puts their value system in the wrong. "To them," Sayers said, "learning is like a horrible heresy, a rival religion, which they dare not allow, because it questions the very foundations of their universe" (*Contempt of Learning* 376–77). Such a view of learning puts pressure on universities to focus on training for specific jobs instead of providing "true learning for genuine scholars" (378). It also leads to the low esteem and low pay offered to teachers. "What is the use," Sayers asked, "of our saying that the future is with the young and that education is the key to reconstruction, if we ourselves pay no honour to those who do the work of education?" (380). She pointed out the unfairness and irony in modern people handing their children over to teachers while at the same time undermining the teachers' prestige by devaluing and underpaying them (381).

Sayers's most important and lasting contribution in the field of education was an address called "The Lost Tools of Learning" (later published in book form). It was, in her estimation, a "little lecture" of slight importance (*Letters of DLS* 3: 323) that she delivered at Oxford in August 1947 to a teachers' conference. In it, Sayers identified the symptoms of educational failure, particularly the inability of people to think critically. She argued that modern education has inadequately prepared people for "disentangling fact from opinion and the proven from the plausible" (*Lost Tools* 4) and diagnosed the problem to be a result, not of what is taught, but of the way it is taught. The modern approach to education, she believed, focuses on teaching students the content of particular subject areas while failing to teach them "how to think" (7).

This address is called "The *Lost* Tools of Learning" [emphasis added] because it argues that students are no longer taught the "tools of learning." Arguing that the modern world has abandoned some of the best things of the past, and has "forgotten its own roots," Sayers proposed that such "lost tools of learning" may be best reclaimed by reviving the approach to education used in the late Middle Ages. The lecture then outlined the effectiveness of the components of the classical education, the Trivium and the Quadrivium, with special emphasis on the essential basis provided by the Trivium, comprised of Grammar, Logic, and Rhetoric.

Sayers concluded her lecture by observing that the efforts of modern education consist of futilely trying "to shore up the tottering weight of an educational structure that is built upon sand" by having teachers do the work that the pupils ought to have been taught to do for themselves. The "sole true end of education is simply this:" Sayers asserted, "to teach men how to learn for themselves; and whatever instruction fails to do this is effort spent in vain" (30).

The proposal to reinstate a medieval approach to schooling was essentially a facetious device. Sayers knew (or thought she knew) that the idea would never be seriously taken up, but she proposed it as a gesture of appreciation, even reverence, for what was best in medieval education. Of her proposal, she observed, "This prospect need arouse neither hope nor alarm. It is in the highest degree improbable that the reforms I propose will ever be carried into effect" (2). Nevertheless, she was bold enough to suggest that "if we are to produce a society of educated people, fitted to preserve their intellectual freedom amid the complex pressures of our modern society, we must turn back the wheel of progress some four or five hundred years, to the point at which education began to lose sight of its true object, towards the end of the Middle Ages" (2).

Astonishingly, Sayers's view that "the old paths" in education deserve to be reconsidered has been thoroughly vindicated, beyond what she ever expected. More than thirty years after her presentation of "The Lost Tools of Learning," the ideas she proposed inspired a new and unusual educational experiment. The growth of the Classical Christian Schools movement in America has shown the value of returning to "old paths" by proving Sayers's backward-reaching idea was more feasible than she or her 1947 audience could have conceived. It was not only feasible; it was immensely successful. Douglas Wilson's book on this educational movement, published in 1991, was called *Recovering the Lost Tools of Learning*. The title in itself indicates the debt to Sayers. The book produced much interest nationwide in a medieval and classical approach to education, and ensured that the movement continued to grow. Since the first such school was founded in 1981 under Wilson's leadership, hundreds of schools have been established that follow a classical model similar to that described by Sayers.

The loss of esteem for learning in the modern world is, as Sayers often observed, closely tied to the loss of accuracy in thinking and in communicating. Her most entertaining and pointed attacks on such deficiencies in contemporary culture took the form of a series of satirical pieces called "The Pantheon Papers," some of which appeared in the magazine *Punch* in 1954.[4] Sayers's satire mimics the style and phraseology of traditional religious writing (hymns, creeds, sermons, and stories of saints) to mock what she identified as the new "religion" of modernity—secular humanism. In one of these pieces, Sayers imitates the rhythm and wording of the well-known hymn that begins "Glorious things of thee are spoken, Zion, city of our God" to expose the shallowness and emptiness of modern rhetoric and the foolishness of modern assumptions:

> Glorious tosh in thee is spoken
>   Babel, city of the glib—
> Sounding brass in accents broken
>   Culled from digest, quiz, and crib;

Where the men who hold the reins trust
 Everything the papers say,
Steered by headlines and the brains-trust
 Down the short and easy way. . . .
. . . .
Bluff and blurbage, garbage, herbage,
 Cats and cans and crocks and cork,
Rag-tag, bobtail, clap-trap, verbiage,
 Drifting down a tide of talk. . . .
. . . .
Babel, home of fond illusions,
 Let us with expanded lungs
Dissipate the world's confusions
 In thy storm and strife of tongues!

May thy shimmering tower of fable
 Soar unchecked to pierce the sky,
And the babblers build up Babel
 Till the springs of speech run dry! ("The Pantheon Papers")

Lewis and Eliot would concur with Sayers's term "Babel, city of the glib" as a summation of the loss of wisdom and integrity in communication, and would equally deplore the foolishness of trusting "everything the papers say," and of being carried away "down a tide of talk," deluded by popular "illusions" and "confusions."

Sayers, Lewis, and Eliot believed that the increasing materialism of the early twentieth century was a serious disintegration of old values because it led to the loss of a right attitude toward possessions. In a foreword she wrote in the 1940s to a book by political economist Garet Garrett, Sayers struck out at the rise of consumerism in England in the 1930s, declaring, "The exhortations to spend became vociferous; the old morality was stood on its head: thrift was no longer a virtue, but a crime against progress—to buy and scrap and buy afresh became the mark of a good citizen" (Foreword to *A Time is Born* vi). She further berated the evils of consumerism in her 1941 essay "The Other Six Deadly Sins," observing that an "odd change" had occurred since the beginning of "the machine age." It is no longer consider a virtue, she pointed out, when one is "thrifty and content with one's lot." Instead, citizens are expected to contribute to their nation's progress by increasing their consumption in every area of life. Such focus on raising one's standard of living, she asserted, raises dissatisfaction with having merely a "decent sufficiency of food, clothes, and shelter." Instead, people are encouraged to strive for much more, and to regard more complicated luxuries as necessities of life (68).

The compulsive consumerism Sayers identified has troubling moral implications. "We need not remind ourselves," she pointed out in the same essay, "of the furious barrage of advertisement by which people are flattered and frightened out of a reasonable contentment into a greedy hankering after goods which they do not really need; nor point out for the thousandth time how every evil passion—snobbery, laziness, vanity, concupiscence, ignorance, greed—is appealed to in these campaigns. . . . It is the great curse of Gluttony that it ends by destroying all sense of the precious, the unique, the irreplaceable" ("Other Six Deadly Sins," 69, 71).

Lewis and Eliot express similar dismay over the changes brought by modernism. A sense of having lost something precious permeates Lewis's poem "A Confession."[5] The specific subject of this poem is modern poetry, but it also bemoans the state of the modern world generally. Lewis declares that he simply cannot perceive things in the way contemporary poets do. He is humorously dismissive of the extreme metaphors of modern poets. Through a mask of self-deprecation (facetiously implying that he is not smart enough to understand these clever writers) he makes fun of the obliqueness and ugliness of recent poetic idiom in general, and of Eliot's style of poetry in particular, citing Eliot's metaphor in "The Love Song of J. Alfred Prufrock," in which the evening is described as "a patient etherized upon a table." In spite of staring his level best, Lewis cannot see how any evening sky could suggest a person lying on an operating table waiting for surgery. Despite the sardonic humor in Lewis's criticism of Eliot's imagery, the dominant tone of the poem is sad and wistful rather than witty. Having dismissed Eliot's image of the "etherized patient," he offers his own—equally poignant—impression of the evening sky: "To me each evening looked far more / Like a departure from a silent, yet a crowded, shore / Of a ship whose freight was everything, leaving behind / Gracefully, finally, without farewells, marooned mankind" (*Poems* 1).

Lewis creates a picture that is less jarring than Eliot's, but both views are equally pessimistic. Eliot's image (although it contrasts in poetic idiom) agrees with Lewis's in its import. Eliot's description of the evening reflects not the appearance of the sky but the helplessness of the observer, who feels himself as incapable of choice and meaningful action as a sedated patient awaiting surgery. Lewis's image is similarly subjective in conveying his despairing sense that everything worthwhile ("a ship whose freight was everything") is slipping away from us with each successive sunset. The fact that the departing ship is "graceful" does not alleviate the sadness. In both poems, mankind is left bereft, marooned from the beautiful and good.

The Naïve Belief in Steady Progress

The kind of modernism that Lewis especially abhorred was the facile belief in progress. In his Cambridge Inaugural Lecture, Lewis discusses the concept of eras—such as medieval and Renaissance—and what divides one era from another. He mentions several things that have caused "the greatest of all divisions in the history of the West"—the changes that divide the twentieth century from the early eighteenth century ("*De Descriptione Temporum*" 17). Chief among these is "the birth of the machines" (20). The "economic and social consequences" of the machine age are enormous, but what concerns Lewis more is its "psychological effect" (20). The human mind has been implanted, he says, with "a new archetypal image"—that of steady, unrelenting technical advance. We are led to assume "that everything is provisional and soon to be superseded, that the attainment of goods we have never yet had, rather than the defense and conservation of those we have already, is the cardinal business of life" (21–22).

Lewis's poem "Evolutionary Hymn" displays another approach to this issue, through its witty mockery of such a blind belief in progress. The poem not only resembles the hymn parodies of Sayers but is probably directly indebted to her.[6] Like Sayers, Lewis imitates hymn lyrics to mock the naïve yet arrogant expectations of endless progress that characterize what he saw as the religion of secularism:

Lead us, Evolution, lead us
    Up the future's endless stair:
Chop us, change us, prod us, weed us.
    For stagnation is despair:
Groping, guessing, yet progressing,
    Lead us nobody knows where.

Wrong or justice, in the present
    Joy or sorrow, what are they
While there's always jam-tomorrow,
    While we tread the onward way?
Never knowing where we're going,
    We can never go astray.

Far too long have sages vainly
    Glossed great Nature's simple text;
He who runs can read it plainly,
    'Goodness = what comes next.'
By evolving, Life is solving
    All the questions we perplexed.

Oh then! Value means survival—
    Value. If our progeny
Spreads and spawns and licks each rival,
    That will prove its deity
(Far from pleasant, by our present
Standards, though it well may be). (*Poems* 55–56).

The poem shows how the modern belief in progress demeaned Nature, ignored the perplexing questions of life, and set the individual up as his own "deity."

In her "Pantheon Papers" Sayers depicts modern egotism through the idea of polarity, playing off the multiple associations of the word *polarity:* oppositional tendencies, isolation, and coldness. In March 1954, Lewis wrote to Sayers that her influence had prompted him to begin "to study polarity." He praises her "Me Meum Laudo" (a parody of a religious creed), which mocks extreme egotism.[7] Of Sayers's whole group of satiric sketches, Lewis comments, "none is without its charm." He then gives her his "effort" along the same lines—the earlier version of "Evolutionary Hymn." He calls it an attack, not so much on "polarity" of the sort Sayers was addressing, but on a "false philosophy" that was not as individualistic as the attitude Sayers depicted in "Me Meum Laudo" (*Collected Letters of CSL* 3: 434–36).

Eliot was similarly concerned about the modern assumption that the new was always better. He observed that "the more highly industrialised the country, the more easily a materialistic philosophy will flourish in it, and the more deadly that philosophy will be" ("The Idea of a Christian Society" 16). He recognized that "Britain has been highly industrialised longer than any other country" and that "for a long enough time we have believed in nothing but the values arising in a mechanised, commercialised, urbanised way of life" (49). One of the worst results of these changes, he said, has been the creation of a very dangerous state in the populous: "bodies of men and women of all classes—detached from tradition, alienated from religion and susceptible to mass suggestion: in other words, a mob. And a mob will be no less a mob if it is well fed, well clothed, well housed, and well disciplined" (17).

Like Lewis and Sayers, Eliot regarded the modern belief in progress as naïve and futile. In his choruses from *The Rock,* he pointed out the tragic irony of "The endless cycle of idea and action, / Endless invention, endless experiment" that brings only empty knowledge—"knowledge of motion, but not of stillness" (96). Continuing this pattern of contrast, he says that endless invention has brought

"Knowledge of speech, but not of silence; / Knowledge of words, and ignorance of the Word" (96). All the newly acquired knowledge fails to provide wisdom; we are "nearer to death, but . . . no nearer to God." And it is not even true "knowledge," but merely "information" (96).

The Church Disowned

During the seventy-five years that comprised the life-span of Eliot, Lewis, and Sayers, the rift between popular culture and orthodox Christianity increased rapidly. Commenting on the Church of England's Lambeth Conference of 1930, Eliot observed that contemporary culture was "trying the experiment of attempting to form a civilized but non-Christian mentality." He knew that it would not work. "The experiment will fail," he said, "but we must be very patient in awaiting its collapse; meanwhile redeeming the time: so that the Faith may be preserved alive through the dark ages before us" ("Thoughts after Lambeth" 377).

In 1939, Eliot spoke again about the changes in culture that signaled a movement away from what the Church represented, but the very title of his talk—"The Idea of a Christian Society"—indicates that he was still hoping that the process of de-Christianization could be halted. He observed that a society is no longer Christian when traditional religious practices are abandoned and when people cease to evaluate behavior by Christian principles. In such a society, material prosperity is the only valid goal. Eliot suggested, however, that the culture of his day had retained some vestiges of Christianity, because it has not yet "become positively something else." He saw the culture as "mainly negative," but having some positive elements, elements that defined the extent to which it is "still Christian." He knew that such a state could not remain static, and that if people did not consciously desire the re-formation of "a new Christian culture" the alternative would be an increasingly "pagan" one ("The Idea of a Christian Society" 10).

In the same essay, Eliot spoke of the insurmountable pressures placed on a Christian living in the modern world by a society that remained Christian only in name. He pointed out that Christians now encounter "the problem of leading a Christian life in a non-Christian society"—a problem arising from the "network of institutions from which we cannot dissociate ourselves" and whose basis of operation is not merely indifferent to Christianity, but specifically non-Christian. Eliot believed that most contemporary Christians had not realized this fact, and that, as a result, they were unknowingly "becoming more and more de-Christianised by all sorts of unconscious pressure." He noted wryly that "paganism holds all the most valuable advertising space" ("The Idea of a Christian Society" 17–18).

Eliot predicted the probable erosion of Christian heritage and Christian traditions within families, and the likelihood that the Church of the future would be made up of first-generation Christians. Warning that the sort of Christian traditions formerly transmitted from generation to generation within families were going to disappear, he suggested that over time "the small body of Christians will consist entirely of adult recruits." He recognized that if Christians became "a persecuted minority," treated as enemies of the state, their situation would be more difficult, but actually simpler. What Eliot most feared was the danger of Christians remaining "the tolerated minority" ("The Idea of a Christian Society" 18).

Sayers was similarly dismayed by the gradual de-Christianization of society. She noted with amazement the widespread ignorance of the basic tenets of Christianity, and pointed out that many people "in this nominally Christian country . . . heartily dislike and despise Christianity without having the faintest notion what it is" ("The Dogma Is the Drama" 24). This came forcefully to her attention in questions she was asked that showed profound ignorance of the basics of Christian belief.[8] She observed that this ignorance was particularly great among the youth. People seemed astonished to hear that "the Church believed Christ to be in any real sense God, . . . [or] that

the Church considered Pride to be sinful, or indeed took any notice of
sin beyond the more disreputable sins of the flesh." Moreover, they
were inclined to regard these ideas as "revolutionary novelties" that
Sayers herself had invented to add excitement to her play (24).

In a series of articles on the challenges that should be taken up by
Christian drama, Sayers elaborated on the seriousness of this problem: "I cannot emphasize too strongly how deep that ignorance goes.
Mediaeval people could not have conceived of such ignorance as surrounds us in England today. We are living in a heathen country: in
some ways it is worse than a heathen country, because for the most
part we have to deal with people who do not bring virgin minds to
the Christian story, but minds filled with totally false conceptions"
("Sacred Plays" 2: 24). She believed that this lack of understanding
of Christianity was the result of "a mass of abominable supersti-
tions" that clouded people's minds, so that they were completely confused by basic Christian concepts that were familiar ideas in earlier
periods. "They do not know what is meant by redemption or atonement," Sayers continued in the same article. She explains: "they have
only the crudest and most distorted notions about vicarious suffering
and substituted love; their ideas of what is meant by heaven or hell
or eternity are of a childish materialism that would have shocked
St. Augustine in the fourth century; not only do they repudiate the
idea of sin—they simply do not know what Christians mean by the
word; and their moral code has in many cases departed so far from
Christian standards that any solution of a moral problem based on
Christian assumptions is merely unintelligible to them" (2: 24).

Eliot was convinced that the rejection of Christianity was tied
to the general disintegration of twentieth-century culture. His choruses from *The Rock* berate the general dismissal of the past that
causes people to neglect their shrines and churches and belittle all
the good the Church did for earlier generations (98).

The play's Chorus, speaking as a prophet would, proclaims "The
Word of the LORD," condemns the "miserable cities of designing
men" and the "wretched generation of enlightened men / Betrayed
in the mazes of [their] ingenuities." The Chorus reproaches the in-

habitants of the cities, saying, "I have given you hands which you turn from worship, / . . . I have given you hearts, for reciprocal distrust. / . . . I have given you the power of choice, and you only alternate / Between futile speculation and unconsidered action" (102). The Chorus proclaims that the great quantity of books being written and published reflect merely the desire of many to see their names in print. People do a lot of reading, but do not read "the Word of GOD"; they do a lot of building, but do not build "the House of GOD" (102). Eliot, through the Chorus, observes that the godlessness of the present generation has surpassed anything that has ever happened before: "Men have left GOD not for other gods, they say, but for no God; . . . [they] both deny gods and worship gods, professing first Reason, / And then Money, and Power" ("Choruses from *The Rock*" 108). The Church has been "disowned," its towers have been overthrown, and its bells silenced. What is there left to do, the Chorus asks, "But stand with empty hands and palms turned upwards / In an age which advances progressively backwards?" (108).

Eliot believed that the brokenness of society after World War II could be mended only by a return to the faith that had defined Western civilization up until the twentieth century. Believing that the situation was redeemable, he said, "We need to know how to see the world as the Christian Fathers saw it; and the purpose of re-ascending to origins is that we should be able to return, with greater spiritual knowledge, to our own situation. We need to recover the sense of religious fear, so that it may be overcome by religious hope" ("The Idea of a Christian Society" 49).

Lies Accepted as Truths

The dismay Lewis, Sayers, and Eliot felt toward modern "improvements" had deep roots. Their love of the past and deep distrust of modernity did not arise merely from personal preference; they believed that the new trends were truly dangerous because they were based on falsehoods.

Lewis's reasons for fearing modernity are apparent in the inaugural lecture he delivered at Cambridge in 1954. Having pointed
out "the great religious change" that had occurred since the early
nineteenth century, when "some kind and degree of religious belief
and practice" had been the norm, he said that he was finding it hard
to have patience with people expressing alarm at the idea that we
seem to be "relapsing into Paganism" (*De Descriptione Temporum*
20). Lewis regarded such a relapse, if it did occur, as having positive
aspects because he found more admirable qualities in pre-Christian
thought than in post-Christina thought. But, he said, such predic-
tions of our reversion to paganism are usually the result of "careless language" (20). If they are anything more than that, they are
an expression of a serious misunderstanding of history: the "false
idea that the historical process allows mere reversal; that Europe
can come out of Christianity 'by the same door as in she went' and
find herself back where she was" (20). Lewis explained that history
does not work this way: "It is not what happens. A post-Christian
man is not a Pagan; you might as well think that a married woman
recovers her virginity by divorce. The post-Christian is cut off from
the Christian past and therefore doubly from the Pagan past" (20).

To Lewis, modernity meant, not progress in understanding, but
deterioration. He saw people becoming increasingly unable to perceive things rightly. His belief that the changes of the early twentieth century had led to a kind of blindness is most graphically expressed in an allegorical poem called "The Country of the Blind." In
this poem, he describes men who have gradually become blind and
maimed and can no longer see the things that had been obvious to
earlier generations. They are a "whole nation of eyeless men," who
are unaware of the long process—the "slow curse"—that blinded
them. But not all of them, the poem tells us, became blind at the
same time. Ironically, a few "luckless" ones had managed to retain
their vision after the majority had sunk into comfortable "darkness." This majority, described in the poem as people of the "up-
to-date" and "normal" type, exist in a cozy darkness, "safe from
the guns of heav'n" (*Poems* 53). This comfortable darkness protects

them from the troubling fear that heaven might contain something
they would be ultimately accountable to, something threatening to
reckon with, a Lion in the Waste Land.

The poem goes on to show that such blindness leads to the abuse
of language, as words that were rightly understood by earlier generations are now unashamedly perverted; even the idea of "light" is
robbed of its potency and corrupted to refer to vague abstractions.
The blind majority use the same words their grandparents had used,
but they abuse them, even speaking of light as if it were something
abstract rather than actual. Worse still, these blind people are unaware of their blindness. Hearing a person with actual sight describe
what he sees, the blind ones do not realize, or at least do not admit,
that they cannot see these things. They do not complain that they
don't understand; they act as if they do, saying, "We've all felt / Just
like that," and the seeing person cannot explain to them that they
are degrading the words he used: "The words— / Sold, raped, flung
to the dogs—now could avail no more." The seeing man is reduced
to silence, and the blind, mole-like creatures go on glibly manipulat-
ing words, "Fools concocting a myth, taking the words for things"
(*Poems* 53).

In the last six lines of the poem, Lewis defends the accuracy of
the picture of modern blindness he has painted:

> Do you think this is a far-fetched
>   Picture? Go then about among
>
> Men now famous; attempt speech on the truths that once,
> Opaque, carved in divine forms, irremovable,
>   Dread, but dear as a mountain-
>   Mass, stood plain to the inward eye. (*Poems* 53)

Lewis, like Eliot and Sayers, was one of those who continued to
"attempt speech," trying to communicate to the blind the absolute
truths—the "permanent things"—that once were so mightily apparent to everyone (Eliot, *Christianity and Culture* 76). These truths,

dreadful and precious, are still as momentous as mountains but are no longer easily perceived by the average person. Once they "stood plain to the inward eye," but now they do not.

Lewis emphasizes again and again the tragic magnitude of this loss of sight, this acceptance of lies as truth, throughout his works of fiction and nonfiction, particularly in *The Abolition of Man,* a book containing three lectures,[9] and the novel *That Hideous Strength.* Lewis regarded *The Abolition of Man* as one of the most important things he ever wrote. Yet, as George Sayer observes, it was not well received initially, and "none of the few reviewers of the first edition seem to have realized its importance" (Sayer 301).

Perhaps the reason for the lack of popularity of *The Abolition of Man* is its vehemence. It is Lewis's most intense reaction to modern wrong-mindedness—a wrong-mindedness that he believed was vividly evident in certain school textbooks. The premise of these books horrified Lewis. They proposed that all value judgments are subjective, and that statements attributing beauty or worth to something simply express the feelings of the observer. In the modern view of life and literature promoted by these school texts, all emotional responses are deemed unreliable because they are "aroused by local association [and] are in themselves contrary to reason and contemptible" (*Abolition of Man* 23). Recognizing that people are "swayed by emotional propaganda" and believing that "youth is sentimental," the authors of these textbooks proposed that the best approach to education is to "fortify the minds of young people against emotion."

Drawing on his own experience as an educator, Lewis strongly refutes this approach, asserting that for "every one pupil who needs to be guarded from a weak excess of sensibility there are three who need to be awakened from the slumber of cold vulgarity." The goal of education should not be "to cut down jungles," he argues, but "to irrigate deserts." He then attacks the assumptions underlying the textbooks in question: "The right defence against false sentiments is to inculcate just sentiments. By starving the sensibility of our pupils we only make them easier prey to the propagandist when he comes. For famished nature will be avenged and a hard heart is no infallible protection against a soft head" (*Abolition of Man* 26–27).

The title Lewis chose for the first lecture in *The Abolition of Man*, "Men Without Chests," alludes to the state of mankind once the capacity for a heartfelt response has been removed. The trends in modern education were, Lewis believed, destroying the very essence of what it means to be human by eliminating the "chest." Lewis's biographers, Green and Hooper, explain that he uses the image of the human chest because of its traditional role as "the seat of emotions organized by habit into stable instincts, and the indispensable 'liaison officer' between man's head (the seat of reason) and man's belly (the seat of instincts)" (219). *The Abolition of Man* asserts that there are such things as stable instincts or "stable sentiments" and that they are connected to basic traditional responses like "magnanimity" and "devotion to truth" and "intellectual honour" (36).

Until recent times, Lewis observes, all cultures assumed inherent values. At the peak of Greek and Roman civilization, in the Middle Ages and Renaissance of Europe, and during the centuries when the great civilizations of Asia were thriving, there was agreement about ultimate values. Introducing the term *Tao*—a word used by the Chinese to mean "the greatest thing"—Lewis uses it to represent "the reality beyond all predicates . . . the Way in which the universe goes on, the Way in which things everlastingly emerge, stilly and tranquilly, into space and time" (*Abolition of Man* 30). Such a term can be used, Lewis feels, to represent "objective value, the belief that certain attitudes are really true, and others really false, to the kind of thing the universe is and the kind of things we are" (31). The existence of such innate and rudimentary values means that calling children "delightful" or the aged "venerable" is not an expression of individual subjective opinion but our recognition of "a quality which *demands* a certain response from us whether we make it or not" (31).

Lewis ends the lecture "Men Without Chests" by observing that, "such is the tragi-comedy of our situation—we continue to clamour for those very qualities we are rendering impossible" (36). Periodicals insist that "what our civilization needs is more 'drive', or dynamism, or self-sacrifice, or 'creativity'" (37). Lewis regards this as a kind of "ghastly simplicity" in which we demand that a bodily function continue after we have removed the organ that makes it possible. "We make men without chests," he says, "and expect of them virtue and enterprise. We laugh at honour and are shocked to find traitors in our midst. We castrate and bid the geldings be fruitful" (37).

Lewis's novel *That Hideous Strength* (published in the summer of 1945) was written soon after *The Abolition of Man,* and grew out of the same fears about the direction the modern world was taking. In that novel, the characters who threaten the very basis of human life are truly and consciously corrupt, and in them we see Lewis's fears about the future of Western civilization magnified and concretized into horror. In a letter written some nine years later, Lewis describes the novel as being about a multilayered conflict: "Grace against Nature and Nature against Anti-Nature (modern industrialism, scientism, and totalitarian politics)" (*Collected Letters of CSL* 3: 498).

In *That Hideous Strength,* the evil regime that takes over a college town represents the extremity that may be reached when the educational ideas that Lewis rebuked in *The Abolition of Man* are given full rein. Lewis said that he was depicting, under "wholly fictional conditions," what he really believed about "a certain type of modern scientific humanist planner" who, though not directly connected with the diabolical, was so unscrupulous that he would be glad to use "diabolical aid" if it were offered to him (*Collected Letters of CSL* 3: 466). Letters from readers confirmed that the evil depicted in *That Hideous Strength* was closer to reality than Lewis had supposed. "The trouble about writing satire," he observed in one letter, "is that the real world always anticipates you, and what were meant for exaggerations turn out to be nothing of the sort" (*Collected Letters of CSL* 2: 672). In another letter, he protested that the detached head in *That Hideous Strength,* kept alive by medicines and infusions of blood, was not as far-fetched as it might seem, arguing, "It's commonly done with cats' heads in Oxford laboratories and was really tried (unsuccessfully) in Germany. One can hardly satirise these people—the reality is always more incredible than what one invents" (*Collected Letters of CSL* 2: 717). Responding to a letter from a reader in Texas, he explained that in *That Hideous Strength* he had taken existing "evil tendencies" to a farther point "to show how dreadful they might become if we didn't take care." He said that the Texas reader's letter indicated that he had experienced "in real life" something astonishingly similar to what Lewis had described in the novel. "That is the trouble," he said, "with satirizing the modern world. What you put into your story as fantastically horrid possibilities becomes fact before your story is printed. The reality outstrips the satire!" (*Collected Letters of CSL* 3: 199).

The Past Disowned

The many declamations against modern culture by Lewis, Sayers, and Eliot support and reinforce one another. In *That Hideous Strength, The Abolition of Man,* and "The Country of the Blind," Lewis grieves for the same disintegration of traditional values that Eliot mourns in *The Rock,* "Thoughts after Lambeth," and "The Idea of a Christian Society." It is the same disintegration that Sayers berates in "The Pantheon Papers," "The Dogma Is the Drama," and other essays. Christianity has been abandoned, what-comes-next is foolishly assumed to be better, and mankind is marooned from the beautiful and the good. All three mourned the egotism of the modern mindset—an egotism which they believed belittles and disowns the wisdom of earlier eras and regards an understanding of history as irrelevant to success in the modern world.

Lewis acknowledged that in his youth he was guilty of using the "names of earlier periods as terms of abuse," because of an attitude he calls "chronological snobbery" (*Surprised by Joy* 206), an attitude that belittles the past simply because it is the past. Such disdain for the past arises from a belief in continuous progress: the belief that everything new improves on what preceded it. This attitude assumes that the ideas, culture, and learning of the present are necessarily superior to those of the past, simply because they arise later in time.

In the second movement of "Dry Salvages, Eliot recorded the same phenomenon, observing that such "superficial notions of evolution" had become "in the popular mind, a means of disowning the past" (*Four Quartets* 132). As Lewis explains, such snobbery involves "the uncritical acceptance of the intellectual climate common to our own age and the assumption that whatever has gone out of date is on that account discredited" (*Surprised by Joy* 207).

Lewis identified his friend and fellow Inkling Owen Barfield as the person who cured him of this sort of wrong-mindedness. Barfield, Lewis explained, insisted that before rejecting an earlier idea, you must find out "why [it] went out of date" and whether it was "ever refuted (and if so by whom, where, and how conclusively)" or if it merely died away "as fashions do" (*Surprised by Joy* 207–8). Once we have asked such questions and found their answers, we are ready, Lewis said, to examine "the truth or falsehood" of an idea assumed to be out dated. We then come to "the realization that our own age is also 'a period,' and certainly has, like all periods, its own character-istic illusions [that] are likeliest to lurk in those widespread assump-tions which are so ingrained in the age that no one dares to attack or feels it necessary to defend them" (*Surprised by Joy* 208).

Like Eliot, Lewis strove to challenge this narrow and arrogant view of history and other unhealthy tendencies prevalent in the modern world. He recommended battling chronological snobbery by reading old books along with new ones. "It is a good rule, after reading a new book," Lewis said, "never to allow yourself another new one till you have read an old one in between. If that is too much for you, you should at least read one old one to every three new ones" ("On the Reading of Old Books" 27). What we need most of all, he said, is "intimate knowledge of the past," because we need "something to set against the present, to remind us that basic assumptions have been quite different in different periods and much which seems certain to the uneducated is merely temporary fashion" ("Learning in War-Time" 35). To illustrate, he observed, "A man who has lived in many places is not likely to be deceived by the local errors of his native village: [similarly,] the scholar has lived in many times and is therefore in some degree immune from the great cataract of nonsense that pours from the press and the microphone of his own age" (35).

Although attempts to disown the past usually arise from chronological snobbery, they can also arise from anger. Sayers's play *The Just Vengeance,* as we saw in chapter 6, deals with the bitterness caused by World War II. It also addresses the larger issue of blaming all our present problems on past events, shifting responsibility back through previous generations. In anger, many people blamed "society" and the earlier events that created the tensions that led to the war. They sought to dissociate themselves from all the wrong-mindedness that the past seemed to represent. When the Airman (the central character), having rejected the creeds of the Church and the formalized ideals of the past, attempts to state his personal beliefs, his "creed" turns out to be the same facile belief in progress that Eliot berated in *The Rock,* and Lewis satirized in "Evolutionary Hymn." The Airman says, "I believe in man, and in the hope of the future, / The steady growth of knowledge and power over things, / The equality of all labouring for the community, / And a just world where everyone will be happy" (Sayers, *The Just Vengeance* 297).

The Recorder asks the Airman to explain what he means by everyone: "Who," he asks, "will be equal and happy?" Does the Airman mean to include the suffering people of Lichfield's past that form the play's Chorus? And they, echoing the Recorder's point, cry out, "Who will give justice to us? / Where is our happiness? Where is our equality?" Disowning them, the Airman responds harshly, "The past is dead. We must turn our backs on it, / Forget it, bury it. I denounce the past. / The past has turned the world to a living hell. / We must build for the future." And he shifts the blame, crying, "I had no time; I was killed; / It was not my fault, but the fault of the old people" (298). The members of the Chorus, speaking individually, one after the other, moving back through the most recent periods of history to the earliest, say, "It was not our fault, but the fault of the old people." Witnessing this backward-moving chain of blame, the Airman finally sees the irrationality of such a view, and realizes that the people of his day and those of the past "are victims together" (299).

Sayers regarded *The Just Vengeance* as her greatest work.[10] A very rich play, it explores many Christian themes, including those examined in some of my previous chapters: the nature of Christ, the process of conversion, and the meaning of suffering. It is also Sayers's most powerful depiction of the impossibility of rejecting the past. In portraying the fallen Airman's bitterness, enlightenment, and redemption, it constructs the basis for making peace with the past. The play makes good the promise of its opening scene when the Airman's feet, heard running into the cathedral, are recognized as "the feet of the fallen, / The feet of the forgetful running back to remembrance, / The feet of the future hurrying home to the past" (283). Written during World War II and performed shortly after its end, the play was a message of hope during a dark period—hope that bitter individuals could be redeemed and time could be redeemed.

Going Back to Find the Freedom of Redemption

The process of redemption includes establishing a right relationship with the past. It is a kind of redemption of time. At the beginning of "Burnt Norton," Eliot says, very cryptically, "If all time is eternally present / All time is unredeemable" (*Four Quartets* 117). This enigmatic statement may be interpreted as meaning that if we live as though the present is all there is, all that matters, we cannot be redeemed and delivered from the bondage of time. This interpretation is supported by the fact that, in the final movement of "Little Gidding," Eliot says, "A people without history / Is not redeemed from time" (*Four Quartets* 144), indicating that redemption of time *is* possible, and that disassociation from history means people will be victimized by time rather than triumphing over it. In movement 4 of *Ash Wednesday,* a poem that explores the process of salvation and the "restoring" of the years, Eliot twice utters the imperative, "Redeem the time" (*Ash Wednesday* 64). The fourth and fifth lines of "Burnt Norton" state "If all time is eternally present / All time is unredeemable" (*Four Quartets* 117). Although, taken in isolation, they seem to imply that the redemption of time is impossible, they actually introduce the theme of the entire four-part work—the theme of the redemption of time. Taken as a whole, the *Four Quartets* show that all time is *not* "eternally present" in the sense that it is fixed and that nothing can be done about it. It can be redeemed.

The redemption of the past operates on a personal level as well as a societal level. The past of an individual life must be accepted, forgiven, and built upon. Eliot's play *The Family Reunion* portrays the truth that "The future can only be built / Upon the real past" (228), as Harry painfully learns the truth about the past, accepts it, and is thus able to forgive it and himself. He realizes that until he faced the past, "all [his] life has been a flight" (280). He acknowledges that he has been "befouled," but now knows that "there is only one way out of defilement— / Which leads in the end to reconciliation" (279). He has embraced the truth about the past. The things he remembers now have a "different sense / That would have seemed meaningless before" (275), but now are part of his reconciliation and redemption. "Everything tends toward reconciliation" (275), he concludes. The reconciliation that Harry experiences comes from a redemptive knowledge of the "real past." Now free of the malignant power the tainted past had held over him, he exclaims, "this is the first time that I have been free" (278).

The four poems of *Four Quartets* explore the paradox of redeeming the past.[11] The third poem, "The Dry Salvages,"[12] deals with recovering the past in a way that connects our personal past with the historical past. In movement 2, it speaks of a common occurrence: we have had a significant experience, but though we recognize its importance, we cannot really understand it. "We had the experience but missed the meaning." But later in time, as we assimilate the experiences of "many generations," and enter vicariously into them, we can begin to better understand aspects of our own past lives. This applies particularly to painful experiences, "moments of agony." In connecting with the "agony of others" we gain acceptance of the pain in our own past, and in embracing the fraternity of suffering we approach something that is "permanent / With such permanence as time has." Even though, in one sense, "the agony abides," the memories are no longer destructive, they are restorative: "Time the destroyer is time the preserver." Painful experiences are comparable to dangerous rocks along the sea coast, "the ragged rock in the restless waters, / Waves wash over it, fogs conceal it." In the "sudden fury" of a storm such rocks are instruments of destruction, but in "navigable weather [they become] a seamark / To lay a course by." It can be thus with memories: when they are unredeemed through being disowned or misunderstood, they will destroy us, but when they are faced and redeemed they bring reconciliation with the past and a connection with "permanent" things. They become a "preserver" of our lives in that they are markers "to lay a course by" (*Four Quartets* 133).

"Little Gidding," the last of the poems in *Four Quartets,* speaks of negative and positive attachments to the past—attachments concerning both the historical past and personal memories. In the third movement, Eliot observes, "History may be servitude / History may be freedom." The wrong sort of attachment to the past is bondage to history in the sense of slavish submission to its tenets and practices. The right sort of connectedness to history is a wise knowledge and understanding of the past. Such knowledge and understanding are gloriously liberating. In this sense, indeed, "History may be freedom" (*Four Quartets* 142).

As movement 3 of "Little Gidding" continues, Eliot speaks of gaining freedom from the past in a more personal sense. Even the untainted things of the past, the precious things, can have negative power over us as we continue to grieve over their loss. The joys of the past drop away from us, "See, now they vanish / The faces and places, with the self which, as it could, loved them." The people and places that "vanish" from our immediate visual field are beloved images that we must let go of—however painful that may be. We must, at certain points, relinquish remnants of people and places and ideas, and let them "vanish" out of our lives. And with that relinquishment we feel ourselves diminished; our former self, the self that loved them, seems to vanish too. We feel depleted and changed, as though we are no longer the same person. But, surprisingly, as the passage goes on to reveal, such relinquishment does not mean a permanent depletion. Although the "faces and places" appear to vanish, they are subsequently returned to us, "renewed, transfigured, in another pattern" (*Four Quartets* 142). The lost "faces and places," and even the best part of our old selves, are miraculously restored to us, "transfigured" into a new "pattern," to become an integral part of our redeemed consciousness, part of the richer tapestry (or "pattern") God is weaving in our lives.

As it draws to a close, "Little Gidding" takes the theme of the redemption of time to an even higher level. In its final movement, all our significant actions are depicted as a kind of death and a step toward personal oblivion: "any action / Is a step to the [execution] block, to the fire, down the sea's throat [by drowning] / Or to an illegible [grave] stone," But, in accordance with the dying-into-life imagery of the gospel, this death is actually a beginning. Eliot declares that self-abandonment is the point from which we must start: "We die with the dying: / See, they depart, and we go with them." But we are also reborn spiritually: "See, they return, and bring us with them." This sort of restorative connectedness to the godly dead was anticipated in the first movement of "Little Gidding," in the depiction of people of faith and prayer being united with us after they are dead. The Apostles' Creed calls this "the Communion of Saints"—a mystical bond of fellowship that unites the godly, both living and dead. In this section, Eliot depicts the saints of the past as surrounding us and communicating with us: "What the dead had no speech for, when living / They can tell you being dead: the communication / Of the dead is tongued with fire beyond the language of the living" (*Four Quartets* 142). Such communication is part of the mystical connectedness within the Church that stretches across time and beyond time.

In movement 5 of "Little Gidding," Eliot continues to explore the redemption from time and of time, alluding again to the communion that exists between people of faith, living and dead. The statement, "A people without history / Is not redeemed from time," does not mean merely that we need general connectedness to history if we are to live well. It means much more than this: it means that a right view of time is a component of redemption. Eliot, Lewis, and Sayers believed that we become rightly connected to history through a redemptive process in which the initiative is God's. "A people without history / Is not redeemed from time" is followed by the qualifier, "for history is a pattern of timeless moments" (*Four Quartets* 144). The "pattern" is not the design of men, but of God; and the "timeless moments" are the moments when frail human beings are brought in contact with him.

The Historical Sense and the Traditional Writer

Eliot's essay "Tradition and the Individual Talent," although written in 1919, expresses the view of the past and of time that Eliot held throughout his entire life. It represents, as Russell Kirk observes, his "literary and social principles from beginning to end." It confirms that Eliot was "not revolutionary, but conservative," and that even in his earliest writings, Eliot was a defender of "what he came to call 'permanent things'" (Kirk 50).

By *tradition* Eliot denotes something very specific. Using the word to mean the best in what is commonly called tradition, he asserts that this sort of "tradition" is crucial in the work of any modern writer. He is not recommending "following the ways of the immediate generation before us in blind or timid adherence to its successes" ("Tradition and the Individual Talent" 14). Tradition, as Eliot understands it, is not repetition; it is "a matter of much wider significance" that requires what he calls "the historical sense" (14). This concept is central to the perspective on time and the past that Eliot shared with Lewis and Sayers: "The historical sense involves a perception, not only of the pastness of the past, but of its presence; the historical sense compels a man to write not merely with his own generation in his bones, but with a feeling that the whole of the literature of Europe from Homer and within it the whole of the literature of his own country has a simultaneous existence and composes a simultaneous order" (14). This historical sense, Eliot explains, allows a person to be simultaneously aware of that which is timeless and that which is temporal, and of the connectedness between them. This, he says, "is what makes a writer traditional." And this historical sense is what makes a writer understand his position in relation to the past, present, and future—makes him "most acutely conscious of his place in time, of his contemporaneity" (14).

Such a consciousness of their "place in time" was one of the most important things that Eliot, Lewis, and Sayers had in common. It was this that caused them to repeatedly "ask for the old paths" (Jer. 6:16). The "historical sense" enabled them to show, in their works, the connections between the things of this world and eternal things. It is in this sense that they were all "traditional" writers, and yet very concerned with what was contemporaneous.

The extensive knowledge of early literature so apparent in all three writers is a necessary ingredient for the kind of good writing that Eliot speaks of in "Tradition and the Individual Talent." He explains that the mind of a culture, including its art, is a current that flows on through the centuries, experiencing changes, but not abandoning anything:

> The poet must be very conscious of the main current. . . . He must be quite aware of the obvious fact that art never improves, but that the material of art is never quite the same. He must be aware that the mind of Europe—the mind of his own country— . . . is a mind which changes, and that this change is a development which abandons nothing *en route.* . . .
>
> Someone said: "The dead writers are remote from us because we *know* so much more than they did." Precisely, and they are that which we know. (16)

Lewis, Sayers, and Eliot are now "dead writers" who form part of "that which we know." By juxtaposing their insights, we come to understand the best that they had to say in new and deeper ways, and to empathize with their greatest concerns.

If Lewis, Sayers, and Eliot are significant individually, they are even more significant when their ideas are set in relation to one another. Eliot believed that a poem should be considered in relation to "other poems by other authors," and suggested that poetry should be approached as something most powerful for its accumulative nature. He said that we should see poetry "as a living whole of all the poetry that has ever been written" ("Tradition and the Individual Talent" 17).

This book is based on Eliot's conviction that literary texts are most valuable when they are set in relation to one another: I believe that the key ideas of Lewis, Sayers, and Eliot are most powerful when considered simultaneously. Eliot said, "No poet, no artist of any art, has his complete meaning alone. His significance, his appreciation is the appreciation of his relation to the dead poets and artists. You cannot value him alone; you must set him, for contrast and comparison, among the dead" ("Tradition and the Individual Talent" 15). Eliot is speaking here of placing new works in the context of older works, works that preceded them in time. Nevertheless, what he says can be applied to what I have undertaken to do in this book, in tracing the similarities in thought of three writers who were contemporaries of each other. None of these writers has his or her "complete meaning alone." We can appreciate the work of each more fully by setting it, "for contrast and comparison," next to the work of the others. When the works of Lewis, Eliot, and Sayers are considered as a complementary body, the significance of individual works is altered and readjusted, and something new and even more valuable comes into being.

For most modern Christians, two of these writers—Sayers and Eliot—are nearly invisible.[13] Of all three, it may soon be said, "See, now they vanish." My intention is to make it possible to say also, "See, they return, and bring us with them" (*Four Quartets* 144). Some aspects of the mid-twentieth century have limited relevance today. Yet what Lewis, Sayers, and Eliot had to say about things of permanent importance—the nature of Christ, the experience of conversion, the ministry of angels, the mystery of suffering, the journey to heaven, and the spiritual loss that came with modern "progress"— is still worth listening to. Through revisiting their work, those of the twenty-first century who find themselves wandering in a Waste Land may better understand the message of redemption and receive it.

Notes

✠ ✠ ✠

1. A Meeting of Minds

1. Although this term is more frequently written today as *wasteland*, both Malory and Eliot wrote it as two words with initial capitals— *Waste Land;* it is therefore appropriate to maintain their spelling throughout my discussion of this image.

2. By this I mean the decades from 1930 to 1960, during which Lewis, Eliot, and Sayers wrote their major works.

3. In *The Company They Keep,* Diana Pavlac Glyer observes that several of the Inklings wrote of "large, symbolic lions," not because they were borrowing from one another, but because "the idea of a lion as an embodiment of strength and royalty is very common, and Christ is designated as 'the Lion of the tribe of Judah' in Revelation 5:5" (37).

4. Lewis grew up in Belfast, Ireland, where the established church was known as the Church of Ireland rather than the Church of England.

5. By this time he had lived outside the United States for more than twenty years and become a British citizen.

6. Barbara Reynolds, in *Dorothy L. Sayers: Her Life and Soul,* gives a full account of Sayers's early life.

7. See Suzanne Bray's *Dorothy L. Sayers: The Christ of the Creeds.*

8. This reminiscence by H. M. Blamires is recorded by C. S. Lewis's brother, Warren ("Warnie") Lewis, in his "Memoir of C. S. Lewis," included in C. S. Lewis, *Letters of C. S. Lewis: Edited and with a Memoir by W. H. Lewis,* rev. and enlgd. ed., ed. W. H. Lewis (1966; New York: Harcourt, 1994), 38; it is also reported by Walter Hooper in *C. S. Lewis: A Companion and Guide,* 20.

9. Rachel Trickett's essay "Uncrowned King of Oxford" is included in the collection *We Remember C. S. Lewis.*

10. J. H. Homes's book review appeared in the *New York Herald Tribune* Weekly Book Review on 26 September 1945.

11. Sayers died in December 1957, and the memorial service was held in January 1958.

12. From the foreword that the Rev. Welch wrote to Sayers's play sequence, *The Man Born to Be King* (1942).

13. Although this poem of Lewis's was not published until 1954, it represents the view of modern verse that he held when he first read Eliot's poetry, and throughout most of his life.

14. The definition by Wordsworth from which Tillyard quotes comes from Wordsworth's preface to the 1804 edition of *Lyrical Ballads.*

15. This essay at first publication in 1930 was entitled "The Personal Heresy," which later formed the main title of the full collection published in 1939.

16. The fact that there was no serious personal animosity between the two should not be surprising in light of the fact that Lewis was in constant, and often ferocious, disagreement with Owen Barfield and J. R. R. Tolkien, and yet these two men were among his closest friends.

17. Lewis's debt to Dante is fully explored in Marsha Daigle Williamson's *Reflecting the Eternal: Dante's Divine Comedy in the Novels of C. S. Lewis* (Peabody, Mass.: Hendrickson, 2015).

18. Lewis's first such letter was written on 19 June 1959 (*Collected Letters* 3: 1059).

19. It is an interesting coincidence that both men married—very surprisingly to their friends—late in life to women who seemed like unsuitable choices, but who brought them great happiness.

20. The passage occurs in the first movement of *Little Gidding:* "There are other places / Which also are the world's end, some at the sea jaws, / Or over a dark lake, in a desert or a city— / But this is the nearest in place and time" (*Four Quartets* 139).

21. This letter to Spencer Curtis Brown, dated 20 October 1960, is in the Bodleian Library's Special Collections, MS. Eng. lett. c. 852, folio 63.

22. In the third movement of *Little Gidding,* the people of the past Eliot most directly alludes to are those on both sides of the conflict in the English Civil War of the seventeenth century, particularly the godly people at Little Gidding who supported the Royalist side, and Milton (equally godly), who supported the Puritan side. The passage reads, "people . . . some of peculiar genius, / All touched by a common genius, / United in the strife which divided them" (*Four Quartets* 143).

23. Charles Williams—who worked at the Oxford University Press and was occasionally a guest lecturer at the university—was the author of sig-

nificant scholarly work on *The Divine Comedy,* as well as very unusual and powerful drama, fiction, and poetry. He was a member of the Inklings from the time he moved to Oxford in 1939 until his sudden death in 1945. He was virtually worshipped by all who knew him. Sayers and Lewis owed much to his encouragement and inspiration. Sayers said of him, "he is a saint without being a prig or an embarrassment, which is so rare; the sort of person who makes the idea of going to Heaven attractive" (*Letters of DLS* 3: 147).

24. Lewis's use of the term *bandersnatch* in reference to Tolkien provides the title for Diana Pavlac Glyer's book *Bandersnatch,* which examines the creative interaction between Lewis, Tolkien, and others. This book grew out of *The Company They Keep,* Glyer's more extensive examination of the mutual influence within the circle of Oxford writers who called themselves Inklings.

25. This review appeared in the periodical *Time and Tide,* on 1 October 1955.

26. This comment on Sayers was made in "Wain's Oxford," appearing on page 81 of the journal *Encounter* in January 1963. It is quoted in Walter Hooper's *C. S. Lewis: Companion and Guide,* 34.

27. The idea of the poetic function inherent in the role of prophet will be explored in chapter 2.

28. This article, first published in London's *Sunday Times* (April 1939) as "The Food of the Full-Grown," was republished in later essay collections under the title "Strong Meat." It is listed by the latter title in the bibliography.

29. In the same letter to Eliot, Sayers alluded to their mutual love of cats, and proposed a social meeting with him the following week. He obviously responded promptly, because four days later she wrote him again, suggesting alternative dates for the meeting.

30. The deep joy Eliot experienced in this marriage was soon apparent to his friends and acquaintances, and was formally expressed in the beautiful poem "A Dedication to My Wife" (*Collected Poems, 1909–1962,* 234).

31. Sayers speaks about the importance of ritual in worship in several contexts, and most directly in an unpublished essay called "Worship in the Church."

32. Though Sayers's work in apologetics and drama was well known in England in the 1940s and 1950s, it was relatively unknown in America.

33. In 1956, Eliot spoke at the University of Minnesota to an audience of nearly 14,000—probably the largest audience ever assembled to hear a lecture on literary criticism. Two years later, he spoke at the University of Texas to an audience of about 7,000. His appeal as a public speaker was less the result of his power as an orator than of his fame as a poet and as a critic.

34. Adrian Hastings confirms Lewis's popularity, pointing out that in the Church of England it was the evangelicals who "came through the sixties in far the best shape," and that it was not a liberal theologian like John Robinson but C. S. Lewis who remained the favorite Christian author (552).

2. Prophets in the Wilderness

1. Evidence of such a sense of prophetic vocation is particularly apparent in John Milton (1606–1674), William Blake (1757–1827), and William Wordsworth (1770–1850).

2. In early life, Lewis spoke often of his ambition to be a poet, particularly in letters to his friend Arthur Greeves. See, for example, his letter to Greeves of 6 March 1926 (*Collected Letters* 1: 926).

3. These radio talks were eventually published collectively as *Mere Christianity* (1952).

4. This book was first published in the UK as *C. S. Lewis and the BBC*.

5. This sermon was preached at Oxford University, in the Church of St. Mary the Virgin, just after the outbreak of World War II.

6. Here she is grandiosely pulling imagery from book 2 of John Milton's *Paradise Lost*.

7. This comes from the undated manuscript (of six leaves) of an address by Sayers entitled "Detectives in Fiction," which forms part of the Dorothy L. Sayers Manuscript Collection at the Marion Wade Center, Wheaton College, Wheaton, IL.

8. I discuss this aspect of Sayers's writing more thoroughly in my book *The Seven Deadly Sins in the Work of Dorothy L. Sayers* (KSUP 1998).

9. The term *apologetics* comes from the larger idea of an *apologia* that has its roots in Latin and Greek, and from which our word *apology* is derived. The term *apology* is now most commonly applied to an explanation of and expression of regret concerning "an action that is open to blame"; *apologia*, in contrast, may be understood to denote "a verbal defense against a verbal attack, a disproving of a false accusation, or a justification of an action or line of conduct wrongly made the object of censure." These clarifying definitions are adapted from the Online Catholic Encyclopedia, available at New Advent, a website making available digitized Catholic documents; see <http://www.newadvent.org/cathen/>. This source observes that some scholars prefer to avoid the term *apologetics* in favor of such terms as *Christian Evidences* or *Defense of the Christian Religion*.

10. "The Food of the Full-Grown" (later retitled "Strong Meat") was first published on 9 April 1939, fewer than five months before the outbreak of the war on 1 September 1939. It is listed under the latter title in the bibliography.

11. Ann Loades makes these observations in the preface she wrote to *The Christ of the Creeds,* a collection of Sayers's wartime broadcasts published in 2008 by the Dorothy L. Sayers Society.

12. *The Christ of the Creeds* is a compilation of Sayers's previously unpublished radio talks and other lectures given during World War II. Suzanne Bray wrote the introduction and notes, providing excellent contextualization and insightful commentary for Sayers's lectures.

13. This society was connected with St. Anne's church, Soho, of which Sayers was a church warden.

14. At this point in time, Sayers had written four works of Christian drama: *The Zeal of Thy House* (1937), *He That Should Come* (1939), *The Devil to Pay* (1939), and *Man Born to Be King* (a twelve-part sequence; 1941–43). She would later write two more: *The Just Vengeance* (1946) and *The Emperor Constantine* (1951).

15. This letter, like the one just discussed, was written in August 1946.

16. *Missioner* is an Anglican term for evangelist.

17. Her current pressing project was the translation of Dante's *Inferno* she was working on for Penguin Books.

18. Sayers responded with empathy and wisdom to Lewis's discouraged feelings about his apologetic writing, as her letter to Lewis of 8 August 1946 indicates (*Letters of DLS* 3: 259–60).

19. This was the first time Eliot spoke from a pulpit during a religious service. He said he had accepted on this occasion only because it was in a college chapel, and that of a college of which he was a member.

20. Successive forms of this journal, under varying names (*Criterion, Monthly Criterion,* and *New Criterion*), were published from October 1922 to 1939. Some appeared quarterly, some monthly.

21. This review by Eliot of works of popular theology by five writers addressed the interchange of opinions, in three small works, between Hilaire Belloc and H. G. Wells, and also considered works by J. Middleton Murry, T. A. Lacey, and Percy Gardner. It appeared in the *Monthly Criterion* 5.2 (May 1927): 253–59.

22. Murry's speculative account of Jesus's life was an attempt to portray him, including his early years, as a universal figure. It was a semifictional work based on artistic license, rather than on the detailed research and reasoned insight normally expected of a biography.

23. This passage from John Middleton Murry's *Life of Jesus* is quoted by Eliot in the review discussed in note 21. The part pertaining to Murry appears on pages 254–58.

24. This review, "Mr. Murry's *Shakespeare,*" appears in the *Criterion* 15.61 (July 1936): 708–10.

25. In the *New Criterion* 4.2 (Apr. 1926): 389–90.

26. In the *New Criterion* 4.1 (Jan. 1926): 1–6.

27. Samuel Butler's *The Way of All Flesh* (1903) is driven by a vitriolic resentment of Victorian religion.

28. "Thoughts after Lambeth" was written in response to the Church of England's Lambeth Conference of 1930.

29. The priest William Force Stead was Eliot's friend and confidant, and an important influence at the time of his conversion (Gordon, *Eliot's Early Years*, 130–31).

30. Eliot's "Choruses from *The Rock*" are excerpted from a pageant play written in 1934 for the churches of London. Eliot collaborated on the play with others, although the choruses and dialogues are his.

31. Thomas Becket was the protagonist in Eliot's Canterbury Festival play, *Murder in the Cathedral*.

32. Eliot's footnote reads, "'Know ye not, that to whom ye yield yourselves servants to obey, his servants ye are to whom ye obey; whether of sin unto death, or of obedience unto righteousness?'—Romans 6.16."

33. Part of Sayers's lecture "Church and Theatre" at St. Anne's House, Soho, was published in *The New Outlook for Faith and Society* in 1952, under the title "Types of Christian Drama." In 1955, the full lecture was published in three parts in *The Episcopal Church News* under the title "Sacred Plays."

3. Christ

1. The term *modernism* is derived from the Latin *modo*, meaning "just now."

2. Translation by Charles W. Kennedy.

3. The original manuscript of this letter, dated 19 June 1943, forms part of the Dorothy L. Sayers Papers at the Marion Wade Center, Wheaton College, Wheaton, IL. It is not included in the four-volume collected *Letters* of Sayers, but is reproduced in *The Christ of the Creeds*.

4. This series of twelve plays was broadcast on BBC radio between December 1941 and October 1942.

5. An indirect, but significant, connection between the image of a lion and the kingly authority of Christ occurs in a passage in Genesis: "Judah is a lion's cub; from the prey, my son, you have gone up. He stooped down; he crouched as a lion and as a lioness; who dares rouse him? The scepter shall not depart from Judah, nor the ruler's staff from between his feet, until tribute comes to him; and to him shall be the obedience of the peoples" (Gen. 49.9–10, *ESV*).

6. "Gerontion" was published in 1920 in Eliot's book *Poems* (New York: Alfred A. Knopf, 1920).

7. Andrewes was a leading churchman during the reign of James I and one of the translators who produced the King James Version of the Bible.

8. The English Standard Version reads, "The light shines in the darkness, and the darkness has not overcome it."

9. The sound effects of the second to last line of this 9-line passage, with its pun-like manipulation of *unstilled* and *still* and of *world* and *whirled*, support the imagery and sharpen the intensity of the passage.

10. The poem "East Coker" was originally published individually in 1940 in the *New English Weekly*. In 1943, it was republished as the second poem of four composing Eliot's *Four Quartets*.

11. The idea that the Messiah would be a suffering servant appears in the writings of several Old Testament prophets.

4. Choosing to Be the Chosen of God

1. The term *conversion* is fairly rare in the Bible and in Protestant confessional documents. Nonetheless, the term does occur, and in something like the sense we now use it, in the Westminster Confession of Faith, Larger and Shorter Catechisms of 1647, adopted and still used by Presbyterian churches in America.

2. Two of these are the *American Standard Version (ASV)* and the *English Revised Version (ERV)*.

3. Gordon, *Eliot's Early Years*, 130–31.

4. Lancelot Andrewes was a highly acclaimed preacher in the time of James I. His influence on Eliot's poem "Gerontion" is discussed in chapter 3.

5. Spurr counters Gordon's assessment of Eliot's movement toward conversion, arguing that this earlier fascination with the lives of mystics and saints was not the most significant stage in the development of his faith. Spurr believes that Eliot's embrace of sacramentalism, at the time of his baptism and confirmation, was the turning point of paramount importance, and argues that Eliot's youthful interest in Christian intensities was a mere preliminary. Nonetheless, Spurr emphasizes the emotional aspect of Eliot's spirituality.

6. In this context, Eliot's calling the gate "unknown" and "remembered" suggests that, though coming to God is like going home (arriving "where we started" [*Four Quartets* 145]), it is also coming to a place we were already dimly aware of, but were unable to find completely on our own.

7. As the first day of Lent, Ash Wednesday marks the start of a period of self-examination and repentance.

8. This is an allusion to the words of the centurion to Jesus, "Lord, I am not worthy that you should come under my roof: but speak the word only and my servant shall be healed" (Matt. 8.8)—words that indicate his great humility and great faith.

9. This line is spoken by the souls that Dante encounters on the level of Paradise described in canto 9.

10. This play and Eliot's next play, *The Cocktail Party*, will be examined in depth in chapter 5.

11. Neville Coghill's note to this passage explains it as "an allusion to Christ's parable of the unclean spirit that returns to a soul it has quitted . . . and the last state of that soul is worse than the first (Matt. 12.43–45)" (219–20).

12. *Prometheus Unbound* 1. 195–99: "For know there are two worlds of life and death: / One that which thou beholdest; but the other / Is underneath the grave, where do inhabit / The shadows of all forms that think and live / Till death unite them and they part no more."

13. The belief that St. Helena, Constantine's mother, was a British princess has been popular in Britain for centuries, but it is more mythic than historical.

5. Angelic Interference

1. Here I am using *myth* in the way Lewis understood it. He said, "The heart of Christianity is a myth which is also a fact. The old myth of the Dying God, *without ceasing to be a myth*, comes down . . . to the earth of history. . . . By becoming fact it does not cease to be myth: that is the miracle" ("Myth Became Fact" 43–44).

2. Malcolm Godwin's book *Angels: An Endangered Species* is an impressive survey of angelology, scriptural and nonscriptural.

3. A houri [sing.] is a mythic nymphlike creature.

4. There are about seventy references in the narratives of the gospels and acts, about thirty references in the epistles, and about seventy in the Book of Revelation.

5. It was translated from Latin in 1549 for the Church of England's *Book of Common Prayer.*

6. Here Sayers may be partly indebted to Milton's similar use of the angel Raphael in *Paradise Lost.*

7. Distinctions between avenging and recording angels are not strictly observed by Sayers. She often overlaps and merges them.

8. A great revival of interest in Platonism occurred in fifteenth-century Florence under the Medici.

9. A footnote to this letter written by Walter Hooper, the editor of Lewis's three-volume *Collected Letters,* indicates that this view of angelic form is found in Aquinas's *Summa Theologica,* part 1, question 50, article 2.

10. In her notes to this line, Sayers explains the wheel as the "combined rotary movement of the planets" (Dante, *Paradise* 60).

11. Eliot's view of Christ as the still center, or axis, is discussed more fully in chapter 3.

12. The dystopian form was made popular by Aldous Huxley in his 1932 novel, *Brave New World,* and by George Orwell in his 1949 novel, *Nineteen Eighty-Four.*

13. This movie was initially released under the title *Foster.*

14. This is a reference to Harry's slight romantic attraction to his cousin Mary, who had been a close friend in childhood.

15. The notable exceptions are E. Martin Browne and Russell Kirk.

16. In Genesis, chapters 18 and 19, and in Judges 13.6, angelic visitors are received as though they were human.

17. The 1974 Faber and Faber edition of *The Cocktail Party* includes thorough notes and commentary by Neville Coghill that draw heavily on the critic's exchanges with Eliot, and on letters by Eliot to which Coghill had access. Coghill was a highly regarded scholar with close ties to the Inklings. His essay "Structure and Meaning of the Play" is included in this 1974 volume.

18. "Burnt Norton" speaks cryptically of the relationship between past, present, and future: "Time past and time future / What might have been and what has been / Point to one end, which is always present," and "Time past and time future / Allow but a little consciousness" (*Four Quartets* 117, 119). This and other aspects of Eliot's view of time will be discussed in chapter 7.

19. This ignorance is a reference to 1 Peter 1.12, in which the "gospel" of salvation is described as something "angels desire to look into."

20. E. Martin Browne, who was intimately involved in the production of all Eliot's plays, comments at length on the shock and dismay with which many audience members and reviewers responded to the play, particularly the last act. "What Eliot wanted," Browne observes, "was certainly not to shock for the sake of shocking, but to make sure that the martyrdom should be realized as actual suffering" (226).

21. Plath's poetry took a form that has been called "confessional"—a form that is largely autobiographical and deals with dark subjects like depression, suffering, and death.

6. Fiery Trials

1. Sayers argued that her play evoked the "spell of poetic speech" and that children will internalize the "mystery and queer beauty of melodious words" even if their brains cannot fully grasp their import. She declared, "It is my business to know how my . . . audience will react; and yours to trust me to know it" (*Letters of DLS* 2: 196–97).

2. The BCC provided news service for other European countries whose own radio services had been curtailed by German occupation.

3. The duty he performed as an air raid warden is evidence of how practically he lived out this principle.

4. This was the church in which, in the sixteenth century, the Protestant reformers Latimer, Ridley, and Cranmer had been tried and sentenced to execution; moreover, John Wesley, John Keble, and John Henry Newman had preached from its pulpit.

5. Eliot wrote this short piece—something between poetry and prose— just after the evacuation from Dunkirk, to accompany a New York exhibition of photos illustrating the war effort in England.

6. From Thomas Gray's well-known poem "Elegy Written in a Country Churchyard."

7. This is recorded by Ralph E. Hone, who edited *The Poetry of Dorothy L. Sayers,* the volume of Sayers's poetry published in 1996. Hone also notes that Sayers was told that Lord Wavell, who was viceroy of India from 1943 to 1947, was heard to recite the whole poem from memory (Hone 122).

8. At the time Sayers wrote this poem, the United States had not entered the war.

9. "We" can refer to those responsible for bombing, on both sides of the conflict.

10. That is, before Germany's aerial bombardment began.

11. The black humor of the egg image is forgivable in view of the many such "baskets of eggs" the Germans had delivered to the people of England in 1940 and 1941.

12. This poem was written for a collection of poems called *London Calling,* published in New York in 1942.

13. This article was published in the *Sunday Times* on 10 September 1939, one week after Britain declared war on Germany.

14. This address was published (almost immediately) in several different venues.

15. These 1943 letters were not included in the four-volume collection of Sayers's letters published between 1996 and 2000; they are, however, in-

cluded *The Christ of the Creeds,* a collection of Sayers's broadcasts edited by Suzanne Bray.

16. This play was examined briefly in chapter 3, in connection with the depiction of Christ, and again in chapter 5, in connection with the depiction of angels.

17. We considered movement 4 of "East Coker" in chapter 3 as a depiction of the redemptive severity of Christ.

7. The Journey to Joy

1. Lewis commented on the third canto of Dante's *Divine Comedy, Paradiso,* in a letter to Arthur Greeves in January 1930, from which this is taken. His numerous appreciative remarks on *The Divine Comedy* in letters of earlier years indicate that Lewis's admiration of Dante was well established before his conversion.

2. This chapter will focus primarily on Lewis and Eliot because imagery of life as a journey to a glorious destination is much less apparent in the work of Dorothy L. Sayers. It is mainly in Sayers's discussions of Dante that the journeying motif is significant. Her view of time and aging does cohere with those of Lewis and Eliot, however, and will be discussed later in this chapter.

3. In the fifth movement of his poem *Ash Wednesday,* as we saw earlier, Eliot describes Christ himself, the divine Word incarnate, as the center or axis about which the troubled world spins.

4. In his Notes to *The Waste Land,* Eliot acknowledged this background material, explaining, "Not only the title, but the plan and a good deal of the incidental symbolism of the poem were suggested by Miss Jessie L. Weston's book on the Grail legend: *From Ritual to Romance* (Cambridge)" (*The Waste Land* 50).

5. The Grail chapel was also called the Chapel Perilous. In legend, it was one of the last stages in the quest, and the place where the knights' courage would be sorely tested.

6. Many commentaries on *The Waste Land,* especially those intended for high school teachers, wrongly interpret *Damyata* to mean "take control of things yourself." To do this is to ignore the point of the passage that immediately follows, a passage that illustrates not *taking control,* but *being controlled.*

7. Eliot, in his Notes, tells us that *shantih* means "the Peace which passeth understanding" (*The Waste Land* 55).

8. We considered this passage in chapter 6 in connection with the Blitz.

9. The image of the Great Dance recurs in Lewis's fiction, particularly

near the end of *Perelandra,* representing the joyous and intricate pattern of the divine will.

10. In referring to the soul as *her,* Lewis is following tradition of referring to the soul using feminine personal pronouns.

11. Lewis taught at Oxford University's Magdalen College for more than thirty years.

8. Ask for the Old Paths

1. The name "Old Possum" originates in Joel Chandler Harris's *Uncle Remus.*

2. The lyrics of the musical *Cats* are taken from these poems.

3. This essay was published in a periodical called *The Fortnightly* in April 1940 and has not been reprinted.

4. The ninety-one-page manuscript of this material is held in the Marion Wade Center at Wheaton College, Wheaton, IL.

5. This poem was considered in chapter 1 as an illustration of Lewis's opinion of Eliot's verse. It also expresses of Lewis's view of modernity in general.

6. Lewis's "Evolutionary Hymn" was published in the *Cambridge Review* in 1957, but an earlier version of it was included in a letter Lewis wrote to Sayers on 4 March 1954—a letter in which he refers to a recent "delightful visit" from her. During this visit, Sayers had apparently shared with him her "Pantheon Papers," some of which had been published the previous month by the magazine *Punch.* See his invitation to her for 18 February (*Collected Letters of CSL* 2: 417).

7. *Me Meum Laudo* means "I exalt myself."

8. These were questions she received in letters from people who had seen *The Zeal of Thy House* (which she had written for the Canterbury Festival of 1937).

9. In 1943, Lewis was guest speaker for the Riddell Lectures at the University of Durham. The three lectures he delivered for that series were published by Oxford University Press the following year as *The Abolition of Man, or, Reflections on Education with Special Reference to the Teaching of English in the Upper Forms of Schools.*

10. She told Barbara Reynolds, "It is the best thing I have ever done" (Reynolds, *The Passionate Intellect* 97).

11. Eliot said of *Four Quartets,* "I'd like to feel that they get better as they go on. The second is better than the first, the third is better than the second, and the fourth ["Little Gidding"] is best of all" ("The Art of Poetry" 64).

12. The poem is named for a cluster of rocks off Cape Ann, Massachusetts, called the Dry Salvages.

13. Many readers are unaware of the Christian undergirding of T. S. Eliot's work, and many have only a vague idea of Dorothy L. Sayers's significance as a Christian writer.

Bibliography

✝ ✝ ✝

Andrewes, Lancelot. *Seventeen Sermons on the Nativity.* London: Griffith, Farran, Okeden, and Welsh, 1887.

Bray, Suzanne. Introduction. *The Christ of the Creeds: And Other Broadcast Messages to the British People During World War II.* By Dorothy L. Sayers. Hurstpierpoint, West Sussex: The Dorothy L. Sayers Society, 2008. 1–30.

Brooker, Jewell Spears. *Mastery and Escape: T. S. Eliot and the Dialectic of Modernism.* Amherst, MA: U of Massachusetts P, 1994.

Brown, Janice. *The Seven Deadly Sins in the Work of Dorothy L. Sayers.* Kent, OH: Kent State UP, 1998.

Browne, E. Martin. *The Making of T. S. Eliot's Plays.* Cambridge, UK: Cambridge UP, 1969.

Bunyan, John. *The Pilgrim's Progress.* London: Penguin Books, 2008.

Churchill, Winston. "Blood, Toil, Tears, and Sweat." Speech to House of Commons, 13 May 1940. *Never Give In! Winston Churchill's Speeches.* Revelations ed. London: Bloomsbury, 2013. 169.

Coghill, Neville. "An Essay on the Structure and Meaning of the Play." *T. S. Eliot's* The Cocktail Party. London: Faber and Faber, 1974. 237–41.

———. "Notes to *The Cocktail Party.*" *T. S. Eliot's* The Cocktail Party. London: Faber and Faber, 1974. 201–33.

"Coventry Buries Her Dead: A Strange, Simple, and Moving Service at the Graveside." *The Guardian,* 21 Nov. 1940: 6.

Dante Alighieri. *The Comedy of Dante Alighieri: The Florentine: Cantica I: Hell (L'Inferno).* By Dante. Trans. Dorothy L. Sayers. 1949; Harmondsworth, Middlesex: Penguin, 1983.

———. *The Comedy of Dante Alighieri: The Florentine: Cantica II: Purgatory (Il Purgatorio).* By Dante. Trans. Dorothy L. Sayers. 1955; Harmondsworth, Middlesex: Penguin, 1984.

————. *The Comedy of Dante Alighieri: The Florentine: Cantica III: Paradise (Il Paradiso)*. By Dante. Trans. Dorothy L. Sayers and Barbara Reynolds. 1962; Harmondsworth, Middlesex: Penguin, 1984.

Donne, John. "Devotions upon Emergent Occasions: XVII Meditation." *The Complete Poetry and Selected Prose*. New York: Modern Library, 1994. 440–41.

————. "Good Friday, 1613. Riding Westward." *The Complete Poetry and Selected Prose*. New York: Modern Library, 1994. 246–47.

The Dream of the Rood. Trans. Charles W. Kennedy. Old English Series. Cambridge, Ontario: In Parentheses Publications, 2000. Available at In Parentheses (web page). <http://www.yorku.ca/inpar/>.

Eliot, T. S. *After Strange Gods: A Primer of Modern Heresy*. London: Faber and Faber, 1934.

————. "The Art of Poetry, I." *Paris Review* 21 (1959): 64.

————. *Ash Wednesday*. *The Complete Poems and Plays, 1909–1950*. By Eliot. New York: Harcourt Brace and World, 1971. 60–67.

————. "Baudelaire." *Selected Essays*. 3rd. rev. ed. London: Faber and Faber, 1951. 419–30.

————. "Choruses from *The Rock*." *The Complete Poems and Plays, 1909–1950*. By Eliot. New York: Harcourt Brace and World, 1971. 96–114.

————. *Christianity and Culture: The Idea of a Christian Society and Notes Towards the Definition of Culture*. 1940; New York: Harcourt, Brace, 1960.

————. *The Cocktail Party*. *The Complete Poems and Plays, 1909–1950*. By Eliot. New York: Harcourt Brace and World, 1971. 295–388.

————. *The Complete Poems and Plays: 1909–1950*. By Eliot. New York: Harcourt Brace and World, 1971.

————. *The Confidential Clerk*. London: Faber and Faber, 1979.

————. "The Cultivation of Christmas Trees." *Collected Poems, 1909–1962*. By Eliot. London: Faber and Faber. 1963. 117–18.

————. "Dante." *Selected Essays*. 3rd. rev. ed. London: Faber and Faber, 1951. 237–77.

————. "Defense of the Islands." *Collected Poems, 1909–1962*. By Eliot. London: Faber and Faber. 1963. 227–28.

————. *The Family Reunion*. *The Complete Poems and Plays, 1909–1950*. By Eliot. New York: Harcourt Brace and World, 1971. 223–93.

————. *For Lancelot Andrewes*. London: Faber and Faber, 1970.

————. *Four Quartets*. *The Complete Poems and Plays, 1909–1950*. By Eliot. New York: Harcourt Brace and World, 1971. 115–45.

————. "Gerontion." *The Complete Poems and Plays, 1909–1950*. By Eliot. New York: Harcourt Brace and World, 1971. 21–23.

————. "The Hollow Men." *The Complete Poems and Plays, 1909–1950.* By Eliot. New York: Harcourt Brace and World, 1971. 56–59.

————. "The Idea of a Christian Society." *Christianity and Culture: The Centenary Edition.* San Diego: Harcourt Brace, 1988. 5–77.

————. Introduction. *All Hallows' Eve.* By Charles Williams. Grand Rapids, MI: Eerdmans, 1985. ix–xviii.

————. "Journey of the Magi." *The Complete Poems and Plays, 1909–1950.* By Eliot. New York: Harcourt Brace and World, 1971. 68–69.

————. "Lancelot Andrewes." *Selected Essays.* 3rd. rev. ed. London: Faber and Faber, 1951. 341–53.

————. Letter to Spencer Curtis Brown. MS. Eng. lett. c. 852, folio 63, Bodleian Library, Oxford University, Oxford, UK.

————. "The Love Song of J. Alfred Prufrock." *The Complete Poems and Plays, 1909–1950.* By Eliot. New York: Harcourt Brace and World, 1971. 3–7.

————. "Marina." *The Complete Poems and Plays, 1909–1950.* By Eliot. New York: Harcourt Brace and World, 1971. 72–73.

————. "Matthew Arnold." *The Use of Poetry and the Use of Criticism.* Cambridge, MA: Harvard UP, 1961. 95–112.

————. "Mr. Murry's *Shakespeare*." Review of *Shakespeare,* by John Middleton Murry. *The Criterion* 15.61 (July 1936): 708–10.

————. *Murder in the Cathedral.* London: Faber and Faber, 1982.

————. "A Note on the Verse of John Milton." *Essays and Studies* (The English Association, 1936). Reprinted as "Milton I" in *Milton: Two Studies by T. S. Eliot.* London: Faber and Faber, 1968. 9–21.

————. "A Note on War Poetry." *Collected Poems, 1909–1962.* By Eliot. London: Faber and Faber, 1963. 229–30.

————. "Poetry and Drama." *On Poetry and Poets.* New York: Farrar, Straus, and Giroux, 1957. 75–97.

————. "Poetry in Wartime." *Common Sense.* Oct. 1942: 351.

————. "Popular Theologians: Mr. Wells, Mr. Belloc and Mr. Murry." Review of *The Life of Jesus* by J. Middleton Murry; *A Companion to Mr. Wells's "Outline of History"* by Hilaire Belloc; *Mr. Belloc Objects to "The Outline of History,"* by H. G. Wells; *Mr. Belloc Still Objects to Mr. Wells's "Outline of History,"* by Hilaire Belloc.; *The Anglo-Catholic Faith,* by T. A. Lacey; and *Modernism in the English Church,* by Percy Gardner. *The Monthly Criterion* 5.2 (May 1927): 253–59.

————. "Preludes." *The Complete Poems and Plays, 1909–1950.* By Eliot. New York: Harcourt Brace and World, 1971. 12–13.

————. "Religion and Literature." *Selected Essays.* 3rd. rev. ed. London: Faber and Faber, 1951. 388–401.

————. A Sermon Preached in Magdalene College Chapel. 7 Mar. 1948. Cambridge, UK: Cambridge UP, 1948. 1–8. Copy in Bodleian Library, Oxford University, Oxford, UK.

————. "The Social Function of Poetry." *On Poetry and Poets*. New York: Farrar, Straus, and Giroux, 1957. 3–16.

————. "A Song for Simeon." *The Complete Poems and Plays, 1909–1950*. By Eliot. New York: Harcourt Brace and World, 1971. 69–70.

————. "Thoughts after Lambeth." *Selected Essays*. 3rd. rev. ed. London: Faber and Faber, 1951. 363–67.

————. "Tradition and the Individual Talent." *Selected Essays*. 3rd. rev. ed. London: Faber and Faber, 1951. 13–22.

————. *The Waste Land. The Complete Poems and Plays, 1909–1950*. By Eliot. New York: Harcourt Brace and World, 1971. 37–55.

Frye, Northrop. *T. S. Eliot: An Introduction*. Chicago: U of Chicago P, 1981.

Gangel, Kenneth. "Angels, God's Ministering Spirits." *Kindred Spirit: A Quarterly Publication of Dallas Theological Seminary* Summer 1995: 5–7.

Gardner, Helen. *The Art of T. S. Eliot*. London: Cresset Press, 1949.

Glyer, Diana Pavlac. *Bandersnatch: C. S. Lewis, J. R. R. Tolkien, and the Creative Collaboration of the Inklings*. Kent, OH: Kent State UP, 2016.

————. *The Company They Keep: C. S. Lewis and J. R. R. Tolkien as Writers in Community*. Kent, OH: Kent State UP, 2007.

Godwin, Malcolm. *Angels: An Endangered Species*. Simon and Schuster, 1990.

Gordon, Lyndall. *Eliot's Early Years*. Oxford: Oxford UP, 1977.

————. *Eliot's New Life*. Oxford: Oxford UP, 1989.

————. *T. S. Eliot: An Imperfect Life*. New York: W. W. Norton and Co., 1998.

Green, Roger Lancelyn, and Walter Hooper. *C. S. Lewis: A Biography*. New York: Harcourt Brace, 1994.

Hastings, Adrian. *A History of English Christianity: 1920–1990*. London: SCM Press, 1991.

Homes, J. H. Review of *Beyond Personality* by C. S. Lewis. Weekly Book Review, *New York Herald Tribune*, 26 Sept. 1945, 12.

Hone, Ralph E., ed. *The Poetry of Dorothy L. Sayers*. Hurstpierpoint, West Sussex: The Dorothy L. Sayers Society, 1996.

Hooper, Walter. *C. S. Lewis: A Companion and Guide*. San Franciso: Harper Collins, 1996.

The IVP Bible Background Commentary: Old Testament. Ed. John H. Walton, Victor H. Matthews, and Mark W. Chavalas. Downers Grove, IL: Intervarsity Press, 2000.

Jones, D. E. *The Plays of T. S. Eliot.* Toronto: U of Toronto P, 1962.

Kirk, Russell. *Eliot and His Age: T. S. Eliot's Moral Imagination in the Twentieth Century.* Wilmington, DE: Intercollegiate Studies Institute, 2008.

Lewis, C. S. *The Abolition of Man: or Reflections on Education with Special Reference to the Teaching of English in the Upper Forms of Schools.* New York: Touchstone, 1996.

———. *All My Road Before Me: The Diary of C. S. Lewis, 1922–1927.* Ed. Walter Hooper. San Diego: Harcourt Brace, 1991.

———. *Collected Letters.* Ed. Walter Hooper. 3 vols. New York: HarperCollins, 2000–2007.

———. *The Collected Poems of C. S. Lewis: A Critical Edition.* Ed. Don W. King. Kent, OH: Kent State UP, 2015.

———. "The Conditions for a Just War." *Theology* 38. no. 227 (May 1939): 373–74. Republished as "To the Editor of *Theology (EC)."* *The Collected Letters of C. S. Lewis.* 2: 250–52.

———. "*De Descriptione Temporum*" (Inaugural Lecture at Cambridge University, Nov. 29, 1954). *They Asked for a Paper.* London: Geoffrey Bles, 1962. 9–25.

———. *The Discarded Image: An Introduction to Medieval and Renaissance Literature.* Cambridge, UK: Cambridge UP, 2007.

———. *English Literature in the Sixteenth Century Excluding Drama.* Oxford: Clarendon Press, 1954.

———. *A Grief Observed.* London: Faber and Faber, 1976.

———. *The Horse and His Boy.* New York: Collier Books, 1970.

———. "It All Began with a Picture." *C. S. Lewis on Stories and Other Essays on Literature.* New York: Harcourt Brace, 1966. 53–54.

———. "Learning in War-Time." *Fern-seed and Elephants and Other Essays on Christianity.* Glasgow: Fontana, 1978. 26–38.

———. *Letters to Malcolm: Chiefly on Prayer.* New York: Harcourt Brace, 1964.

———. *The Lion, the Witch, and the Wardrobe.* New York: Collier Books, 1970.

———. *Mere Christianity.* San Francisco: HarperCollins, 2001.

———. *Miracles: A Preliminary Study.* 1947; San Francisco: HarperCollins, 2001.

———. "Myth Became Fact." *God in the Dock: Essays on Theology.* Ed. Walter Hooper. Glasgow: Collins, 1979. 39–45.

———. "On the Reading of Old Books." *First and Second Things: Essays on Theology and Ethics.* Ed. Walter Hooper. Glasgow: Collins Fount, 1989. 25–33.

———. *Out of the Silent Planet.* New York: Collier, 1965.

————. "A Panegyric for Dorothy L. Sayers." *C. S. Lewis: On Stories and Other Essays on Literature*. Ed. Walter Hooper. New York: Harvest-Harcourt Brace, 1982. 91–95.

————. *Perelandra*. New York: Collier Books, 1965.

————. *The Pilgrim's Regress: An Allegorical Apology for Christianity, Reason, and Romanticism*. 1933; Glasgow: Collins Fount, 1977.

————. *Poems*. Ed. Walter Hooper. New York: HarperCollins, 1994.

————. Preface [1941]. *The Screwtape Letters*. By Lewis. London: Geoffrey Bles, Centenary Press, 1942,

————. Preface [1962]. *The Screwtape Letters*. By Lewis. New York: McMillan, 1963.

————. *A Preface to Paradise Lost*. Oxford: Oxford UP, 1975.

————. *Prince Caspian*. New York: Collier Books, 1970.

————. *The Problem of Pain*. Glasgow: Collins Fount, 1979.

————. "Rejoinder to Dr. Pittenger." *God in the Dock*. Grand Rapids, MI: Eerdmans, 1970. 177–83.

————. *The Screwtape Letters*. Glasgow: Collins, 1956.

————. *The Silver Chair*. New York: Collier Books, 1970.

————. *Surprised by Joy: The Shape of My Early Life*. New York: Harcourt Brace, 1955.

————. *That Hideous Strength*. London: Pan Books, 1983.

————. *Till We Have Faces: A Myth Retold*. New York: Harcourt Brace, 1984.

————. *The Voyage of the Dawn Treader*. New York: Collier Books, 1970.

————. "Wain's Oxford." Letter. *Encounter* Jan. 1963: 81.

————. "What Are We to Make of Jesus Christ?" *God in the Dock: Essays on Theology*. Ed. Walter Hooper. Glasgow: Collins, 1979. 79–84.

————. "Why I am not a Pacifist." *The Weight of Glory: And Other Addresses*, by Lewis. Rev. pbk. Ed. New York: HarperCollins, 2001. 64–90.

Lewis, Warren. "Memoir of C. S. Lewis." *Letters of C. S. Lewis: Edited and with a Memoir by W. H. Lewis*. By C. S. Lewis. Ed. W. H. Lewis. Rev. and enlgd. ed. 1966; New York: Harcourt, 1994. 21–46.

Loades, Ann. Preface. *The Christ of the Creeds: And Other Broadcast Messages to the British People During World War II*. By Dorothy L. Sayers. Hurstpierpoint, West Sussex: The Dorothy L. Sayers Society, 2008.

Malory, Thomas. *Malory's Le Morte d'Arthur: King Arthur and the Legends of the Round Table*. Ed. Keith Baines. New York: Mentor, 1962.

Milton, John. *Paradise Lost*. Ed. John Leonard. London: Penguin, 2000.

Moorman, Charles. *The Precincts of Felicity: The Augustinian City of the Oxford Christians*. Gainsville: U of Florida P, 1966.

Murry, John Middleton. *The Life of Jesus*. London: Jonathan Cape, 1926.

The 1928 Book of Common Prayer. New York: Oxford UP, 2007.

Nott, Kathleen. *The Emperor's Clothes: An Attack on the Dogmatic Orthodoxy of T. S. Eliot, Graham Greene, Dorothy Sayers, C. S. Lewis, and others.* London: Heinemann, 1953.

Phillips, Justin. *C. S. Lewis in a Time of War.* New York: Harper Collins, 2002.

Plath, Sylvia. "Black Rook in Rainy Weather." *Crossing the Water: Transitional Poems.* New York: Harper and Row, 1977. 41–42.

Raine, Kathleen. "The Poet of Our Time." In *T. S. Eliot: A Symposium.* Ed. Richard March and Tambimuttu. London: PL Editions Poetry, 1948. 78–81.

Reade, Herbert. "T. S. E.—A Memoir." *T. S. Eliot: The Man and His Work.* Ed. Allen Tate. New York: Dell, 1966. 11–37.

Review of "Beyond Personality" (series of broadcast talks), by C. S. Lewis. *Times Litereary Supplement,* 21 Oct. 1944. 513.

Reynolds, Barbara. *Dorothy L. Sayers: Her Life and Soul.* London: Hodder and Stoughton, 1993.

———. *The Passionate Intellect.* Kent, OH: Kent State UP, 1989.

Sayer, George. *Jack: A Life of C. S. Lewis.* Wheaton, IL.: Crossways, 1988.

Sayers, Dorothy L. "Christianity Regained." Rev. of *Surprised by Joy,* by C. S. Lewis. *Time and Tide* 1 Oct. 1955: 1263–64.

———. *The Christ of the Creeds: And Other Broadcast Messages to the British People During World War II.* Hurstpierpoint, West Sussex: The Dorothy L. Sayers Society, 2008.

———. "The Contempt of Learning in Twentieth-Century England." *The Fortnightly* 147 (Apr. 1940): 373–82.

———. "Creed or Chaos?" *Creed or Chaos?* New York: Harcourt, Brace: 1949. 25–45.

———. "Detectives in Fiction" (address). Undated, handwritten ms. DLS / MS-66, Dorothy L. Sayers Manuscript Collection, Marion Wade Center, Wheaton College, Wheaton, IL.

———. *The Devil to Pay. Four Sacred Plays.* London: Victor Gollancz, 1948. 105–212.

———. "Devil, Who Made Thee?" *World Review,* Aug. 1940: 35–39.

———. "The Dogma Is the Drama." *Creed or Chaos?* New York: Harcourt Brace, 1949. 20–24.

———. *The Emperor Constantine.* London: Victor Gollancz, 1951.

———. Foreword. *A Time is Born.* By Garet Garrett. Oxford: Basil Blackwell, 1945. v–ix.

———. *Four Sacred Plays.* London: Victor Gollancz, 1948.

———. "The Greatest Drama Ever Staged." *Creed or Chaos?* New York: Harcourt, Brace, 1949. 3–7.

————. *He That Should Come. Four Sacred Plays.* London: Victor Gollancz, 1948. 213–74.

————. "How to Enjoy the Dark Nights." *The (London) Star,* 14 Sept. 1939: 2.

————. Introduction. *The Comedy of Dante Alighieri: The Florentine: Cantica I: Hell (L'Inferno).* By Dante Alighieri. Trans. Dorothy L. Sayers. 1949; Harmondsworth, Middlesex: Penguin, 1983. 9–66.

————. Introduction. *Great Short Stories of Detection, Mystery, and Horror.* Third Series. Ed. Sayers. London: Victor Gollancz, 1934. 11–14.

————. Introduction. *The Man Born to Be King.* By Sayers. London: Victor Gollancz, 1946. 17–40.

————. *The Just Vengeance. Four Sacred Plays.* London: Victor Gollancz, 1948. 275–352.

————. *The Letters of Dorothy L. Sayers.* 4 vols. Ed. Barbara Reynolds. New York: St. Martin's Press, 1996–2000.

————. "The Lost Tools of Learning." London: Methuen, 1948.

————. *The Man Born to Be King. A Play-Cycle on the Life of Our Lord and Saviour Jesus Christ.* London: Victor Gollancz, 1946.

————. "Notes on the Way." *Time and Tide,* 15 June 1940: 633–34; 22 June 1940: 657–58.

————. "The Other Six Deadly Sins." *Creed or Chaos?* By Sayers. New York: Harcourt, Brace: 1949. 63–85.

————. "The Pantheon Papers." DLS / MS-163. box 1, folder 4, undated drafts of the Pantheon Papers; and folder 5, drafts of the Pantheon Papers dated 1953–54. The Marion E. Wade Center, Wheaton College, Wheaton, IL.

————. *The Poetry of Dorothy L. Sayers.* Ed. Ralph E. Hone. Hurstpierpoint, West Sussex: The Dorothy L. Sayers Society, 1996.

————. "The Religions Behind the Nation." *The Christ of the Creeds: And Other Broadcast Messages to the British People During World War II.* Hurstpierpoint, West Sussex: The Dorothy L. Sayers Society, 2008. 43–48.

————. "Sacred Plays," Parts 1, 2, and 3. *Episcopal Churchnews* 9 Jan. 1955: 20–22, 35; 23 Jan. 1955: 24–25, 34; and 6 Feb. 1955: 24, 31–33.

————. "Salute to Mr. G. K. Chesterton: More Father Brown Stories." Rev. of *The Scandal of Father Brown,* by G. K. Chesterton. *Sunday Times* 7 Apr. 1935: 9.

————. "Strong Meat." *The Whimsical Christian: 18 Essays.* By Sayers. New York: MacMillan, 1978. 17–22. Originally published as "The Food of the Full-Grown." [London] *Sunday Times* 9 Apr. 1939.

————. "The Technique of the Sermon." Review of *The Art of Preaching.* *The Spectator.* 2 Feb. 1940: 150.

————. "What Do We Believe?" *Sunday Times,* 10 Sept. 1939. Reprinted in *Unpopular Opinions.* By Sayers. London: Victor Gollancz, 1946. 17–20.

————. "The Wimsey Papers—II." *The Spectator* 24 Nov. 1939: 736–37.

————. Worship in the Church (address notes). Undated ms. DLS / MS-245. Dorothy L. Sayers Manuscript Collection, Marion Wade Center, Wheaton College, Wheaton, IL.

————. *The Zeal of Thy House. Four Sacred Plays.* London: Victor Gollancz, 1948. 7–104.

Shelley, Percy Bysshe. *Prometheus Unbound: A Lyrical Drama in Four Acts.* Bartleby.com. <http://www.bartleby.com/139/shel116.html>.

Spurr, Barry. *Anglo-Catholic in Religion. T. S. Eliot and Christianity.* Cambridge: Lutterworth Press, 2010.

Thompson, Francis. "The Kingdom of God." *The Works of Francis Thompson. Poems:* Vol. 2. London: Burns, Oates, and Washbourne, 1913. 226–27.

Tillyard, E. M. W., and C. S. Lewis. *The Personal Heresy: A Controversy.* Oxford: Oxford UP, 1939.

Trickett, Rachel. "Uncrowned King of Oxford." *We Remember C. S. Lewis.* Ed. David Graham. Nashville: Broadman and Holman, 2001. 61–64.

Vanauken, Sheldon. *A Severe Mercy.* San Francisco: Harper and Row, 1977.

Welch, James. Foreword. *The Man Born to Be King: A Play-Cycle on the Life of Our Lord and Saviour Jesus Christ.* By Dorothy L. Sayers. London: Victor Gollancz, 1946. 9–13.

Williams, W. E. "The Spoken Word." *The Listener,* 15 Aug. 1940, 248.

Williamson, George. *A Reader's Guide to T. S. Eliot: A Poem by Poem Analysis.* New York: Farrar, Straus and Giroux, 1953.

Williamson, Marsha Daigle. *Reflecting the Eternal: Dante's Divine Comedy in the Novels of C. S. Lewis.* Peabody, MA: Hendrickson, 2015.

Wilson, Douglas. *Recovering the Lost Tools of Learning: An Approach to Distinctively Christian Education.* Wheaton, IL: Crossways, 1991.

Wordsworth, William. *The Borderers.* Ed. Robert Osborn. Ithaca, NY: Cornell UP, 1982.

Yeats, William Butler. "Among School Children." *The Collected Poems of W. B. Yeats.* Wordsworth Poetry Library. Ware, Herts.: Wordsworth Editions, 2008. 183–85.

Index

✠ ✠ ✠

Works by C. S. Lewis (CSL), Dorothy L. Sayers (DLS), and T. S. Eliot (TSE) are indexed under title; other literary works are indexed under author.